The Pathways Home
A Memoir of Sisters on Both Sides of Addiction

Lenaya Andersen and Larissa Cherpeski

With love,

Lenaya Andersen

ISBN-13: 978-0692560716
ISBN-10: 0692560718

DEDICATION

For Mom and Dad

To Dad; for teaching us we could be *anything* we wanted, and for making us believe it.

To Mom; for sacrificing *everything* to teach us, and for doing so without complaint.

CONTENTS

ACKNOWLEDGMENTS

Lenaya

Thank you to my husband, Brian, for choosing and loving me. And for being brave enough to share me and my story with the world. To Xiana, for giving me purpose when I had none. To Ekco, for excitedly asking about progress month after month for years. To Kolton and Argenta, for letting mommy write even when they wished to hear a story. To Mom and Dad, without whom I would not be; for unconditional love, broken hearts, and infinite prayers. To Cami, for tirelessly editing the whole book without complaint. To Cami, Nic, and [Jed], for sacrificing much of their own lives in order for Mom and Dad to tend to me. To every single friend along the way who lifted me, reached out to me, encouraged me, and finally motivated me to write this book. To Larissa, for never giving up.

Larissa

Nathan has ever supported and loved me on our path together. My children, Brandon, Andrew, Connor, Nicole and Danielle molded me into who I am. My greatest hope for them is that they have beautiful paths in their future. I thank my family for their patience with my distraction. I was blessed to grow up in a close family, and I count my siblings among my best friends. Cami's hours of editing transformed a manuscript into a book. The time I spent at the Center For Change provided insight and inspiration. My Read the Book Bookclub was invaluable in the insight and feedback they provided. Finally, I have special thanks to Gary Morgan who planted the seed of this creation.

I. Beginnings

Lenaya

All my life people have both encouraged me to write this, and then later, begged me not to. It doesn't matter; I was always going to write this. However, after I had a child, the details and the point of telling my story changed. No longer did I feel the need to go into graphic details of my sordid past. Instead, I find myself wanting, no needing, to tell my story of recovery, redemption, and fulfillment......ultimately, my story of hope. So, gory details aside... here is my story.

It's like a dream. I close my eyes sometimes and vivid memories flash like pictures on an electronic frame. Sometimes I can't grasp what my memory tells me, others, I feel as if those memories are actually recollections of a movie I watched a long time ago. I am not a participator, but rather a voyeur. I see what is happening, but I cannot come to terms with those pictures being me. They are some other girl; or not a person at all; some actress, with memorized lines and no real-life consequences. Surely that person is dead. Surely something terrible happened to her. Surely, positively, absolutely, that person is not me! My memories are as intangible as a dream. Often I can't pull them from my brain on demand. At other

1

times, they will pop into my head so suddenly and dramatically, they can be all but debilitating, paralyzing. Many memories are gone—lost to the world where details float around like bubbles. Somewhere in my brain are a million memories kept secret, protecting me from anguish. Unfortunately, so many positive memories are gone as well. There likely are portions of my brain which are permanently damaged due to years of substance abuse. Though I consider myself intelligent, I wonder what would my brain would be like without the barrage of misuse. Certainly my brain would be different in more ways than one had I gone down a different path, lived an alternate life, had revisionist memories. But I didn't; and that's okay.

It's challenging to determine where this story begins. I've had so many life-defining moments in my past. I can't articulate a specific, 'this is the moment it all changed' experience. It was more imperceptible than that; more gradual. It sounds so cliché, but it truly was this slippery slope where once I set foot on the edge, I just slid down. In many respects it was impossible to prevent. My parents have asked multiple times what they could have done differently, how they could have prevented this. My answer is, and always will be: "nothing." There is absolutely nothing they could have done differently. There are plenty of things that I could have changed, but I was utterly unwilling. Also, it couldn't have been, *I* couldn't have been without those choices; so many choices.

By fourth grade, the social hierarchy was already set in place. The most popular kids hung out on the grass and at the swings. The next caste was banished to the monkey bars. If ever I got into a fight with my so-called popular friends, I would be banished also, sheepishly making my way over to the monkey bars in hopes that the second most popular girls would let me hang with them until whatever infraction had been reversed, enabling me to return to my coveted spot at the swings. On one day I remember the air was warm, the sun shine kissing my skin like little rays of happiness. I had never intentionally sworn before. I was swinging, feeling the air at my front and my back. I felt like I could truly fly. I *loved* that feeling, that excitement, that exhilaration. Swinging to me felt so free. A lot of the other kids had grown past that rush. They used the swings as a socializing spot. Dani taunted me as I sat there. "Just say it," she cajoled, "I've never heard you swear before." It didn't help that it was Dani-Freaking-Smith. She was the coolest girl, the ring leader of the popular kids. She was my best friend...some days... or even weeks. I'm not sure why, but from a young age I was obsessed with popularity. I wanted to be the first one picked; the first one confided in; the first one wanted. I was the most confident, self-conscious person I have ever met. Some people build walls or reject others first as a preemptive strike to avoid rejection. I did the opposite, people-pleasing from the gate, boisterously pleading, 'pick me, love me, desire me, choose me.' I built no walls around me which, in turn, became my walls. I can trace this anxiety about missing something back to my earliest childhood memories. For someone as outwardly confident as I am, I have spent my life utterly dependent on being irreplaceable. I have always wanted to be the first guest invited, and the last to leave; the one person privy to all the entertainment and present for every exciting thing that takes place. When I first got hooked on meth, one of the things I loved the most about it was that I never slept. All my life I had felt left out when I went to sleep because I knew somewhere, someone was doing something, and I was missing it.

Call it peer pressure if you want, but I find self-pressure to be a more truthful term. Still, this moment in time might have been it—the beginning of my downward spiral, the moment when I chose popularity over integrity. I said the F-word, out loud, with emphasis. "Give me a break, like I don't swear anyway. I swear all the time just not around you." I needed her to know that I wasn't doing what she asked; I was simply doing what I always did... except I didn't. She seemed pleased; truly pleased. It was strange: this thrill I got from pleasing her. She was, after all, the queen bee. She was in charge, and she was impressed with my ability to spout profanities. More importantly, *I* was pleased. I couldn't believe how freeing it felt to say those words, the words that I had never before uttered, but many times thought. In my mind, the utterance of those words was the equivalent of damnation. This did not feel like damnation. No, this felt invigorating. I was *so cool*. I was swinging, no flying, and my friends were impressed with me, and I could say anything I wanted.

A year later, in fifth grade, I had a slumber party at my house. My parents were great; they supervised until bedtime and then left us to our own devices. Our own devices were some travel bottles of liquor one of my friends had smuggled from her dad's suitcase. We all drank some. One of my friends acted quite drunk, spraying

3

whipped cream on my dad's speakers. I didn't get drunk, not even a buzz, but I acted like I did. To be honest, I didn't really feel anything and found it hard to imagine why people liked the toxic stuff. Plus, it tasted horrible. Later that night, we would all take showers at 3 am and head down to the park to meet up with some boys. This was my drug. I French-kissed my little boyfriend (probably a foot shorter than me as all boys were at that age) long into the early morning when we walked home. It felt so devious, so adult. I felt I was the oldest, wisest, girl in the world. We wouldn't get caught I was certain. We were invincible! Plus, the boys thought we were oh-so-impressive to be drunk in the early hours of the day. I can't remember the next time I drank. I can't even remember the first time I got drunk. It's all a blur. From that day forward, if there was alcohol, I drank it. It didn't matter anymore once I had tried it the first time. I wish I knew exactly when I first decided it was a feeling I liked, but I do know that it was a feeling I liked. Like the swing, I could fly. I was invincible. I was articulate. I was the one that everybody wanted to know. I was euphoric. I was the best.

Later, therapists and counselors would constantly seek the source of those choices. Did I have a bad home life? Was I abused? Molested? Traumatized in some way? I wasn't. I have the most amazing parents in the universe. I was raised in a loving, happy home. My childhood was exceptional. My parents checked up on me and watched over me. Countless times I had friends' parents lie for me in order to attend parties, get-togethers, and ridiculousness that my parents would never have approved of. Also, I mastered the art of lying at a very young age. I was convincing. I was the first girl to answer questions in Sunday school and volunteer to say the prayer. I lived a duplicitous life. Oddly, it wasn't very confusing at the time. Years later as I would try to dredge through those years, experiences, and choices, the hypocrisy would floor me; but not then. I was proud of my ability to live separate lives. I was horrified to ever think of my naive parents finding out about my other life. I wasn't interested in open rebellion but in satisfying my curiosities and experiencing everything. As early as first grade my answer to the question, "What do you want out of life?" was, "Stories to tell." I was insatiable.

Ironically, it was much easier for me in those early years to get drugs than it was to get alcohol. Drinks are controlled substances; drugs, on the other hand are capitalism at its best. I always found it strange that I couldn't buy cigarettes, but I could shoot meth into my veins...of course, that would be much later.

The first time I smoked weed was much like the first time I drank. I didn't feel anything. I pretended to be high because I also pretended that it wasn't my first time. None of my peers were pressuring me, but I desperately wanted to be cool. I was at a house party in the sixth grade. I heard that there were some high-schoolers in the back room smoking pot, and I sought them out. When I found them, I pretended that I smoked weed all the time. I didn't know how to smoke out of the bolts and screws they were using so I acted like I was a much more posh pothead, only smoking out of glass pipes in the past. They taught me how to use their contraption. I hit it, but nothing. Looking back, I probably didn't inhale. Plus, it's not that uncommon to not get high the first time you smoke. Still, like vodka, from there on out, if there was weed present, I found it. Unlike being drunk, I absolutely remember the first time I got high. To say I loved it would be an understatement. I lived for it. To me, it felt like this was the culmination of my entire life. This was where I was supposed to be. This was what life was. I felt so philosophical, genius, wise. I remember talking and laughing for hours, musing about life, the world; solving everything in this universe in a matter of a few short hours. I felt like I was flying and falling, and nothing mattered. Weed was my metaphorical swing. I loved that feeling. Marijuana would always be my drug of choice. For the next fifteen years it scarcely mattered what other substance I was addicted to, pot was always present.

Dragon's Scent

You come to the dragon, he's calling to you,
He looks so sweet, what's said can't be true,
You breathe in the dragon, happy and pleased,
And just for the moment, you feel at ease.
The hurt of your problems a thing of the past,
The happy confusion, you wish it would last,
But as you come down from this chemical high,
Look at the dragon. Stare him straight in the eye,
His eyes mock your feelings, a secret hides deep,
He knows you'll be back the next time you can't sleep.
Once you've inhaled him, you're never the same,
You'll always be near him, you can't stay away.
Without his strange scent you're alone and you're lost,
But with him so near, you're in a happy box.
You're content where you're at for the moment it seems,
But you just can't see what this dragon eye sees.
He's laughing at you, spitting right in your face,
He's watching the people call you a disgrace.
He knew from the start, you'd be addicted at once,
But he stood by and watched, as you breathed in his ounce.
Your mind's gone forever, your brain cells are dead.
You sit there and breathe him...to clear up your head.

-Lenaya Frey 1993(14-yrs-old)-

I've always heard the term "gateway drug" referencing marijuana. I remember scoffing at the term, consistently making the joke about the drunk driver and the stoned one. The drunk blows a red light while the pothead waits for the stop sign to turn green. I never imagined a stoned driver to be impaired. I still worry less about the dirt-heads of the world than the drunks in a lot of ways, but rather than scoffing at the term gateway drug, I find it's absolutely and irrevocably true. Weed is a gateway drug, not only because it decreases sensitivities and preconceived notions about drugs, but also because of its ability to influence choices. While stoned, most teens are more likely to try other substances than if they had a clear head. Everyone is a little slower to respond, a little less likely to be alarmed, and a little more prone to make poor choices. Many people argue the contrary, but in my experience; Marijuana led me to other drugs. My early drug use meant I didn't have the maturity or the experience to help dictate what paths I should take.

It would be a cop-out to blame weed for my choices. It helped, but I was always drawn to the dramatic. I always fantasized about tragedy. After school specials were lost on me because I was envious, not of the hero that got the teenage swimmer off cocaine, but of the swimmer herself. I wanted to be the girl in the bathroom with a bloody nose, struggling with my oh-so-dramatic addiction to coke. I wanted to be the one everybody talked about, and worried about. Not an uncommon teenage experience, I used to daydream about my loved ones, or myself, suddenly finding out about a terminal illness. In my mind, I was dying of kidney failure with my true love holding my hand and sobbing as I lay on my death bed. Sometimes, when I would reverse roles and pretend a loved one was dying, I would cry. I wasn't so sadistic that I actually wanted to die, but the drama of fake tragedy was alluring. I read and re-read the saddest, most traumatic books I could get my hands on. I loved nothing more than an irreversible conflict, ambivalent ending, or no-resolution solution. I remember in the fifth grade making up tragedies in order to get attention from my friends. 'Please coddle me,' I would silently beg, 'everyone pay attention to poor me who, with such strength, is getting through this challenging experience'… except that I typically wasn't. Like I said, life was pretty good to me. I was inwardly and outwardly very happy. I laughed a lot and had a lot of fun. I never took no for an answer, and I enjoyed my time; too much sometimes. Most of the drama in my life was self-induced. Because of this, it was difficult to figure out who to blame… for all of us. The irony is that years later when I really would become the after school special, it was no longer the least bit appealing to me.

Larissa

"…For unto such shall ye continue to minister; for ye know not but what they will return and repent, and come unto me with full purpose of heart, and I shall heal them; and ye shall be the means of bringing salvation unto them" (Book of Mormon, 3 Nephi 18:32).

It is impossible to describe the exquisite pain that comes from watching a loved one stray from the path. When someone you love dies, you have hope to see them again someday. When someone is "dead" spiritually speaking, you live with the fear that they may be lost to you forever. For many years I searched for a magic word that would somehow transform my sister. There must be some single act that would help her see the light and turn her into a new person. If I could just have the perfect conversation, then she would have clarity and change. This feeling was perpetuated by the shows I watched and books I read where everything could be resolved in 60 minutes or under 300 pages. I came to understand that ministering is unique to each situation. It is not one action but a multitude of actions over an indefinite period of time. The creation of a true relationship is inherent in ministering. While I thought that I was working to change my sister, I came to ultimately understand that I needed to change myself to be able to help her.

I didn't come pre-packaged with all the skills that I needed to minister to my sister. I needed to develop a new sensitivity and ability to relate to her, even when she was living a life opposite of mine. I needed to learn where I would set my boundaries but all the time our situation required unconditional Christ-like love. The process of ministering to her actually changed me and made me a better person. It turned me toward the Lord, and sent me to my knees in my hours of anguish.

I finally learned that nothing I said could change my sister. She could only be changed by turning to the Lord, and that would happen in its own time and in its own way. I could minister to her, but only Christ's atoning power would have the ability to heal her.

Our sibling relationships have the potential to be the longest and strongest relationships we will ever have. We will generally outlive our parents. We will not know our spouses or children for as long as our siblings. We come from the same background which brings with it a special bond and understanding. Our relationship as siblings tends to endure longer than other friendships that may come and go. During this mortal life, we are brothers and sisters longer than we are sons and daughters, husbands and wives, fathers and mothers, or friends.

Cain posed the question so long ago, "Am I my brother's keeper?" After much consideration, I believe we are truly their keeper and can reach our siblings in ways that our parents may be unable to do. What I have learned from, "Keeping my sister," was that she in turn has helped to "Keep me."

The question that haunted me for years after my sister became wayward was, "Why?" I wanted to understand why she would make choices that would hurt herself and the people she loved. Didn't she see the harm she was causing to our family? Wasn't she aware of how one person affected many? I wondered why she felt the need to turn to drugs. She had to know the physical effects of drugs and alcohol and yet still made those choices. I conjectured about possible past abuse that could have led her to this path. Sometimes I asked, "Why?!" with an angry fist. I felt anger toward her and furious at my own helplessness to do anything. Other times I asked it with intense guilt, when the question changed into, "Why didn't I know before now?" I wondered if I wasn't worthy of receiving guidance, or if I wasn't obedient enough to have the Lord give me the answers.

A close cousin to the question, "Why?" and perhaps even more destructive was the other question that often went through my mind, "Who is to blame?" In my distorted thinking, I would have peace if I could just know the cause and perpetrator. Sometimes I blamed peer pressure, claiming that sleepovers and bad friends had brought her to this point. I spent a lot of years subtly blaming my parents as I saw them fall apart over their agony. I spent a lot of time angry that they were blind to what she was doing and decided to take matters into my own hands. I turned into the private detective who was going to sniff out the truth and fix things. Ultimately, when I failed to change her, I would blame myself.

My mom later told me an interesting story about how she felt an emotion close to rage that was directed toward someone who she thought was supplying my sister with drugs. She wanted to go to their parents and accuse them of failing to stop their child from destroying my sister. She later came to find out that my sister was the one who was supplying the drugs for this person. It was a stunning discovery and very humbling.

These questions I asked were agonizing. They put me in a place where I became stuck. Looking back, I can't see how these questions served any useful purpose. All they did was fill me with a sense of helplessness and despair. The questions, "Why?" and "Who is to blame?" were the wrong questions to ask during this time. Ironically, the answer to the question, "Why?" only came long after I had stopped requesting an answer.

Other questions I asked were helpful. One that probably helped me the most was, "What shall I do?" That question allowed me to put my trust in God. I admitted that He knows better than me. By asking this question, I became more hopeful that things could be changed in the future, and that I could play a role in that change. The experiences that I went through changed me as a sister, daughter, friend, wife, mother, and child of God. I was put in a position where I needed to work hard to be receptive to the Holy Ghost. I was forced to strive continually to be a receptacle to answers that might help my sister. They came.

They came, but not in the time frame or the way that I imagined.

Lenaya

In those early years there were ever so many firsts. The first time I smoked a cigarette I was at a friend's house. Her mother had lied for me and promised my parents that there would be supervision for our sleepover. Instead, my friend's older sister was having a get-together with some of her friends, and their mom was nowhere to be found. My friend, who smoked quite regularly by the ripe age of 11, asked if I wanted to smoke a cigarette. Meanwhile, her sister and their friends were snorting lines of what I would later learn was cocaine, off the glass coffee table. My friend and I sat on the front porch with a pack of menthol lights out of her mother's purse. We used matches to light them. I remember the burn of the sulfur as I attempted to both light and inhale at the same time. I tried to resist the burning tickle in my throat, but I coughed. I stopped inhaling it because it kept making me cough. I was filling my mouth with smoke and then blowing it out. Eventually, I got the hang of it. I inhaled deeply, then exhaled. The stars in the sky and the dark, night air, swayed a bit around me as I felt light-headed. It tasted awful, but I enjoyed the buzz. Like many other substances, I would have to teach myself to crave this… it was not an immediate addiction. It would be one of my longest lasting addictions, and also one of the hardest to overcome. Minus two failed attempts of long-term quitting when I was fifteen and nineteen, I smoked for sixteen years. That's a long time for someone who quit by the age of twenty-seven.

Arguably the longest lasting addiction, and one that greatly influenced my poor choices, although more imperceptibly, was my eating disorder. I assume it can be called an addiction because it was something that I scarcely felt I had control over for more than half my life. I began struggling with my weight far too young. The overpowering call of media, society, and peer groups felt suffocating from the time I was as young as eight. I played the typical comparison game where I never could come out on top in appearance, comparing my weaknesses with others' strengths. In the third grade I remember being at a friend's house when her mom weighed us. She weighed fifty-one pounds. I weighed seventy-one. I was probably a foot taller than her, but my young mind couldn't grasp the difference. Instead, I remember being embarrassed and vulnerable about my size. For the first time my insecure feelings about being bigger than other girls seemed to be more than my incorrect perception. I wanted to weigh fifty-one pounds! I wanted to be the *petite* one! Later, I began to put on some weight. My cheeks rounded, and my body became softer, less angular than it had been when I was a child. I remember taking a bath lying on my back. I looked down and, for the first time I discovered my round belly. It wasn't flat. Instead, I could see dimpled layers of flesh. I could squeeze them between my fingertips. I was disgusted. Again, I felt self-conscious and insecure about my size. What was even more discomforting to me was that I simply hadn't noticed. How long had I looked like this? How long had I been *fat*? I lacked the information necessary to remedy my growing size or the understanding, that putting on weight as you begin puberty is completely normal. I didn't know how to eat healthily. I had learned tiny pieces about the food pyramid, but what nine-year-old understands healthy eating habits? When I look back now it's appalling the things I would consume for the sake of losing weight. Once, I went a good year living off of Mountain Dew and Airheads because they were fat free. Pure sugar. Another time I survived on bagels and white rice… also fat free. But At nine, I ate whatever Mom made… and candy bars. Once, I asked if I could have a Snickers from the giant box and my mom said "No." I began sneaking candy bars and dry cereal ever after. Of course, this led to more weight gain, and I recognized further that I was bigger than my friends. They were all skinnier than me! Eventually, I was introduced to even more unhealthy methods of weight loss.

At cheerleading practice a few years later, there was a girl on my squad who had recently lost all of her round edges. It had been a noticeable and instant transformation particularly because I was already body-conscious. We were exercising strenuously for cheerleading, and I thought that was the source. I too was losing weight, but not at the pace she was. One evening, at practice in a field, she informed the coaches she needed to use the bathroom. Not wanting her to walk across the street to the empty building alone, they asked me to accompany her. While there, she let me in on a little secret. She stuck her fingers down her throat and made herself throw up. I had been jealous of her weight loss, but even more so of the attention she was receiving because of it. For me, this was a great revelation. 'Oh, I get it now. Eat what you want, then make yourself throw up and it all goes away without having to deprive yourself of anything.' This was such a foreign concept. I genuinely had never even considered the fact that vomit prevented calories. I was so utterly naïve; I didn't understand calories at all. I did understand trying to refrain from eating candy bars without success. Without hesitation I began copying her. Because I had never even heard of this disorder, I also had no concept of the damage, both physical and psychological, it could do. It wasn't like me to weigh the consequences before making drastic decisions anyway, but that was the beginning of a life of throwing up, starving, taking any number of diet pills, and later laxatives. Like my friend, I immediately saw results. I was reliant on instant gratification and nothing in my world had to change, except knowing the location of every bathroom in every place I would visit for the rest of my life. I knew what sounds best disguised the vomit hitting the toilet water, what gums best hid the smell, and what angles best prevented the bile from hitting my clothes or face. It wasn't pretty, positive, or anything I could ever be proud of; it was hideous, embarrassing, and frightening. But it was also effective, and that was the beginning of the end for me.

Due to my body image, my absorption with popularity, and my self-destructive tendencies it shouldn't come as any great surprise that I lost my virginity when I was thirteen-years-old. It wasn't to some predator preying on younger girls. It was to my boyfriend. We were in love of course, and we were going to be together forever. To say I was emotionally unprepared would be a serious understatement. Almost all of my friends were having sex. I genuinely thought every thirteen-year-old was sexually active. Reality is what we see and what we know. I was one of the last of my group of lemmings, so it didn't seem age inappropriate. Still, I had no idea what was happening. I was so immature. We set up a time and a place to meet, similar to the first time I French kissed a boy, and then we had sex. Only I didn't really know what sex was. Mine wasn't a home of open birds and bees talks. I knew a moderate amount from sex education; but truly, I was clueless. It didn't feel intimate, like an intense expression of love. It was awkward and confusing and staged. Afterwards I didn't feel more mature or more deeply enamored like my friends articulated. I wondered if there was something wrong with me. My friends said they had enjoyed it, continued to enjoy it. Me? I was ambivalent. I didn't feel like I needed to start wearing a scarlet letter either. I didn't feel particularly guilty, yet I knew sex before marriage was wrong. I'd been indoctrinated about purity and chastity in my Sunday school classes since I was a little girl. Shortly after, while reading the scriptures as a family, we came across 3 Nephi 18:28-29: *"And now behold, this is the commandment which I give unto you, that ye shall not suffer any one knowingly to partake of my flesh and blood unworthily, when ye shall minister it. For whoso eateth and drinketh my flesh and blood unworthily eateth and drinketh damnation to his soul; therefore if ye know that a man is unworthy to eat and drink of my flesh and blood ye shall forbid him."* The words, "damnation to his soul," coursed through me and chilled me to my very core. I believed this to be the word of God, and I didn't doubt for a second that this was true. I remember asking my older brother to help me hide the fact that I was no longer taking the sacrament on Sundays. Knowing what was true and adhering to those standards were two different things. My testimony was a major inconvenience, one which I would spend years numbing, ignoring, and disregarding. I believed the teachings of the Mormon Church, but I had no desire to follow them. I know now that it was this testimony, and the foundation laid by my parents that would be rungs on the ladder that saved my life.

I didn't have to evade the bread and water for long because, by then, my parents were concerned about me. Through my thirteen-year-old eyes I continued to feel an invincible child without a care in the world. I felt that I successfully tricked my parents on a daily basis. I didn't think they had any clue I was making these choices. Apart from getting caught ditching a church youth activity, being discovered in a major lie, and being discovered having boyfriends before the parent-approved age of sixteen, there were very few altercations. I'm sure I was more transparent than I perceived because it wasn't a coincidence that they read my journal. My disposition had suddenly changed shadowing my characteristic zest for life. I was a faithful journal keeper. I wrote in it diligently almost daily from the time I turned eight. My parents gave me my own scriptures and journal for a baptism gift. They let me pick a beautiful maroon leather-bound journal with my name inscribed in gold embossed letters on the front. I treated it like a trusted confidante, writing lengthy descriptions of all my recent escapades.

It was unusual to find my dad home during daylight when he greeted me at the door after school and asked me to come in his room for a talk. This wasn't entirely suspicious because it wasn't uncommon for Dad to have father-daughter meetings. I prepared my best face and readied myself to lie with a smile. My heart skipped a beat when I saw the level of formality with three chairs set up in a circle and my parents' grave expressions. I began to panic, 'what do they know? What are they going to ask me about? What loose ends do I have?' I felt my world closing in on me. My dad spoke and directly asked me about smoking marijuana. I tried denying it but quickly discovered they had read my journal. I argued that everybody was doing it and that it wasn't a big deal. I vowed never to do it again and pleaded to be forgiven. Then my dad said, "What about the more serious matter of the sex?" I don't think there's a more awkward sentence ever to be uttered from the mouth of a Mormon father. I. Was. Shocked. I was also a little confused that to them the more serious crime was the one which was not illegal and didn't involve jail time if caught. To this, there was no more pleading or apologizing. I was mad, fuming, seething. How dare they read my journal? How dare they breach my privacy and read what was sacred to me; what was mine and mine alone! I can't remember in great detail the way the rest of the conversation went. I know we talked, argued, and cried for a long time. It was probably a crushing decision for them to make to read my journal in the first place, but I had no room in my heart for allowances. I was embarrassed, and angry; oh-so-angry. A small piece of me let go of pretenses that day. The worst had been found out. My parents were no longer the innocents I needed to protect, but rather the enemy. They had openly defied my privacy, and for the next year and a half, we were at odds. We were on different teams. And yet, through all of it, I was never openly rebellious. I never came out and said, "Deal with it"—the route of many of my friends. I continued to be very careful about phone calls and communication with my friends but now less for my parent's protection than for mine. I also punished them dearly by sticking firecrackers in my journal and blowing it up. *I sure showed them.* What I wouldn't give for that journal now, all these years later when my memories are fuzzy. This is only the first small casualty in the long list of things I lost or destroyed.

Part of our resolution in that talk was my parent's insistence that

I go meet with the Bishop. In the LDS church, there are Bishops who preside over each congregation unit called a ward. Every responsibility in the church is by calling—none receive financial compensation for any job they have. I had a lively and friendly Bishop whom I liked. Nevertheless, I had no interest in talking to him about things I wasn't at all repentant for. I met with him, confirming about a million times that he couldn't tell my parents anything. I pretended that I would take the necessary measures to ensure repentance. I considered him my friend. I was fortunate that way. I am grateful that he loved me, didn't judge me, and was genuinely interested in my peace. At the time though, our definitions of "peace" differed. I remember thinking that, though he and my parents were kind, they all had it wrong. *They* were missing out. *They* were out of touch with reality. *They* didn't realize the true definition of peace which was excitement and fun. In short, *they* were naive. I felt superior to my superiors because of what I deemed their lack of experience. Truly, I thought I was the happy one. I found them to be delusional and clinging to something that wasn't real. I never doubted they meant well, but was bitter towards the church. I justified my ideology feeling like my parent's many responsibilities at church took time away from my family, which ironically, I didn't want anyway. By then, I wanted to spend every waking moment with the most important people: my friends. I felt like my parents' strict rules and outdated morality were a result of a religion that didn't bring happiness. My friends' parents always agreed with me. As did the many counselors I insisted on seeing. I refused to consult anybody that was Mormon because if they were, they sided with my parents, if they weren't, they typically sided with me. Fortunately, my parents gave me opportunities to feel the spirit from a young age, so despite my resentment, rebellion, and disdain, I never could deny God was real. Ironically, I spent many drunken nights defending Him.

Another repercussion of the fateful journal reading was that my parents forbid all contact with my boyfriend and transferred me, in the eighth grade, to a different middle school. I had long since been secretive and calculating, but this began a longstanding relationship with the freedom of the night. I would sneak the phone downstairs, lying on the burnt orange carpet with my legs propped against the sliding glass door and talk to my prohibited boyfriend all night long.

When the sun rose, I would quickly hang up and head to the shower. Later, when I began sneaking out, I knew well the sounds, the lifelessness, and the liberties of the wee hours of the morning. I had found a great freedom in my ability to survive on minimal amounts of sleep. When the sun went down, the vampires came to life.

Despite the adjustment to my new school; it didn't matter where I went, it wasn't long before I found what I was looking for: *wild* teenagers. They were all having sex and experimenting with alcohol and drugs. I was drawn to one girl in particular, Rae, who would be my best friend for a long time. We would experience lifetimes together and suffer serious loss together. And when I got sober, I would watch and encourage her efforts in and out of rehab, long after I was clean. She was never as eager as I was about trying new drugs. She was always a bit more hesitant, a fragment more afraid. The moments I yelled, 'let's do this for the rest of our lives!' she was often yelling, 'let's never do this again!' In my life I would often experience friends hitting the brakes just as I was slamming on the gas. Yet, in the end, I was the lucky one. I was the one who got out. It's unfair in so many ways, and I still wonder why I got to have such a beautiful life. I recognize one of my major fortunes in life is having a network: family and resources, lost or never there for so many others.

Rae and I clicked instantly and were inseparable. Her mom thought my parents were overly protective and would more often than not side with me when we fought. Later, she would become their unlikely ally when we were both so out of control they were paralyzed. Her mom treated me like her own. In turn, I was polite, articulate, and animated... always animated. Rae and I betrayed her affections by sneaking out immediately. I landed a new boyfriend who was in high school and he brought friends to set up with Rae. We met on the corner of my *cul de sac* every night at 1 am. I grew intensely familiar with house and night-time noises. Initially, I went right out the front door. I slowly crept out of my bedroom, stuffing pillows under my covers and noiselessly turning the doorknob. Tip toeing down the hallway, I listened for the familiar sounds of my parent's part breathing part snoring before venturing farther. If they startled awake, I could always pretend to be using the bathroom. Confident that they were, indeed, sound asleep (with earplugs in no less) I would step right, lunge left, then holding my breath, put my weight on the railing and bypass the bottom squeakiest steps. My system wasn't foolproof; it was an old house and it creaked, but it was vastly better than the no holds barred method of my inexperienced trials. When the air hit my face, it smelled of freedom won but never paid for. My feet pounded the cement as I ran to get wasted all night until 5:45am… just in time to sleep before getting ready for school. I was tired, but not as tired as I should have been.

Eventually all the sleepless nights, the lack of nutrition, and the destructive behaviors began to take their toll on my body. This led me to the discovery of Mini Thins. Initially created as an over the counter asthma medicine, these little white pills did the trick. They enabled me to live off of absolutely no sleep, and… they suppressed my appetite! They were $5.49 a bottle at 7-11. I have no idea how many times I emptied the vase filled with change downstairs in order to buy bottles of Mini Thins, but I never ran out. From the time I discovered them until a decade later, I had them on me at all times. I remember after taking a handful of them, the feeling of being high, but not burned out at all. I would touch my scalp and it would send shivers down my spine. I would get goose bumps on my head. But most importantly, I got skinnier and was awarded more late night hours. Plus, they sobered me up in a pinch, so I rarely had to deal with anyone when I was in a mind-altered state. My poor mom had to drive me all the way across town every morning to my new school. It must have been a serious hardship on her time. I insisted on playing the radio stations I wanted to listen to both ways. I would sing every lyric to every song. Perhaps my mom wanted to use that time to get to know me better. Or, perhaps she was every bit as scared to know me as I was.

In due course, my parents began clueing in to my sneaking out. They never confronted me about it, but I noticed little booby traps: strings, tape, objects strategically placed in front of the door so that there would be an indication that it had been opened in the night. I was fairly meticulous. I paid attention to the smallest of details always making sure to put *everything* back where I found it. After they had exhausted all other resources; my parents installed alarms that would beep loudly if the doors were opened. That was when I began going out the window. The details are hazy, but I know I shared my room and had to be extra careful when climbing out the window; it was trickiest when it was no longer my room. After climbing out the window, I scaled the roof to the edge where the fence met the side yard, reached my tippy toes down until at least one foot had ground, and then climbed down the fence. I got pretty professional at it. Once, I fell…hard…I bounced on the fence and smacked the pavement so hard I thought I was broken. I had a gnarly bruise and hematoma wrapping all the way around my upper thigh. To this day the lump protrudes hideously about an inch from my body. It was impossible to hide, so I made up a story about running and falling on a stick. I'm sure I was dramatic and had all the embellishments to make it believable. Writing this I realize what a ridiculous explanation that was. Surely the necessary doctor visit would have uncovered my deceit. Over the years I would sustain and ignore many injuries due to my secret life. I never once thought of the far reaching impact. I never once thought to be concerned. I never stopped going out that window… even when I was sure I would get caught.

Larissa

When I was a little girl, I woke up to sunny skies, the crescendo of messy noise from my younger siblings, and the faint smell of high desert foliage. My first salient memories were located in Sparks, Nevada. This was a place of slot machines in every gas station, nearby legalized prostitution, bountiful breakfast buffets and Sagebrush boasted as the state flower. Nevada was originally a temporary stop on a long-term plan for my debt-laden parents who had bounced from Idaho to Provo for college and then to Salt Lake City for Law School. Our first house was purchased after the heavy inflation of the early 1980's and was almost more than they could manage. By then my parents had four children, all roughly 2 years apart: me, my sister Camella, my brother Nicholas, and my youngest sister, Lenaya. We were surprised with my youngest brother Jed six years later.

The houses in our middle-class neighborhood were squeezed together. We lived on a busy street a block away from a shopping center and our elementary school. The dollar theatre was located in the shopping center, and was a great treat in a time before VCR's. We could always scrounge some change to walk down the block to 7-11 and debate between blowing it all on a candy bar or penny candy. I usually went for quantity rather than quality. We had a string of cats that descended upon our home. I always took a running leap at bedtime to avoid their ambushes from under my bed. We rode our trikes and ordered endless milkshakes and hamburgers from the rosebush in the side yard we pretended was a drive-up window. We loved to swing from the branches of our Weeping Willow in the backyard and climb high into the tree, until my dad spotted us and cut the branches to where we couldn't reach. We roller-skated on the patio or the driveway and ran with the neighbor kids.

My birthday was in October, and I had started school in Utah where the cutoff was later, so when we moved to Nevada I had to test into my grade. I was always bright, and that was an easy task, but as a result I was always the youngest one in my grade. I confess to being a bossy oldest sister. My mom had to go to work after Lenaya was born. Their medical bills had become challenging due to complications at her delivery as well as several early illnesses and hospitalizations. I was often in charge at home when my mom worked at a nearby casino as a seamstress. They had good benefits, which my father's work didn't provide and helped with all the medical bills that accompany a young family.

Both converts to The Church of Jesus Christ of Latter-day Saints, my parents were deeply immersed in their church work as well as social structure. Church attendance was more than a Sunday event. The charge to look after the flock was a group responsibility, and I felt comfortable surrounded by the community of worshipers who lived and believed in unity. The family joke was that we would come home from church an hour late, because my dad liked to talk to everyone. I inherited this same social nature from my dad.

Unlike my father, my mother was less social, though she did enjoy socializing with smaller groups of friends. My father was an eternal optimist, while my mother was the self-avowed pessimist. There were many differences in their natures, but they had quite a bit in common. They shared a love of learning and the same faith. Both came from poor homes where hard work was valued. They had similar tastes in literature, music, and art. My father was physically active and had always enjoyed playing sports. My mother claimed that her only grade that was lower than an A was in P.E., but she loved hiking, biking, camping and walking. They shared a love of music and were in a band for several years until life became too busy. They had little financial or emotional support from their parents, and I know they struggled monetarily for many years, working extra hours at a gas station and cooking the cheaper cuts of meat. My mom cut herself more than once deboning a whole chicken.

While they both valued education, my mother, typical of that era, sacrificed her formal education, so my dad could pursue his. She gave up a National Merit Scholarship. She joked that every time she went back to school, she got pregnant, but with sad irony it was usually true. She was a devoted mother who nursed us back to health when we were sick with cool hands and a chicken noodle soup. She pushed us to do well in our school and finish what she was only able to start. She also valued independence and gave us a lot of latitude. We had plenty of freedom to explore our neighborhood and were not highly dependent on her. She was only a touchy-feely mother with us as young children, but was very hands off as we grew older. I think she was strongly influenced by her parents who were older than most. Her father was 50 when she was born and was older than my father's grandparents.

My dad was driven and a hard worker. He was in the white collar version of a sweat shop where he worked millions of hours to make the partners in his firm very wealthy, while he still drove a Volkswagen Bug and dreamed of the good life. He also was generous almost to a fault. Never a great money manager, he was nonetheless always a great man and willing to share all he had with whomever had a need. When he managed to spend time at home, he loved to read us nursery rhymes and play The Three Little Pigs. We used our brick fireplace as the third pig's home and would race across the room with squeals of terror as he played the Big Bad Wolf chasing us. Together my parents didn't have a perfect marriage, but they had the same goals and ideals and woke up the morning after their fights still loving each other. I felt safe in our home and cared for.

Once I started school, I entered my own world. I only wanted to play with my friends, forgetting that my siblings could be good friends until I was an adult. I was more of a second mother to Jed and thrilled when he took his first step or pulled all the books out of the bookcase. The last year my mother worked, I took the place of our babysitter and watched my siblings from after school till my dad got home from work near bedtime. One night, Jed wouldn't stop crying, and I was beyond my limits. A family friend stopped by and seeing my plight helped comfort him until my dad came home.

We soon became crowded in our house, and my parents took the plunge and upgraded to a nicer neighborhood. At the same time, my mom quit working. I had to adjust to a new school between middle school years. I liked the extra space though, and we all loved the stairs. I also appreciated coming home to fresh cookies. Life seemed to be getting easier for our family.

One early spring afternoon before we moved, I was at my best friend's house playing in the barn on a pile of mattresses. Our other friend was over, and she had managed to pinch a few of her dad's cigarettes. They were working up the nerve to light up, while I was working up the courage to be strong against peer pressure. Up to that point, I had walked with them to the nearby candy store after school and bought candy cigarettes that blew powder out of the wrapping, but this felt much more sinister and heavy. I had been taught that smoking was wrong, but at the same time my position as best friend could be threatened, and I didn't want to be seen as a goody-goody. After wavering for some time, I knew in my heart that I had to choose the right. They mocked and teased me and then they were genuinely angry at me for putting them on up to that point. I slowly walked home, sadly knowing that life would never be the same again. There was always a gulf between me and my friends after that. We stayed friends, but I felt more excluded.

Moving to a new school was a fresh start, and it started out with enormous promise. There was a cute and popular boy who seemed to like *me*, of all people. We flirted together for several weeks and I enjoyed the positive attention. In the late fall when the weather was still warm we sat next to each other in science class. He leaned over during a lecture and asked me in parochial terms to, "Go out with him." To this day I'm not sure what caused me to answer, "No," but I did. Known for my stubbornness, I was unwilling to back down from my original answer even when he asked me again on the bus-ride home. I was shunned the rest of the year. It was one of the loneliest and hardest years of my life, but my direction was set. I was started on my path.

Looking back, I can see that if I had done anything differently, my course could have been no different from Lenaya's. I got through those years and had a pretty solid relationship with God by my sophomore year of High School.

Around that time my sister came home from school crying because her friends had turned on her. She wanted desperately to fit in and be popular, and I understood her pain, having been through it recently myself. We sat in the downstairs family room, our hideous 70's orange carpet filling the space, and I talked to her and tried to comfort her over the noise of our siblings watching cartoons. I walked her into the bathroom and turned on the curling iron to give her a special makeover to try and boost her confidence. I talked to her as the steam rose from the heated iron wrapped around her long blonde hair. After I finished, she had calmed down and looked nice. I hoped that maybe I made a difference in how she would be able to cope.

This memory stands out as an experience that I looked back on many times. I often wondered if this was the moment that she made the decision to turn from the safe path. Or maybe she already had plunged into the deep.

Lenaya

Because of Rae's hesitancy when we first began smoking weed and drinking, she insisted that we make a pact: nothing chemical and we would never snort anything up our noses. We broke that pact within the year. I remember more than once attributing the demise of our friendship, ourselves, and the world around us to that pact. We promised our lives if we broke that pact. I'm not a superstitious person, but even now I can't deny that in more ways than one, we gave our lives for breaking that pact.

Though I take accountability for my choices and behavior, sometimes I feel like part of my desire to escape was because I was born overly sensitive. I vividly remember as a little girl, maybe five-years-old, seeing an old man shuffling down my street, pushing a shopping cart. My heart felt heavy with his burden, with the injustice of it all. I wanted to march over to him and ease his suffering. I couldn't understand why life should be so hard for this man. I was empathetic to a fault. I carried the weight of the world on my shoulders. Despite my charmed life, I ached for the injustices of the world; and they were all around me. When I was six, I memorized the entire soundtrack to *Les Miserables*. I wanted to suffer like Cosette, and, like Marius, I wanted justice.

My first experiences with mind-altering drugs were positive and enjoyable. I sought the feeling of escaping, of being out of control. I relished slowing down my busy mind, not obsessing; worry-free. Ironically, it also was thrilling to feel I was expanding my mind when in fact I was doing the opposite. The first time I did acid, something that was so clearly chemical and a blatant violation of our pact, was no exception. We went to a reservoir called Pyramid Lake with our boyfriends. We dosed at 7 pm which was a growing concern to me with my curfew and the knowledge that this would be a long trip. Had I been the least bit prudent, I would have declined, but I never was the prudent type. Acid is the epitome of mind altering— changing the way I viewed *everything*. Giggling uncontrollably, I attempted to catch the vibrant, palpable, and colorful air. I could *see* oxygen. I could *feel* it. When we got out by the lake, the rocks were Native Americans with infinite wisdom and encouragement. Their voices rang with stereotypical Native American accents and lingo.

Movies do a decent portrayal of an acid trip. The neon lights, the moving inanimate objects, the bubbling sand, the windows transforming into water are very like what I experienced. However, the movies fail to depict the confusion. On the way out to the water, we got a flat tire, but none of us realized until it was decimated. We stopped, but we were on a dirt road in the middle of nowhere; surely there wouldn't be a soul to help us. We should have panicked, but we didn't. I ceased to be aware that I was supposed to be home, and time meant absolutely nothing. There was a rabbit running in the headlights that caused us to begin a philosophical commentary on our way of life. We repeatedly talked of how the little rabbit just kept running but couldn't figure out how to get out of the way. Instead of running to the side out of danger, it couldn't leave the brightness of the headlights. It kept running in the worst position possible: directly in front of the car. At the time, the irony was lost on me, but years later I can more fully appreciate this analogy and how it applies to my own actions and choices.

Beyond all reason, a semi-truck was traveling on this remote dirt road. When it came barreling towards us, we suddenly thought it was a train...headed straight for us! We ran to the sides concerned about how to get our car off the tracks that weren't there. Thunderous horns boomed in my ears while the perceived train-engine sounds eerily crept up on me. I could see lights and a hazy cloud of smoke billowing around what could only be the engine. There was no way we would ever get away in time! We abandoned all hope and ran like orphans to the sides of the railway. We speedily ducked, covering our ears as we cried out in horror just in time to see the truck slow to a stop. We were shocked and a new fit of hysterics caught us. They offered us a ride. We huddled in the truck where there was a husband, wife, and three kids. I thought the woman was preaching religion to us. Perhaps she was. I remember laughing and saying way too loudly that she was a crazy Christian woman; hiding my face in my hands, like a toddler with no object permanence. I evidently thought the same about their ability to hear because I didn't silence nor edit my words. The man asked our names and my boyfriend couldn't remember his... Genuinely forgot. I imagine the couple was afraid. I can't believe they picked us up! They took us to the main road where we began walking when a reservation cop pulled over. This was frightening enough to sober most of us up, but my boyfriend still did not know his name which was cause for great alarm for the police officer. I tried to be as friendly as I was capable. Mostly I tried not to hysterically laugh. Rae's boyfriend commented that the bars between the front and back seats of the officer's vehicle weren't very substantial; he could break through them easily. The cop turned around and snarled, "Try breaking through them with handcuffs on." This sufficiently scared us into silence. He dropped us off at a pool hall where we used the payphone to call one of our friends to come pick us up. We began playing pool, feeling self-conscious with the members of the reservation staring at us stonily. They were nowhere near as nice as the rock-Indians we had previously encountered. We must have been quite the side-show playing with the pool table for what felt like minutes but had to have been at least an hour. Then, suddenly, a maroon Mazda 929 pulled into the parking lot. That was strange considering the only person I knew with such a car was my dad. And then, my stomach dropped. It *was* my dad—and my mom. To this day I'm not sure how that came to be, but we embraced it, thanking them for rescuing us. I know I lied to them. They never would have allowed me to go out to the lake with boys on a school night. We all squeezed into the backseat and my boyfriend kept uttering, "and the poor little rabbit just kept running," making the rest of us burst into laughter. We commented on the vibrant, talking moon as well. My parents must have thought we were crazy or drunk because they had very little knowledge of acid and its effects. I got home and put marshmallows in the microwave tripping out on the bubbling, browning mass. I let them burn and then left them in the microwave all under the watchful eyes of my parents. I imagine I got grounded or scolded or something, but I don't remember any of that. Instead, I remember watching the flowers on my wallpaper dance as I bounced on my water bed I believed was a yacht until the sun came up. All night I smoked, dropping the butts out of the hole I had long since cut in my screen. It was a horrible circumstance, but I scarcely noticed. Like most of my experiences, it would be a decade before I would consider the fear and heartbreak my parents were experiencing two doors down in their bedroom.

Regardless of repercussions, I always had fun, always felt alive, always felt the tickle of the thrill in my stomach residually left over the next day, until I didn't. Though I don't remember the first time I got drunk, I do remember the first time I blacked out. I excitedly went to a high school party with one of my friends. I told my parents that I was going to pizza after a game with my cheerleading team. Instead, we went with unknown older guys to a trailer in the middle of nowhere fully stocked with kegs, beer bongs, and boys... lots and lots of boys. One boy began feeding me beers. I have no idea how many I had. I have vague flashes of throwing up multiple times, getting a ride home from this boy, and throwing up in his car. I know I came home very late, but I don't remember my mom's reaction. She was waiting up by the door when I clumsily attempted to sneak in. I remember the next day being grounded and making up some story about having a Pepsi drinking contest in an effort to explain the throw up all over me. I have no recollection of what really transpired. Surely I smelled like alcohol, but I was so young that it might have been hard not to overlook what was right in front of her. Having been grounded so often, it wasn't a major deal. The major deal was the backlash the next day. My "friends" informed me the following day that I was a slut, and that everybody at the school thought I was a whore and hated me. My friends chastised me for being so drunk and embarrassing. The more they filled me in on my actions from the night before, the more devastated I became. Surely I would be outcast for this. I would never be invited to a party again because of my ridiculous behaviors. I was mortified, ruined. I felt a gnawing pain in the pit of my stomach around the clock. Both my friends who went with me were cold and catty to me for a long time after. Yet my pariah status did little to curb my self-destructive path. Instead, I vowed to control my drunken behavior. What should have been a great deterrent to my destructive behavior instead resulted in a decision to cultivate the control to party as much as I desired. Surprisingly, this is something I mostly accomplished; not to say that I didn't embarrass myself, but I presented myself in such a way as to be cool, not naïve, wild, not unable to handle my liquor. I would rely on this image for the rest of my life. And then later, I would have to pick up the pieces and try to find an identity other than "superior addict."

Larissa

I entered high school nervous but confident, and eager for a fresh start. I became consumed with friends and finding my place in the world, a typical egocentric teenager. Needing to find my niche and improve myself, I tried out different clubs and activities to see where I fit in. I wanted to run for freshman class president, but our adviser talked me into running for Secretary, since no one else had signed up. It felt like a sellout to me, but I knew that I wasn't likely to win and agreed to it.

Music had always been a central part of our home. Both my parents sang and played instruments, and I had followed their lead and picked up the flute. In an effort to improve myself and compete in school, I became much more serious, taking private lessons for many years. Each week my mom drove me on the belt-route to the opposite side of town for flute lessons she financed waiting patiently in the car for me to finish. Some weeks she listened as I wailed about how hard my teacher was on me, making me change my embouchure. One thing I have always appreciated about my mother is that she is not one to give advice. She values independence and put no pressure on me to achieve; my drive was completely self-imposed.

We had a highly competitive, talented band in Nevada which brought out the competitive side of my nature. I challenged my classmate every week for the chair ahead of me and every week she beat me. After I started taking lessons I moved to the first chair. From then on she challenged me every week, but I don't remember ever letting her beat me. Music became my place where I felt at home; thus, band became the center of my social life. I busied myself with marching practice, traveling for competitions and a full schedule of football and basketball games, where we performed. In the winter we switched to concert band and went through another round of rehearsals, performances and competitions. I built within myself an internal metronome and recording device that has carried me through the years. To this day, my ear hears the music, the melody, the beat, but the words are lost to me. I worked hard to qualify for Honor and All-State

Band and achieved all of the goals that I set for myself. I learned that if I worked hard enough I could accomplish whatever I desired.

Those years were marked with both excitement and anxiety throughout the world. We watched in astonishment as the Berlin wall came down and hailed better times ahead. Yet, one mild day in January, while I was walking our dog several blocks from home I heard shouted into the streets that the United States had declared war on Iraq. Soon after my friends were enlisting in the military and later shipping off. Suddenly the future was perilous. We discussed in classes at school the possibility of WW III. The future felt very fluid and precarious; nonetheless, I was young and hopeful.

Most of the time in high school I felt pretty ordinary and plain. I had average brown eyes, average brown hair, an average body and was treated as the dependable and unremarkable teen that I was. It was a time of intense emotions bouncing all over the place and also plenty of lonely moments. A high-achiever, I combated loneliness by throwing myself into academics.

Those high school years were filled with many influential men and women who stood in my life as pillars of strength marking a long-lasting impression upon my character. During my sophomore year, my maternal grandmother had a stroke, leaving her paralyzed and speechless, not expected to live more than 24 hours. My mom left for Utah that same day, and 24 hours turned into 4 years. Mom spent many weeks helping her out, which left me in charge of more at home. I sunk into a depression during those months falling to a low point spiritually, mentally, and emotionally. It didn't help that my best friend had moved away that year. Overwhelmed, I turned to prayer in my bedroom one night after everyone else had gone to sleep. Pleading for strength and happiness, I wanted to be more than an ordinary girl, but felt that I was not special enough. After my prayer, I heard the rain falling outside, a rare occurrence in our high desert, but more importantly, I felt a sense of sadness from my Father in Heaven. I felt love from Him, that he cared for me and was sad that I was struggling. I felt a warmth inside, assuring me of my importance to God and encouragement to continue on, that things would work out for the best. This defining moment kept my feet firmly planted on the path I had started on. Growing, "line upon line, precept upon precept," I was developing faith slowly but surely.

As part of our church youth group I was working on a program called Personal Progress that consisted of making goals, working on accomplishing them, and reporting on the outcome. My Senior Year, I decided I wanted to volunteer at the Reno Suicide Hotline for one of my Young Women's Personal Progress projects. I persisted through forty grueling hours of training, which were required before I could answer phones. These fascinating classes opened my eyes to all the ills of society and bred a strong desire to make a difference. My first call on the Crisis Line was from a popular young man at a nearby high school. I was shocked that someone so likable and seemingly successful had just attempted to take his own life. I also felt overwhelmed by the task of attempting to help him. I stumbled through, but felt elated at the end of the call, feeling that I had been able to help him. I knew from this point on, that I wanted to do something like this the rest of my life. Volunteering there the rest of the year, I learned through first-hand accounts about the effects of addiction, gambling, sexual abuse, domestic violence, depression, and downright despair. Ironically, I was concerned about people in our community, but interacted very little with my own family members.

I survived the rigors and social challenges of high school, and graduated in June of 1991. My parent's financial situation had eased, and my mom had traded her past employment to be a permanent taxicab for all our lessons and events. This was a busy season when all my siblings were pursuing their chosen interests, making life hectic.

I was accepted into BYU. Elated, I prepared to leave for college. Around that time on a beautiful, blooming spring weekend, Elder Henry B. Eyring, then in the Presiding Bishopric of the LDS church, came to reorganize our Stake Presidency. To my amazement, my father was called as a counselor in the new presidency. The president of a stake and his two counselors are responsible for presiding over the dozen or so wards, or congregations, in a geographical area. They administer the church

31

programs, train the members and regularly spend time interviewing and sometime giving counsel to people in the Stake. His work was still quite demanding, and this calling ramped up the number of hours that he was away. I was both proud of him but also at times resented the time taken from our family, though I was less personally impacted than my younger siblings.

The month before I left for college, I received my patriarchal blessing. In the LDS church a patriarchal blessing, sometimes known as an evangelist's blessing is given by a patriarch, which is another calling that is given for life. It is a special one-time blessing, recorded and written down for members to keep and refer to throughout their lives. Containing the individual's lineage, it offers counsel and potential blessings and is viewed as a personal message from God. My patriarchal blessing answered several questions I had been pondering including giving me an answer that a mission was in my future. The only chink in the perfectness of my blessing centered around my future children. I was told that I would have a challenge in raising my children in righteous paths. Those words haunted me for many years, especially when I witnessed what my parents went through with my sister.

Though challenging at first, I have always felt that my life started when I embarked on college. My first year was filled with the typical early adult angst over dating and school. I scheduled my classes on opposite ends of the campus and would have to jog back and forth, only to run into my classroom catching my breath. Not being used to so many people, I fell into the trap of comparing myself with my peers only to fall short. I gradually overcame my fears and reveled in the wonderful teachers and experiences I was having as well as keeping busy going on group dates. I oscillated between being homesick, stressed, exhilarated, overwhelmed, and grateful. BYU campus provided regular meetings where the presiding Apostles of the Church of Jesus Christ of Latter-day Saints came to speak to the student body. It was thrilling to have access to so many presiding officers of our faith, and I even had the opportunity to shake President Thomas S. Monson's hand after a devotional, who later became the Prophet of the church.

Managing to find a ride home from Thanksgiving, I realized how much I really loved my family and was thankful for my upbringing. College was humbling for me, initiating the process of removing my blinders of self-centeredness.

At the end of my first semester I was worn down from the last few days of finals and drove home for Christmas break in a car of stranger. I was glad to have found a lift from the ride board; for the price of gas money, I would be able to spend two weeks at home. We left in the evening for the nine hour drive traveling into pounding snow. I was a little nervous that there were no seat belts in the back seat, but huddled into my jacket trying to relax and sleep. The snow let up a couple miles out of Battle Mountain, and we sped up closer to the speed limit. Without warning the car started spinning wildly out of control on a sheet of black ice. Right before a bridge we careened off the road and plowed through a fence. The car came to a stop upright, narrowly missing the icy stream ahead. My head ached dully from the suitcase that flew up from behind, but I knew that our lives had been spared. Hours later a highway patrolman helped fill our blown tires and followed us as we made our way back to Battle Mountain. We sat in the Owl Café the rest of the night. In the early morning hours I opened my scriptures and started where I had left off the day before in the *Book of Mormon*, coming to an epiphany:

"I say unto you, [Larissa], that if you should render all the thanks and praise which your whole soul has power to possess, to that God who has created you, and has kept and preserved you, and has caused that ye should rejoice, and has granted that ye should live in peace one with another—I say unto you that if ye should serve him who has created you from the beginning, and is preserving you from day to day, by lending you breath, that ye may live and move and do according to your own will, and even supporting you from one moment to another— I say, if ye should serve him with all your whole souls yet ye would be unprofitable servants. And behold, all that he requires of you is to keep his commandments..." (Mosiah 2:20-22).

I emerged from this event changed and more committed to following and obeying God. I looked for more ways to serve in the community around me during my second semester. I finished up my freshman year of college and came home for the summer changed. Lenaya finished up sixth grade right after I came home for the summer and was headed to middle school, where all of her undertakings would soon come to the surface.

Lenaya

I was avoiding a relationship with God, but still my parents tried all they could to help me feel the spirit. They insisted on scripture study when I was home. They expected me to go to church on Sundays, youth activities during the week, and Church Girl's camp. I resented them for it, though I still didn't feel like I could simply decline. That notion felt far more perplexing to me than to jump out my window and run; perhaps forever. Instead I kept up appearances which I often thought was the only thing of importance to my parents. Looking back I realize this is a justification; another way for me to feel traumatized and dramatic. I swore I wouldn't set foot at Girls' Camp without Rae. Though a nonmember, she often attended my mandated meetings with me, though more regularly we skipped them. She went to camp with me my second year.

Unfortunately, we were there looking for mischief and making a stab at pre-high-school popularity. There was no shortage of very popular high-school girls in my stake. Rae had them all dialed in by the time we arrived. She knew who was who at which school and we carefully treaded in close-proximity to these queen bees. Interestingly, with a few exceptions, these were nice, spiritual girls. Often I wonder at my inability to see that they were leaders without compromising their morals or lifestyles. Still, I was oblivious and instead tried to impress them with my rebellious, cool ways. We partied a little, sneaking off when we could to smoke a joint or cigarette, but at girl's camp, they keep a pretty close watch so our setting was often compromised. Something that will always stand out to me about that trip was that, despite my bad attitude, deceitful intentions, and poor priorities, I still felt the spirit. There were countless moments during that week when I had to fight the tears stinging at my eyes because the Holy Ghost was so present, and so powerful. I knew what this felt like. I recognized these promptings even if I couldn't articulate them. I also understood what I was certain I didn't: the gospel brings happiness. For several moments, a warm and soothing sensation tickled away my defiance and seized my emotions offering me a glimpse into the experience many of the other girls must have felt the entire time. I fought these feelings, and it would take many years before I could be certain that the glimpse was true, that righteous living does bring peace. But I am still incredibly surprised that those young girls had enough faith for the spirit to penetrate even my thickest walls. The Lord made Himself known to me, even when I was in the grips of Satan's clutch.

Larissa

"True doctrine, understood, changes attitudes and behavior. The study of the doctrines of the Gospel will improve behavior quicker than a study of behavior will improve behavior. That is why we stress so forcefully the study of the doctrines of the gospel" (Boyd K. Packer).

Last night my two-year old burst into our room, stumbling through the dark with shouts of, "Pee pee's coming!" I groaned inwardly as my comatose body refused to budge. I heard my husband struggle out of the bed and relaxed into my pillow, safe in the knowledge that he would deal with this episode. From our bathroom, I heard her screams of, "JUST ME! JUST ME!" She insisted on asserting her independence even in the middle of the night and didn't want help pulling down her pants or climbing onto the toilet. In the very same moment she was reaching out to us, she was also pushing us away.

This isn't much different than an addict. The first time that I had any inkling that Lenaya had a problem was when I talked to her on the phone around her 13th birthday in early November. I called home from my college dorm to talk to my parents. They were gone, so I had a conversation with her instead. She was suddenly on my radar. I wrote in my journal that night that I knew she was a good enough girl but her friends weren't the best influence, and she was too swayed by their opinions. She confided to me that she had some bad grades but hadn't shown my parents her report card yet.

The previous summer break I had been home in name only. Between my seasonal job and a pretty serious summer romance, I slept in my bed and ate only a few meals at home, probably adding to my parents' worry. Back at school with the summer over and my romance cooled, I began to see beyond myself with a little more clarity. My *New Testament* class journal filled up with the spiritual strength I was gleaning through life and my classes. In contrast, I could feel that things were slipping at home. My dad had started working at a new law firm with a significant increase in salary. I felt some of my younger siblings had become more materialistic, and there was a strained spirit in the home. I blamed this shift on a sense of entitlement or prosperity, but later came to understand that the secrecy and stress of Lenaya's actions were taking their toll.

My second year, I felt more at home on BYU's campus. I looked people in the eye while walking to class. I anticipated the ringing tones of the Carillon Bell Tower. I spent more hours studying in the Library and stopped for ice cream occasionally at the Creamery. I was also lonelier that year. Many weekends I walked across campus to the bus stop and made the three hour, $3 bus ride to Clearfield, which led to my extended family. I found comfort visiting my aunt, uncle and cousins, usually staying with my grandpa in his nearby trailer. I always tried to visit my grandma at the rest home. Her stroke had left her permanently paralyzed, losing nearly all her speech.

I enjoyed visiting my grandpa. He was fifty when my mom was born, living a colorful life before he married and had two daughters. My favorite story he told was of breaking horses until a horse named Kit broke him....literally. He lay in a hospital for nine months. When gangrene set in his leg they almost amputated. But they decided to drip a new medication called penicillin on his wound that saved his leg, though you could see the indentation on his leg where doctors had cut out much of the bone.

That year was an important one for me because it was the year I met my future husband, though I didn't know it at first. We met in a dance class. Nathan noticed me from the start and asked me to dance the first dance of every class. I was flattered but also a little wary. He was a year younger with a mission on the near horizon, and that made him feel a little safer to me, as I was determined to go on a mission.

My grandma passed away soon after we met. Nathan took me to the World of Dance performance and then partway through brought me back to my dorm to meet my parents, so they could drive me to my grandma's funeral. They liked him from the start and I enjoyed chatting with them on the drive up to Clearfield.

Funerals are always hard, but I was relieved that after four years of suffering her anguish was ended. "Her missionary," Melvin Farnsworth spoke at her funeral. He told the story of her legacy to us. My grandma was living in a small town in Nebraska. There were no missionaries or branches of the church in her town, but he and his companion were visiting on a preparation day when they felt impressed to go tracting. They met my grandma and gave her a copy of the Book of Mormon. She started reading it that night and didn't sleep the rest of the night so she could finish it. While reading she felt impressed that she should quit smoking, and she did permanently. When the missionaries returned the following preparation day they were shocked to see her absolutely converted. They taught her all the missionary lessons during the next few weeks and baptized her. Just a month after she was baptized, the mission president closed her area, and she had no contact with the church for an entire year.

After that year, they moved to a larger Nebraska town where there was a branch of the church. She was active the rest of her life. My grandpa soon followed her example and served in leadership. My mom and her sister both were baptized when they were eight, and my mom never doubted the testimony of her mother and was always a believer. They retired to Utah where she was able to work in the temple up till her stroke. Her actions laid a strong foundation for my family as well as me personally.

At the funeral I worried about Lenaya. She was trying to grow up too fast and appeared to be influenced by her friends. I worried about Nicholas. He seemed so depressed and pessimistic about everything. I worried about my mom. She lacked the capacity to cry through her sadness but seemed more angry and resentful. I didn't know how bad things would ultimately be, but I could see trouble was brewing.

Lenaya

When I started high school a few months later, it didn't take Rae and me very long to establish ourselves among the cool, older, wild crowd. We were as unmanageable as ever. Rae started to gain more sense for a while, but most of my friends would turn a blind eye to me before long. There was distance between me and my old friends because we had been separated for the last year while I attended a different Middle School. Perhaps they couldn't bear to see what I'd become, or our friendships weren't as strong as I had believed. Whatever the case, I didn't care because it was Rae and me against the world. Except that wasn't true; I still wanted to be popular, no matter what I pretended. I didn't want anyone to have fun without me. I still don't! It was easy for me to make new friends; I have the gift of friendship. One of my talents is to make people feel special. Even as a little girl I could make others think they were the most important to me. The flipside of that of course is that it's always been extremely important to me to be known, and recognized as a good friend. So losing my old group of friends should have wounded me more than I remember it hurting. Looking back I realize, that must have been because I didn't feel much at all.

Reckless doesn't begin to describe the great lengths I went to in order to get wasted. I would stop at nothing. On a family trip to Utah I managed to meet some shady looking guys at the neighborhood pool in my grandpa's trailer park. I convinced the gangsters (about fifteen years my senior) to pick me and Rae up down the street from my aunt's house. We went to parties where we got utterly decimated night after night. I was promiscuous, and even managed to get shot with a bb gun. I didn't care; it was all in the name of fun. I felt utterly invincible. I think back on my life now and cringe in horror as I imagine all the possibilities of what might have been. I truly am a miracle with no reason to be alive.

The sneaking out and doing whatever I pleased worked for a time until I yearned for the freedom my friends had in the daylight hours, so I ran away. I guess at fourteen everything is much more dramatic than when you're older, but it felt so permanent. I brought a bag with my makeup in it and any money I could scrounge up. Then, after much persuasion from two of my girlfriends, I walked

out the front door. I remember how my feet felt pounding the
pavement. They seemed to slap anxiously with every step. I
wondered if this was the beginning of a new life. In my mind I
would never return home: a life of dumpsters, brown bags, and
dreadlocks loomed in my future. I ran to a friend's house
breathlessly; afraid, relieved. I felt like a child once out of my home.
My parents wasted no time contacting the authorities whom I
attempted to dodge at first. Frustrated, I wished my parents would
just leave me alone, but they would never give up, and for that I was
bitter. How many children are there alone in this world? Neglected?
Abused? Completely invisible? And there I was, attempting to force
my parents to let me go. I yearned to have the freedoms of my
friends with divorced parents, who lacked parental supervision. I saw
nothing as it really was. I couldn't for an instant fathom why it was
preferable to have a stable home and family. I envied wild eyed
rebellious teenagers and cloudy, listless bums. I was turned around
and incapable of recognizing it. I stayed at random houses, hooked
up with random guys, and chopped my blond hair off dying it brown
in an immature effort at disguise. Tears of indignation, fear, and
vanity slowly rolled down my cheeks as my friend took the kitchen
shears to my beloved blonde locks. It was exciting, but I was annoyed
that my parents kept looking for me. Many friends' parents didn't
want to turn me in, but refused to harbor me as well. I spent a lot of
time at houses with single, working parents. I bounced around a lot,
but my only concern was not being able to get party products. I was
used to smoking weed in the parking lot or hooking up with alcohol
and drugs outside of school and church hallways. I had to rely heavily
on my friends, and not all of them thought partying was as important
as I did. I would get to a friend's house and immediately try to figure
out the best way to get high without it seeming like I was a fiend.
This demon crept up on me so subtly that I didn't even know it was
there. I always tried to play it cool for fear I would seem like a junky.
Years later, when I realized that was what I had become, I no longer
confused the horror with happiness.

After about a week, Rae convinced me to go to the McGee
center —a runaway shelter. I was promised that they couldn't contact
my family without my permission. I thought I could just go there to
live and hang out. Well, that was a lie. In actuality, once there I was
stripped of my clothing, my makeup, my friends; and my family was

contacted. We had bed time, and we were locked in. While in the processing room, Rae told me to run for it, but we were surrounded. Once I had willingly gone inside, there was no way out. I was less than thrilled at the prospect of being stuck in there: nasty food, sanitarium bedrooms and living rooms. I recall there were some board games and a TV... though nobody had free reign of it. I also met people who were there due to *real* hardships and true homelessness. I felt like a phony. As usual, I implied a much harder existence than I had ever actually had. Our long-time home teacher (a church calling where men and women are assigned to visit and check up on multiple families to make sure there aren't needs not being met) Brother Loveland came to the McGee center and talked with me. He was so kind. He expressed great love for me while both encouraging and facilitating my return home. I was met with both angry hostility and fawning love when I came home. I had learned a few things while away. I knew never to return to that halfway house. I also learned that I could leave. I could always leave.

Larissa

"And now, my brethren, I wish from the inmost part of my heart, yea with great anxiety even unto pain, that ye would hearken unto my words, and cast off your sins, and not procrastinate the day of your repentance. But that you would humble yourselves before the Lord, and call upon His holy name, and watch and pray continually" (Book of Mormon, Alma 13: 27-28).

Both Lenaya and Nicholas had become very rebellious, and I didn't like the way they were changing. My sensitivity to the Spirit was changing, and I wanted to share what I had learned with them. My third and as it turned out to be final year of college was much more comfortable. I shared a room with my cousin, where we had a wonderful camaraderie. I was more familiar with the workload and enjoyed the daily trudge up the hill to campus.

Just a couple months into the year, I sat in a basketball game with some friends and felt my head start throbbing, my muscles start aching, and my throat become sore. I crashed into bed that night but only felt worse the next morning when I awoke. I debated all morning whether I should go to the health center and finally decided to call my mom to ask her advice. When my father answered the phone at 11:00 am on a workday, I instantly knew something was wrong. He was home discussing Lenaya's situation with my mom. Her grades had gone down, and she had gotten into trouble with some friends recently, though he was vague about what kind of trouble.

My heart sank as they discussed their options of homeschooling or transferring her to another school. They had already started dropping her off at school and picking her up at lunch. She had lost all phone privileges. She was so good-natured at home that it was difficult to comprehend some of the things she was doing. I was also upset, because the family cat, Boo had died that morning. I was flooded by happier memories, and I cried the rest of the morning.

I got into a doctor the next day and finally started to feel better with antibiotics. I spent some time pondering where I was at in my life and feeling truthfully it was the happiest and most peaceful I had ever been. I talked to Lenaya the next day to see how her birthday was. She told me she was switching schools and couldn't ever see her friends again. I worried that she would completely rebel, but I didn't see what other choice there was.

I came home for Thanksgiving break soon after. We did some fun activities as a family, but to say that it was a happy vacation would have been a lie. My parents were heartbroken, and their emotions affected everyone, though they purposely tried to suppress it. I experienced more sorrow that week than I ever had before. One night I was alone in my room crying and emotionally drained. I felt as if there was no hope for my family and that all was lost. I prayed for courage and comfort. As I was praying, I suddenly felt as if someone was hugging me. I finally understood what it meant to be encircled by the love of God, and to feel His comforting embrace. All was well, though I would have more trials ahead.

Back at school, I wrote essays, took tests, attended concerts, and played with my friends and roommates. Being away from the contentious spirit in our home, I started to feel happier.

Christmas was right around the corner, and again my parents worked hard to make it fun. They took us to see *Cool Runnings* and planned family outings. One night when my parents had meetings, I went jogging with Lenaya. She talked about her new school. She didn't like it very much even though she already had a lot of new friends. She told me stories of her friends that were in a big fight, and I was scared for her and the people she hung out with. Still, she had a good heart.

One bleak windy day, an older man knocked on the door asking for work to earn some money. My mom said they didn't need anything done and turned him away. My siblings and I pleaded with her to find something for him to do. She finally consented, and we ran to find him. He and his wife raked and cleaned up the back yard, and Lenaya made them lunch.

I had a chance over the break to talk to Nicholas about the types of families we wanted to have one day. I worried less about him. I didn't know until decades later, that he was always aware of what my sister was up to. They were best friends, and he covered for her. He must have been so torn up with anxiety for her, but his intense loyalty kept him silent. He also questioned the existence of God for many years and had many unhappy years, before he came to know of His reality.

We were all affected by her choices. Cami was increasingly independent, and Jed complained to me one night, "Everybody fights, and I'm getting sick."

The next couple of semesters flew by, and before I knew it I was graduating from college. The day before I graduated I received my mission call to Alaska. I was so excited and anxious about what the future held. I had three months before the start date, so I went home to recuperate after a grueling year.

My body was worn down after working a night job my last semester, and I slept twelve hours nearly every night. I hadn't felt that rested in years. I read a few books, worked on a counted cross-stitch, and took some ceramics classes. Though I felt sorrow over some of the attitudes of my brother and sister, I still had many sweet times with them and hoped they would mature over time. These positive interactions started to wane the longer I was at home.

One night we were sitting around the dinner table for a hurried dinner, before dad headed off to stake meetings and mom went to her church meetings. Lenaya announced that her friend Shannon invited her to go to a birthday dinner with her family. Shortly after, my parents head to their meetings, and dad discreetly pulled me aside and asked me to make sure and meet Shannon's older brother, a student at UNR, who would be picking Lenaya up.

Soon after they left, Lenaya informed me that Shannon's brother didn't know which house it was, so she would wait outside. I decided that it was a good time to go through some boxes in the garage and followed her out. Not soon after, she told me that she should probably go wait at the end of the court, so they could see her. I asked her to help me carry in some of my boxes and she willingly agreed. After that, I sat myself down in the front yard with a complete view of our cul-de-sac announcing how beautiful the weather was and started telling Lenaya stories that I had heard about Alaska. She conveniently heard the phone and ran into the house, though she must have had better ears than me.

She came back out and told me that Nicholas wanted me. "What for?"

"He wants you to walk to the Chapin's house with him." Amazing that he had never in his life made that sort of request before.

"No way. I'm not walking all the way over there." I returned to my stories.

A couple of minutes later a truck pulled up with two boys in it. She seemed to recognize them, though she claimed to have never met them before. I followed her to the pick-up to ask them a few questions. One of the boys was holding a cigarette which he discreetly hid under the seat.

"What school do you go to?"

"Sparks High,"

"Reed High," they answered nearly in unison.

"Where are you coming from?"

One of the boys sneered, "From home." What? Not the tutoring session that Lenaya had described. I started to feel confused and had a sick feeling in the pit of my stomach.

"Lenaya, you absolutely are not going with these guys!"

She proceeded to throw a tantrum. Before they even pulled out of the court, another vehicle drove up and a girl jumps out whom, "just happened to be passing by." She and Lenaya both give the boys a look of, "Sorry" and walked into the house together. They hid out in her room over furtive secret phone calls. Then Lenaya received a phone call and proceeded to talk very loudly and clearly, so that I could hear, "Shannon's mom was going to meet us at the restaurant. My sister is so untrusting that she didn't believe it was her brother picking me up! I was mixed up about what school he goes to, but for some reason he got a variance to Sparks. Yea, I can't believe that Shannon showed up at the same time. It was perfect timing!"

I wasn't stupid, and I didn't like to be deceived. It only made me trust her less. I hated being the mean "babysitter." I just felt sad.

Two days later my dad took Jed and me camping to the

beautiful grass and wildflowers of Jackson Meadows. The view was stunning, and we cooked some tasty food over our campfire. We fished and hiked. The next day we drove home and went to Jed's soccer game. We came home to the shocking news that Lenaya had run away. She was grounded as usual, and at 3:30 she went outside for a minute and never came back. She called at 7:00 pm and said, "You don't need to worry about me, I'm okay," and hung up.

At first, I felt numb from shock. Then I became so angry that I physically started shaking, but I vented by furiously storming around, cleaning the house. That passed, and I had a fit of sadness weeping for a long time. Finally, I just waited, sick inside. We sat at home, until the police arrived and filled out a report. I had a huge headache, but I couldn't sleep. I felt a massive, almost unreasonable, responsibility to fix everything. It was hard to live with the uncertainty. I couldn't imagine what grief my parents were feeling. My mom especially was having a hard time.

Days passed and every time the phone rang, I jumped. Every slamming car door commanded my attention. When I went to the grocery store, every face seemed to resemble Lenaya's. My hands never stopped shaking, partly from fatigue. I felt like throwing up from the sick feeling in my stomach. I had a throbbing headache from crying, but at each thought tears welled back up in my eyes. It was hard to imagine that this grief was nothing compared to the sorrow that Heavenly Father and Jesus Christ felt.

All we knew about Lenaya was from Rae, her friend. Rae finally called after the police persisted in questioning her and told them some story. I knew she was lying. The stake presidency came over and gave us each some great blessings. Mine was for peace and comfort. I was told to continue being an example and working toward righteous goals. I just needed to relax and get some sleep.

I was most worried about my mom. She didn't want to go with me to the temple that weekend, when I was going to go for my first time. I'm sure she didn't want to be out of town, where she couldn't be reached if Lenaya was found. I was physically and emotionally depleted, but I still felt peace from the Lord.

After a few days, my brothers went back to school and a detective was finally assigned to the case. Both he and the school guidance counselor pulled Rae out of every class asking, "Where's Lenaya?" Rae finally convinced Lenaya to call the counselor, who persuaded her to go to a half-way house. Lenaya didn't realize that she couldn't talk to her friends when she got there and had to be checked out by her parents. She reluctantly met them with a counselor and worked through things.

The biggest shock to me was that Lenaya cut her hair five inches and dyed it brown. When she saw me there she called me vulgar names and told me that she hated me. She was glad that I was leaving, because our parents were too "stupid" to catch her. I was furious at her and cried at odd times. I found myself staring at her picture thinking about how she used to be. She really was always a loveable person. I loved her and wished I could make her see that.

Unsure how I would react when Lenaya finally came home; I just gave her a big hug and said I was glad she was home. There was an uneasy truce in our home, though it was very strained.

A week later someone stayed with the younger kids, while my parents and I went to Oakland for my first visit to the temple. It was wonderful, especially when contrasted with the previous weekend. We shopped at Burlington Coat Factory for the rest of my mission clothes. A few weeks later we celebrated my 21st birthday and then in November I entered the Missionary Training Center.

It is difficult to describe the pain I felt watching a loved one stray. Especially when I was younger I lacked perspective and saw very little beyond the situation. The Lord tells us to "wait upon" Him and then he will come to us. I sometimes think that the Lord answers our silly little prayers, so that we keep on praying for the big things when they seem like they aren't being answered. I often felt that my prayers and fasting for Lenaya were not answered. The situation was hopeless in my limited sight. I wanted an instant answer to prayer. I wanted an Alma the Younger conversion that was immediate and complete. My faith was tested when the answer didn't come when or how I wanted it. My prayers changed over time, but I never stopped praying.

Only later would I discover that our prayers were answered daily and sometimes minute by minute.

I also wondered about how my prayers could be answered without taking away Lenaya's agency. I feared that she would never choose to change. We hear David O. McKay's oft-quoted standard, "No other success can compensate for failure in the home," and believe that our wayward child represents a failure. I consider failure as giving up on that child and giving up on the Lord in our prayers.

Lenaya

I ran away any time I didn't get my way from then on. My parents literally had no control of me. I knew it; they knew it. If they grounded me, I'd walk out the front door. If they told me no, I'd walk out the back. No matter what, I felt I was in charge and they could no longer dictate anything about my life. Once, I had run away telling my parents that I wouldn't return unless I no longer had to take piano lessons. Imagine the insanity. It was around Christmas and I called my parents from a pay phone to conceal my location. By then they had evolved in the technological world and bought a caller id. It was the first I'd ever seen supplied for just such an occasion. As a result, I had to be careful to use unidentifiable phones. Sometimes I'd simply say, "I'm fine," and hang up. I suppose it offered some kind of a crutch from the guilt that was ruining my vacations. My dad whispered that Christmas would be here soon, and my friends wouldn't be able to buy me nice gifts the way that my family would. He desperately clung to a rope that I was hanging from. In his anxiety he attempted anything he believed would successfully bring me home. I was irate. I remember yelling at him on the phone and, later, scoffing to my friends about how my dad thought he could *buy* my love. In reality, I knew him. I knew his heart. I knew he would have done anything in the world for me. But I also knew that it was much easier to justify my actions if I could hate him, for any reason. If I could only convince my heart that *his* priorities were messed up, it would make hurting him so much less painful. Of course, there were always drugs. I always could numb the sorrow welling up within my soul. I could squelch the sadness with a defiant puff of a pipe or a cigarette. I could pop pills and call it family. I could inhale deeply and call it love. I could jump on a motorcycle and call it happiness. There was no shortage of the things I could do... particularly when I was a runaway. I had quickly made connections with some meth "cookers" who kept me in constant supply so long as I sold. I was able to earn a little money and have a never-ending supply of drugs.

Another time I had agreed upon a meeting place and time to return home because I had run out of places to hide. Through our conversation, my parents discovered where I was and came to get me. Unfortunately, Rae and I had recently dropped three hits of acid each. Rae got into it with her mom, who was in failing health. She pushed her down as we jumped out the window and tried to make a break for it. My parents were coincidentally in the driveway right at that moment. We tried to fight, to run, to escape. It didn't work; they held us there on the dilapidated cement of Rae's driveway of the house her parents had purchased for the sole purpose of enabling her to attend school with me. My parents turned into hideous monsters right before my eyes. Yet, all I could do was laugh. I found it hilarious that these beasts were my parents. They threatened to have me arrested. In fact, Rae did get arrested and taken to juvenile hall. But I didn't. My parents took me home. I wonder what the conversation was like while we drove. A decade later, my older brother Nic told me that my little brother, Jed, made the distinction to him after school one day when I'd left: "Lenaya is gone… you know, the kind of gone when she doesn't come home and the police come over." It must have been very confusing for the then 7-year-old. Beyond that, it must have been intensely disheartening to Nic who so loyally covered for me probably often squelching his own broken heart. He dealt with me running away so many times before he got fed up. I ran into him at our high school's graduation while an escapee. He wouldn't talk to me. I was indignant, outraged, hurt. I couldn't believe he would take *their* side. How could he? He was supposed to be on *my* side! Of course by then, there was no such thing as my side anymore. He had wrecked my parent's car by then and done some serious soul searching. Right when he began dangling on the fence of rebellion with me, this accident saved his life. I remember him telling me that he spoke with God while he waited for the police to arrive on the scene. I didn't know what that meant exactly, but I was pretty sure he would no longer be straddling the line of righteousness. I still considered him my best friend though. He was the only one who knew all of me and had to love me anyway. Everyone else knew pieces, but not me in my entirety. Recently I found a letter written to him long ago. In it I tell him,

"Nick, First off, I just want to let you know that I love you and I miss you. I really wish you could put yourself in my shoes and try to understand the way I feel about things. I also wish I could put myself in your shoes and learn what you're feeling and what's in your life. Unfortunately, neither of us can do that, so

the best I can do is to write to you what's on my mind. I'm sorry I'm not the way you want me to be. Believe me, it's not the design I'd hoped for myself. But you can't hold a grudge against me for that forever. Everybody has problems, some more than others, and everybody deals with those problems in different ways. It's not fair to hate somebody because of the way they deal with things. If I learned anything of importance while I was gone, it's that you can't live without a family. They are your entire support. They are a part of your life and they make you who you are. Without them, certain characteristics begin to wither away because your family isn't there to nurture them. And eventually, you have no sense of who you are and what you're all about. If you continue to shut me out of your life and blame me for all of your problems then we'll both lose. You've always been a part of me and the only family member I really turned to. I'm not asking you to forget, I'm only asking you to forgive."

I don't remember writing it. I scarcely remember the circumstance except that my brother was angry, and hurt, and wasn't allowing me to play the accustomed victim. I genuinely believed that I was happy and my family was my obstacle to truly free bliss. Yet, even in this bipolar letter, I can see that I knew. I recognized that I was hurting my family. I felt the disorder in their lives: *my* disorder. I pointed the finger at my brother so that I didn't have to feel the blame, to see that it was *I*, not them, that was doing the punishing. It must have been intolerable not to tell on me, which eventually he did. I tarnished our relationship along with any closeness Jed might have felt to me at the time. He was only eight-years-old when I left. With a child that age now, it's alarming to realize how much was expected of him to understand. I was oblivious to the situations of my loved ones.

Often, the only thing keeping me alive was the prayers of family and friends; wings softly holding my head up and maintaining my heartbeat for the next long decade. After returning home from being a runaway once again, I decided to climb *in* my window and awaken to normalcy. I scaled the fence stopping on the shingles I knew by heart. I looked out over our safe *cul de sac* and felt something close to invigoration coupled with rage. The street light flickered in the crisp, inviting air. I was hallucinating, envisioning something of the injustices of the world; the easy trials for some while others suffered. I felt like a drug induced vigilante. I gazed at the pavement and felt the weight of all things beyond my reach buckle over me. I felt ever so sensitive; fragile. I silently crawled to the window and heard my family in there talking; waiting in my room for my return; talking about how clueless I was. The intensity of the situation was unbearable; once more I felt trapped and hopeless. I ran to the edge of the tiles on the roof envisioning myself jumping, taking flight, a bird freeing myself from all the hurt, the injustice, the web I had spindled around myself. And then, a voice urgently yelled in my head, "LENAYA!!! REALITY CHECK!!! THIS IS REAL!!! YOU CANNOT FLY!!!! I sat on the edge of the roof, dangling my legs as I sobbed with the realization of what I had almost done. I wasn't suicidal; though I'm not sure anyone would ever have believed that had I truly been a bird that night. Exhausted, I decided it didn't matter that my family was waiting for me. I boldly ambled to the window and, without hesitation, slid the window open. When I climbed in, the room was empty; the house silent with the exception of the familiar noises of deep breathing, ticking of clocks, and the careful "tch tch tch" of the refrigerator downstairs.

The first time I ever tried crank (methamphetamines) was early in my freshman year of high school. The weather was cooler than summer, but warm like spring. The air was sunny but had the first crisp indication that fall was coming. The weather is so ingrained in my mind that for a decade every time the season changed I would fiend. The start of a new season persistently makes me feel a little jittery and anxious. Rae had met a guy, a junior, who had some "peanut butter crank" and offered to let us try it on our lunch break. We went near the school to his apartment. I crossed my arms and hugged myself feeling intense anticipation and distress. I uncomfortably shifted my eyes around the room that seemed to meet the kitchen, living room, dining room, and bathroom simultaneously. I briefly wondered about the lives in this house. How did we come to be here? How did this boy manage to find himself snorting lines of meth off of his family's kitchen counter? Our benefactor eagerly chopped some lines and placed them across the counter top. Rae and I were moderately stoned, about to come down and get the munchies. I was taking Mini Thins to try to assuage the hunger. We each put our heads down with half straws in our hands and snorted a line. It burned like habanero peppers being forced down our gullets. My eyes watered, my nose ran, there was the most disgusting taste sliding down the back of my throat. I tried to swallow; I tried not to puke; I tried to look halfway cool while doing it. It tasted like exhaust and antifreeze burnt together in an unalterably horrific concoction. Then, I began to feel…high. so. very. high. He offered a rock on tin foil for us to smoke. He taught us the art of not holding it in as long as you would a hit of weed or hash. With each exhale I felt my brain rushing out of my head. I felt light-headed, and airy, and fast, and invincible, and wonderful. I began singing, "Raindrops on roses and whiskers on kittens." I laughed, and the munchies that had been chasing me only moments earlier disappeared. The crash I had been expecting vanished. When the euphoria from the marijuana wore off, I got out my glass pipe and brought the euphoria back to my cloudy mind. I relished in the dawning comprehension that I could smoke weed for the rest of forever and not experience any of the negative side effects. I would never have to come down again!!! I chain smoked cigarettes until my throat swallowed itself leaving burnt powder in the place of flesh. I drank a bud light and felt every bubble produced from the carbonation as it wetted my sandpaper mouth. We were awake for fifty-two hours. I remember telling my older brother. I remember his dismay. The expression on his face was haunting and yet, I remember not… caring…at…all. Rae called later the first night of being awake. She was paranoid and agitated; I was scrubbing my room thrilled with a task to complete besides the hours of solitaire, and Pink Floyd on repeat. She told me that she never wanted to do it again. She hated it and was so disappointed in herself. I made a split second decision that if she truly wouldn't do it again, we would no longer be friends. I would *never* stop. Panicked, I called another friend to see if she was consumed instantaneously. She loved it; she was my new best friend. How fickle it sounds to me as I write this; how disgustingly inconsiderate, but I felt as if my dreams had come true. I dropped seven lbs. in three days. I didn't come down off my high, and I never had to sleep again. I painted and listened to music and dreamed with my eyes awake. Eventually, it wore off and I welcomed slumber after three satisfying days of ecstasy.

I don't want to downplay the role my eating disorder played in all of this. Many of my addictions were a direct result of being consumed by losing weight. For fourteen years I was utterly devoured with the desire to be skinny. Every night, as soon as I spotted the first star, I would say, "Starlight star bright first star I see tonight, I wish I may I wish I might have the wish I wish tonight. I wish I was skinny. Please let me be skinny," even when I was 110 lbs. I thought of nothing else at times. Always, somewhere in the back of my mind I thought of ways I could eat and still be skinny. I would plan my binges around parties, weddings, etc. I would eat, throw up, then go outside and smoke a cigarette. My mom caught me once (probably knew all along) and pulled me into her room to confront me about how unhealthy it was, this pattern I was in. I bold faced lied and denied all allegations. She assured me that I wasn't in trouble, but I had no room in my mind for anyone to know about this embarrassing pastime. Plus, I worried that she would find ways to control my eating patterns. She said, "You need to eat something." I refused explaining I'd already eaten. "You've thrown it all up!" she retorted. I assured her I had eaten lunch. "It doesn't work that way!" But it did work that way…that was the *only* way it worked. I refused to hear anything she said, panic stricken as I plotted ways to prevent her from hearing what I thought I was so carefully hiding. I wish I could convey the sadness, the heartache, the physical and mental anguish associated with these years. It's next to impossible to truly understand what it's like to have stabbing pains every waking moment in your abdomen, rushing to make it to the toilet before you have an accident, never being able to tell a soul. I can't say how many thousands of times I put on a happy face and pretended nothing was wrong, when really; I was excreting blood by the bucketful and in agonizing pain. For years I ate nothing but rice and toast and then took thirty to fifty laxatives a night. Truly, it felt like I was dying. I had no regard for my body. I thought it, along with food, was the enemy; the most pernicious kind because you simply cannot live without them. And the pangs of hunger grew so familiar; I detested drinking a glass of water for how it dismantled my flat, empty belly.

Crank was fixing my incessant need for food, but I hardly recognized the extreme weight loss I was achieving. One day I entered a nameless class. The season was changing; the days were still hot, but fall was upon us. I'm not sure I had attended the class yet a single time. I had smoked weed all morning while snorting lines of crank around the clock for countless days. I was wearing blue denim overall shorts with a navy blue and white striped tank top that exposed my midriff. Hoops in varying sizes peppered the seven holes in my ears. I had chugged vodka and cranberry in a bathroom stall prior to entering the room, and one of my best friends from seventh grade sat next to me in a class full of strangers. She looked at me with pure horror on her face; an expression that will forever be etched in my memory. Tears welled in her eyes as she said, "What's happening to you? You're shriveling up!" I looked down at my crossed legs and, for the first time in all of my recollection I could *see* myself. I looked like a skeleton; after a lifetime of only seeing fat. It was shocking, jarring, wildly surprising. But instead of being horrified, I was relieved. I felt victorious, but I also felt so out of touch with reality having never seen before what she pointed out to me; what everyone must have seen for so long. I got up and walked out of class never to return to it.

Final Escape

The people look and see a looser,
A teenage drugged out, smoking boozer,
But their eyes tell lies and not the truth,
Their suspicions are their only proof.

They don't see the girl she used to be,
Smart, religious, a good family.
She was sweet, cheerful and tried to be nice,
That first try at drugs, and she paid the price.

Addiction seemed to take over her mind,
She couldn't stop at one little line,
It got worse and worse 'till that's all she had.
At first it was fun, in the end it's just sad.

She sits alone in her room filled with hate and rage,
Wanting to scream 'cause her room's like a cage.
Same life, new day, the same harsh blow.
The pain inside her seems to grow.
She'll let no one hear her screams for help,
She needs a way to be herself.

She dreams of a place where no one knows her name,
With different people things won't be the same.

She's lost all feeling and has no care,
She finds emotions with drugs and stale beer.
A little more pot and a little more crank,
She smiles and says, "that's all it takes."

Some time has gone by, she's alone again,
Sniffing cocaine through her new silver pen.
She looks out the window, wanting to fly,
To spread wings and soar, alone in the sky;
To escape all the jails that exist in her life,
And start somewhere new, in a world that she likes.

The desire is more than she can bear,
She looks around at the only thing there.
She weighs her options, but her mind's not clear.
She chops one more line and drinks one more beer.

She does more and more, drug after drug,
Tears spill out as she falls on the rug,
Her little brother comes in to play,
He silently watches, her final escape.

-Lenaya Frey 1994 (14 yrs. old)-

Because of the ridiculous amount of absences (my attendance indicated I made it to class a grand total of twenty-seven days that semester) my mom and dad threatened the most fearful of all punishments: homeschool. I pled and begged and cried and promised that I would go to school. They agreed on the condition that if I missed any more school, they were pulling me out and homeschooling me. The following Monday I was dead set on going to all my classes. I was genuinely afraid of the repercussions if I didn't make it. I got dropped off at the church for seminary; walked in the front door and out the back to smoke weed with my friends on the way to school as was my usual routine. I had already snorted lines in my room before leaving the house so I was euphoric and fast.

If I squeezed enough partying in between classes then surely I would be able to stay for the duration. I went to first period: math of some sort. Years later one of my friends would tell me how the teacher made it a running wager if I was going to make it to class or not. I went to second period too, I think it was biology. On nutrition break I went out to the parking lot, smoked more bowls, smoked cigarettes, and then my new best-meth-loving-friend asked if I wanted to go get high at her house. All my resolve immediately disappeared. Not only was I an addict, but my fundamental character traits of constantly feeling like I was missing out on something and never wanting to be left out were far more than I could withstand. I left with her and didn't return. I remember what I was wearing only because it would be several weeks before I would change. I wore a white wife beater tank top with a denim collar and buttons down the front bearing a flat almost indented stomach and pushed up breasts. I had on baggy, short, sky blue denim shorts. I think the last time my tummy had been so flat was when I was six. By the time I changed from the outfit, it was fit to be burned due to smell and stains. After school that day, the same friend was driving me home. We were listening to one of our favorites: Pink Floyd's "Mother."

Mother do you think they'll drop the bomb? Mother do you think they'll like the song? Mother do you think they'll try to break my balls? Ooooh aah, Mother should I build a wall?
Hush now baby, baby don't you cry. Mama's gonna make all of your nightmares come true. Mama's gonna put all of her fears into you Mama's gonna keep you right her under her wing she won't let you fly but she might let you sing. Mama will keep baby cozy and warm
Ooooh Babe Ooooh Babe Ooooh Babe you'll always be baby to me.....
Mother, did it need to be so high?

The haunting melody rang out with the triumphant crescendo while Roger Waters bemoaned this hardship… this life where, in my mind, mother did her job and loved you right into a cage. Once again, the story of my life, I felt trapped. I didn't know what to do. I felt euphoric and philosophical and caged and muddled. Panic set in as I realized my parents were serious. They would try to homeschool me now. I was fairly certain I could evade them, but I dreaded the encounter. I was quickly trying to think of a way out of this particular cage when my friend spoke up that she, too, was in a world of trouble at home. "There's a Grateful Dead show in Santa Cruz this weekend. We could go there instead." Her words were sweet victory. Her willingness to go on an adventure of massive proportion with me on this doomsday was beyond comprehension. What began as heart palpitations in preparation for an unpleasant particularly feeble battle evaporated and were replaced with a steady rhythm of excitement and freedom. This bird was going to fly. *Mother, did it need to be so high?*

We hit 1-80 with a half tank of gas, $12.00 cash, an eighth of weed, and a quarter of crank. We may as well have been royalty for how concerned we were with our supplies. The drive is vague. I remember putting my face out the window, feeling the breeze blow onto my cheeks. The air smelled of fresh trees and an approaching salty ocean. She must have known where we were going because I was incapable of navigating. I don't remember how we got there, but I will never forget when we got there. As we pulled into the city block already bombarded with hippies and buses and patchouli oil, the sky was dusk. We searched for somewhere to park blocks away next to a grassy field. We got out and saw generations of families: grey haired tie dyed bandanas, middle aged overalls and maxi dresses, and toddlers frolicking on the grass in hippie rompers with multi colored fringe. They caught smoke rings and danced to the beat of distant drums while they all smiled, laughed, sang songs, and looked happy. They were idyllic. I'd always had an affinity for hippies and bums. Even as a child, I was always the first to strike up a conversation with a woman in a flowing skirt, flower in her hair. I loved bel bottoms and tie dyed clothing. When I was in the gifted and talented program in elementary school, I used to go to a theater for music and acting. There was a bum who lived outside of the stairs to the theater. Every day on my way to and from the program, I'd talk with him. I asked him about his life, his boundaries, his choices. Even then, I yearned for what I deemed his liberties. I envisioned his life as being so romantic compared to the steady flow of horns, feet on the pavement, and money I felt motivated the rest of society. It was clear that this man chose this life because he loved it. He had stories to tell and was one of the most fascinating people I'd ever met. I was envious of the "dead heads'" freedoms, and their complete antiestablishment lifestyles, and of what I perceived as their immense and overflowing love towards one another: judgment free. As we entered the gates I thought this must be what heaven was like. People walked up and down the temporary roads passing out acid oranges, pot brownies. They were on a complete bartering system. I scarcely heard anyone ask for money. It was on your honor; pay it forward. There were men with huge burlap sacks at the end of each makeshift road (there were dozens of them; an entire community) passing out "free hugs." They were the good kind too… those where you genuinely feel enveloped in warmth and tenderness. That was it. No ulterior motives. Just hugs. There was incense burning as far as the eye could see. Drum circles under dozens of trees where naked people danced with no embarrassment or regard for anything other than their own intensity; their own feelings of rhythms and chords and beauty. Everyone smoked weed out of bongs and pipes fearlessly as police weren't allowed inside the gates of a Grateful Dead show. Dreadlocks hung to dancers' calloused feet as they navigated this little city barefoot and unafraid. Everywhere we went people shared their drugs with us, talked, hugged, sang, replenished their own ill-nourished souls with the vibes and energy of those around them. There was no such thing as a stranger.

We ate mushrooms and tripped out throwing a glow-in-the-dark Frisbee on the beach with a bonfire next to us and the calming sound of waves crashing on the shore. We wrote: "TEST THE BOUNDARIES" in 6-foot letters in the sand with others who shared our thoughts, our feelings, our needs. We followed a mountain lion to its lair and were shocked when it cried out and charged us. We ran into the ocean utterly surprised that this mountain lion didn't feel the connection that we shared. When the bonfire became a pile of coals, lit up in beautiful hues of reds and yellows and oranges, I had to stop myself from touching the gorgeous, living creature. I hallucinated that I was a bird long into the night, and began to feel much the way you do after bouncing on waves in a boat for an extended period of time. I grew weary from the flying and tried to sleep in the sand. For the hours I slept I continued my hallucinations and never ceased being that bird; flying, flying, flying. When I woke, I was in a tent. My latest boyfriend was there. I didn't have any idea how or when that happened. Frankly, I didn't care. My brain felt like oatmeal. My throat felt like I had eaten an ashtray. And yet, I still couldn't overcome the feeling that it had all been worth it. The experience was somehow bigger than me; somehow bigger than us all.

We continued to get high and decided that it would be a great idea to eat some hits of acid. We asked for some change outside of a McDonalds and tried to convince the employees to sell us sausage biscuits when there were serving only lunch. They wouldn't relent so we ate 39 cent cheeseburgers that tasted heavenly as they hit our empty stomachs. The truck had broken down, so we were no longer traveling in it, but in a rust colored car instead. We were on a confusing freeway where the navigator was giving the driver a "test." It seemed to consist of seeing how many lanes of traffic the driver could cross to exit at speeds far above the 65 mph speed limit. We got off the freeway to use the bathroom at what appeared to be a miniature amusement park. I believe our intentions were to go inside, but my friend and I got stuck. They say you should never look in a mirror when you're on acid. That's probably good advice. We got stuck in the bathroom watching our faces melt, laughing uncontrollably into the toilet; memorizing the marble pellets ever moving as we attempted to make our way through this obstacle course known as a two stall restroom. I don't remember anybody coming in. Perhaps we locked the doors. It's amazing nobody called the police. We were in there for what felt like an hour, perhaps longer. When we finally emerged our eyes were blinded by the sunlit skies we thought had surely disappeared in our absence. The boys were wandering around some statues; amused, lost... just as stuck as we were. In an ironic twist of fate, I didn't feel trapped.

We made it back to the car and began traveling again; presumably to the next Grateful Dead show, though at the end of several hours we ended up back in Reno. My boyfriend and I sat in the back seat. He had a goofy grin on his face and his arm was around me when, suddenly, this hilariously stupid acid trip went down. Down. Down. All at once he looked like a caveman: barbaric and ignorant and somewhat frightening. He reeked of B.O. and his facial hair seemed to be growing right before my eyes. I told him he looked like a caveman. I yelled at him to not touch me. He had been doing disgusting amounts of acid in the previous months and was deteriorating right before my eyes. I couldn't get away from him. I didn't want him near me. I hid inside my own mind for what felt like an eternity. My skin crawled everywhere he touched it and I began to wonder if this was the reality of the entire trip. I began to panic, wondering about reality while simultaneously loathing him for being the one to ruin my high. The words coming out of his mouth were foreign. He was speaking some kind of nonsensical, extinct caveman language. I was the girlfriend of this Neanderthal. What did that make me? Fortunately, the radio blared in the front seat, and he got lost bellowing tunes the remainder of the trip. When we returned to Reno, it was far too dangerous for me to stay with him as that was the first place the police always looked. What was first a relief immediately transformed to intense anxiety. Where would I go? What would I do? While my friend went home to face the music and sleep in her own bed in her apartment with her far more understanding single mom, I had nowhere to go. We arrived at a friend of a friend of a friend's house. They wouldn't let me stay. The police were everywhere. Nowhere was safe. A group of strangers far more menacing than those from the show turned on strobe lights while throwing knives in the air. I don't know if I played it cool or not. In my mind I did, but I was terrified. I was shuffled from house to house to house. Finally, I was left at a little house in the middle of nowhere with two hippie men. They must have been in their early twenties while I was fourteen. I'm certain they didn't know that. They offered, or perhaps demanded a shower. I smelled bad enough to be offensive to these men who presumably lived almost completely off of the land. They were nice enough, much less intimidating than the last bunch. Still, with the weight of an acid trip gone bad barely off my shoulders, a lifetime of sleep deprivation and not knowing a soul, I was apprehensive. I took a shot of Goldschlager and curled into a ball of blankets on the floor like a little cat and slept restlessly while the party commenced around me.

Eventually I had to leave that house, but not before having sex with one of the residents. I wasn't pressured, and I didn't feel obligated, but I had the sour stench of my caveman boyfriend living in my nose, it was an attempt to sever emotional ties with him. I was transported from place to place sometimes in trunks of cars. When I finally returned home, I was completely fried. My brain hurt, my heart was empty, and all sense was dead. I don't remember anything about how things went or what prompted me to finally return. I only remember what a sensation the Grateful Dead had left on my impressionable mind. At church the following Sunday, I felt judged and knew there were hushed whispers everywhere I went. Perhaps I was being overly sensitive, but I couldn't make sense of the judgment and scorn from this society that, according to my parents, was of Christ. When these "terrible people who were out to kill me" conveyed nothing but unconditional love, why would those who were "here to help" so merciless? I was confused and disheartened. I felt certain that I understood what my parents did not: the true definition of happiness. I felt the only people on this earth who were kind, loving, and generous were the dredges of society. I couldn't trust parents I found so incredibly misguided. I simply couldn't fathom how my reality could be wrong and theirs right. It makes me think, now, of Jesus and those he surrounded himself with. Truly, we all need to be Christ-like and judge righteously. Otherwise, we run the risk of teaching the world that good is bad and bad is good; that righteousness is wickedness and vice versa. I was fourteen. I was confused. I felt justified in all I was doing. And yet, I was trapped.... Again.

The semester was nearing a close by then. The fact that I failed every class didn't come as a surprise to anyone. As a result, I was sentenced to summer school which wasn't as terrible as I anticipated. In the mornings, I would snort lines of crank in my bedroom, push my glass picture with my razor, straw, and white powder in a miniature plastic bag under my dresser. My ride was a junior boy I had a crush on, and we smoked insidious amounts of weed on the way across town. I would be comfortably numb all through the English writing prompts. We had one break where we went outside and smoked cigarettes. Because it was far more contained than the regular school year, there was less room for my escape making it easier to maintain attendance. I didn't know then, but my world was about to drastically change. When I had returned home from my Grateful Dead tour, one of the conditions was that I took a drug test. I wasn't concerned because I knew that acid didn't show up on urine tests, and I hadn't had access to meth for most of the time I was gone; spending my time on hallucinogens instead. When the results came back that I had a "serious drug problem," I was more than a little taken off guard.

It was a school morning; I had just snorted a line and was awaiting my ride. My parents, who weren't always up by the time I left for early summer school both came into my room. I nonchalantly brushed my hair annoyed at the invasion. They sat down with grave faces and broken hearts explaining that my drug test results indicated that I needed help. They told me to pack a bag for two weeks. I threw my brush at the mirror with anger and confusion overtaking me as I screamed, "The experts don't know what they're talking about!" I swore at them while I freaked out. My mind spun in circles: how could they know? What could have shown up on that test? How can I possibly be in trouble? They hadn't done a spinal! How on earth could they know that I was on anything besides marijuana? No expert alive would call smoking weed a "serious drug problem." As I panicked, my parents hedged me in my room eliminating the escape I was plotting. Desperate, I begged to call my ride and tell him not to come. They hovered at the door as I continued my attempt to find a way out. I called several friends pleading for help, but what could they do? Finally, someone answered. I told her through tears that my parents were sending me to rehab. I hoped she could come break me out. "Oh, don't worry!" she said, "It's not a big deal, and you can still get drugs in rehab. Plus, I met some of my best hookups there. It's only two weeks. Seriously, I promise it's not a big deal." Well, okay then, I guess. Next I called my ride and told him, again through sobs, not to come pick me up. I angrily packed opting against my drawer full of bikinis that I would never lay eyes on again. I was making a mental list of every stash I had hidden in my bedroom. Fortunately, I had just snorted my last line; due to pick up a new bag that afternoon. I had a mirror and straws under my dresser and half an eighth in the pocket of a jacket hanging in my closet. That was all I could come up with, so I felt relatively safe. I was so naïve. I genuinely believed that my parents still had no clue and were simply overreacting about weed in my system. I assumed rehab was going to be a simple moment where the experts, like my previous counselors would think my parents were being overprotective. My parents strong-armed me into my dad's maroon Mazda, their eyes glued to me like paranoid vultures. As we began driving, I argued and cried, pled and yelled until I lost stamina. When we started heading east on I-80 I became suspicious demanding they tell me where I was going. They solemnly explained that we were going to a rehabilitation facility in Utah. They were cryptic about where in Utah, not that I would have had any understanding anyway. I pleaded with them to at least stop for cigarettes and let me smoke. They wouldn't relent, though later, much later, a time would come when they would suffer through that disheartening act. I stood on the corner of the gas station parking lot, angrily drinking a coke. There was a Hell's Angel type getting off his motorcycle. I was still plotting my escape looking like a deranged child, I pled with him to take me with him... anywhere. He looked at me like I was crazy, which I was, and wordlessly disappeared. We got back in the car, and I slept off and on as we drove and drove and drove until the streets of my past gave way to the mountains of my future.

After what felt like eternity, we arrived at a big house in the middle of nowhere. There were horses and fields of what appeared to be hay or alfalfa. We went inside where another girl with shiny long jet black hair looked up at us, hesitant, distrustful but inviting. My parents went into the director's office and the girl instantly began talking to me like we were old friends. Our first stop certainly wasn't the hospital I was expecting. Instead, it was a beautiful and eclectic home; antiques spilling over carved tables, shelves and intricate rugs climbing down the walls and ceiling. Dejectedly, I sat down next to the girl. "So, what are you in for?" she asked. I told her I was there for two weeks because of drugs. "Gangs too?" she asked.

"Umm, far from it" I answered. She laughed then a deep, head-thrown back in the air sort of laugh.

"I remember being told that I would be here for two weeks. That was two years ago." This girl clearly knew nothing of my family, *my* life. My parents would *never* leave me for two years. They scarcely let me leave for two hours without the gestapo on my tail. She was friendly. She spoke highly of Joe (the director's nickname) explaining it would just take some getting used to, but really, "it's all right." Reality began to sink in. I began to feel claustrophobic, terrified, and seething with rage and feelings of betrayal.

"I need to smoke a cigarette. Where do you smoke?"

"We don't."

"How can that be? That's impossible! It's gotta be illegal or something to take drug addicts completely off their drugs and take away cigarettes at the same time! This can't be the case. I'll just have to explain to this Joe person that I *have* to smoke. My parents will have to explain that *I can.*" Again, she gave the head in the air laugh and said, "Yeah, good luck with that. I promise you will be quitting smoking way sooner than you think." I panicked. What will I do?

How will I ever make it? All I could think about was not smoking cigarettes. *What will I do?*

After meeting with Joe and being introduced to multiple kids in the program, we loaded up the car once again and drove to a second location. The feeling was indescribable as the woman of the house showed us to my room in the basement. There was concrete on the ceiling and floors alike; bars on the window, and a crack in the ceiling directly above my bed. Mom and dad carried my bag down steep, dark, narrow stairs. I was still in shock not believing that this was going to last longer than two weeks. My mom put her arms around me and, with the only tear I had ever before witnessed in her eye said, "Get better and come home to us soon." They left. I lay on the bed and sobbed deep powerful, gut wrenching cries until long into the night. By the time I awoke, I was unrecognizable with my lobster face and disfigured eyes. The withdrawals were a demon indescribable to mankind. I wished for death; indeed, I felt that was death. The cravings sent physical pain throughout my body. It felt like someone was sticking lightning rods in my stomach and connecting live wires to my head. I was in unqualified agony. The anguish was almost more than I could bear. The tears were an endless fountain of desperation and fatigue. It was my darkest hour so far. It would get darker.

Larissa

Dear Larissa,

...The days go ticking along, and here it is already nearly time for you to leave the MTC and to go to Alaska. Well, on Christmas, don't miss what you don't have, but enjoy and drink in the new experience you are having. The time will go so fast. Have a merry Christmas and know that we adore you and never miss a day thinking of you. Go get 'em!

Merry Christmas! Love,
Dad

Sunday, Jan 1, 1995

Dear Larissa,

Happy New Year! You were probably sound asleep when the year changed this morning. We have been thinking about you and how strange New Year's Eve must be in the mission field....

Lenaya, of course was much too cool to go to a boring church dance and talked us into letting her go with her friends to a small get together at Dani's house. We even checked with Dani's parents to make sure they were planning to be there all evening and I told them I would be home too if they needed any help. Well, at some point they told her parents they were all coming over here to watch a movie. Of course, where they went was downtown Reno to see the New Year in, in the casinos with people who really know how to party. They got separated somehow from Dani and the guy (nameless, of course) who drove them downtown, so Lenaya and Rae had to bum a ride home with some guy they had just met at the party. Those stupid girls! But he was perfectly safe, because he was from Carson City and he knew the Cherpeskis and anyway Rae sort of knew who he was. They got home about 1:30 and helped Dani's dad call some people who might know where she was. She finally showed up about an hour later, drunk and hysterical. (I could be wrong, but I don't really think Lenaya had been drinking. She and Rae seemed perfectly lucid and didn't seem to have any trouble remembering all the telephone numbers they had to come up with in their search for Dani.)

So, Lenaya starts the new year grounded and without telephone privileges and I am back to being the warden. Rae, of course, is not in trouble since she had her parent's permission in advance to go downtown and to spend the night anywhere she wanted to, which happened to be at our house....

We look forward to hearing of your first experiences in the mission field. I will get this in the mail right away even though the post offices are closed tomorrow for the holiday. We hope you don't feel lonely or forgotten. Please know that we love you and miss you.

Love,
Mom

January 18, 1995

Dear Larissa,

....Lenaya has been having a serious feud with some of her friends that has escalated to the point she is afraid she might get jumped. Lenaya has been just terrible this last week, getting in trouble in school for her rudeness to teachers, not coming right home after school (and that's even with me picking her up every day—some days she simply can't be found), leaving her Young Women's activity to go do something with her friends. I really don't know what we are going to do with her, she is so out of control. She seems really unhappy all the time, too.

We trust that things are going well for you. We certainly enjoyed our last letter from you and we relistened to your Christmas tape this weekend. You are meeting and working with a broad cross section of people up there. I had never thought of Alaska as a place that was so ethnically diverse.....I talked to my dad last week. He has had a few more bad spells but is doing well on the whole. He always asks about you.

This is a very boring letter because I haven't gone anywhere or done anything for the last two weeks except for stuff around the house. I'm not even sewing or crafting, partly because I'm too tired from not sleeping night after night. I know this bad spell will pass, they always do, but at the moment it doesn't feel like it. I think your dad has been feeling a little down, too. This weekend was Stake Conference and he had more than his usual trouble getting his talks prepared. Conference went well.

Well, I'd better close and get dinner in the oven. I certainly miss you, but know you are exactly where you ought to be.

Love,
Mom

Thursday, February 2, 1995

Dear Larissa,

Here it is almost the weekend already and I am just now getting around to writing you. It sounds as if you are really, really busy there if you are even teaching discussions on your prep day. Do you ever get any time to relax? And how have you been doing with sleep? Are you getting enough to stay well?

It's been a particularly stressful week here because Lenaya decided to disappear again last Saturday. We should have known something was going on because she was actually being nice to us. She had been in trouble earlier in the week for going in the front door of the church for Young Women and then right out the back. She says she and Rae were "just walking around", but I sincerely doubt that—for one thing, it was raining and they didn't look very wet to me. (First they had told us they were over at a friend's house jumping on the trampoline, but we checked and found that was untrue.) But she seemed really sorry and willing to make restitution, so we let her go to a party on Friday night. The invitation said there would be parents present all evening, but the parents left so she and her friends went to pizza instead, or so the story goes. Saturday night Dad and I left her to watch Jed while we went out to dinner and when we came back (early, luckily), she had sneaked out. Rae and her boyfriend whom she introduced to us as her cousin had been there earlier that evening, so we assumed she was with them.

She called late Sunday morning from a blocked number to flippantly say she had decided to go to a Super Bowl party and would be home "sometime." Sunday evening she called from Rae's house to announce she was spending the night there because she was "too tired to fight and needed some time to think." We nearly broke Rae's door down, to the surprise of her parents who had just arrived home, then had to bodily drag Lenaya out to our car. We took her straight to the police station, which calmed her down considerably, where they officially called off the search for her and had her cited. We chose to have her cited, which means she will have to have a hearing with a judge at juvenile court in a few months. They would have just released her to our custody if we had asked them to, but we didn't think she deserved to get off that easy. On the other hand, they also would have booked her and taken her to Whittenberg if we had requested that. Maybe next time. I don't know if anything good will come out of her hearing. She will probably be put on some sort of probation, and will (hopefully) be sentenced to some hours of community service.

As hard as it was for me to believe at first, it appears that she really was not with Rae. It makes me feel a little embarrassed about some of the wild accusations I made on Sunday night; I was fairly angry. Lenaya's story is that she was picked up by some friends (nameless, of course) she hadn't seen in a long time to go four wheeling up in the hills. They got stuck in the mud too far from civilization to walk back in the dark and had to stay in the truck until morning. Anyway, Lenaya is grounded and has lost phone privileges for a couple of weeks and we have cancelled her membership at the YMCA. (She has also been disappearing with her friends when I drop her off there to work out.) She's in trouble at school too. She failed Algebra, because of 12 absences and got a D- in something else. I suppose that means she has been cutting. She says she can do extra credit to buy back some of the absences in both those classes to bring them up to C's and maybe she can. But we have a really tough new attendance policy that started this year.

Sorry. You don't need to hear me go on and on about his, but I can't seem to snap out of it and let it go. I also haven't been able to sleep this week: two nights not at all and two others I have been asleep for less than three hours when the kids woke me up to drive them to seminary. I'm kind of a wreck, so if my thought processes seem a little disjointed....

Nicholas and Dad went to a special recognition dinner tonight put on by the stake for all the boys who have earned their eagle in the last two or three years. I begged out on the ground that someone needed to stay home to supervise Lenaya, but I really didn't want to go very badly. And now I don't have to make dinner. Jed will open a can of soup and Lenaya is glad to eat one of my Healthful Gourmet frozen entrees when she gets a chance. Nicholas had a perfect 4.0 this semester with good citizenship grades too, and he is enjoying weight training and track. He was so mad at Lenaya this weekend that he punched a hole in her door with his fist. (Now we can spy on her.)

Dad has been extremely busy and is completely stressed out about some cases he is working on. I think that means they are not going well.... I am taking that Thursday morning institute class at the Rock building, you will be happy to hear. It's on the Pearl of Great Price and is very interesting and even entertaining although, for some reason, I usually come home feeling a little depressed. Maybe it's the thought of all those worlds without number....

We love you and know you are accomplishing so much good. Please don't worry about us here. We will just take things one day at a time and do as much as we can. Stay warm!

Love,
Mom

March 5, 1995

Dear Larissa,

How's life in Alaska? Every thing here is fine....
    Dad bought me a Alaskan flag. I could eat a horse I'm so hungry. (It's because I'm fasting). Lenaya stole 18 green bucks from me. It's dinner time so I have to go. Lots and lots and lots and lots and etc.

                       Love,
                       Jed

Dear Larissa,

    I apologize for having delayed so long in writing. I have held a copy of my journal entries to use to catch you up on what I have been doing. It was sure a joy to speak with you on Sunday. There was more that I would have liked to ask you and say to you, but I suppose 3 hours was pushing the limit. Later in the week, we received a letter from your mission president stating that you had been assigned to train a new missionary. Congratulations! We assume you are still in Anchorage.
Well, let me catch you up on some of the things I have been doing here. I was busy during the week of April 3rd, but I left work each day around 5:30. On Monday, we watched home movies as a home evening activity. I spent Tuesday and Wednesday evenings at home. I pitched to Jed on Wednesday and we read together most evenings. I tried to spend time talking to Lenaya and Nicholas. I wish Lenaya would do more than merely answer my questions. We received a very nice letter from you.
On Thursday, the 6th, I handled my usual interviews and returned home. We got to bed early but mom was awakened by a sound and we discovered that Lenaya was not home. She had sneaked out with her friends. What a night that was. The next day, I purchased some door alarms and we talked with Lenaya on Friday and I installed the alarms. I felt pretty much like a failure as I installed them. What a thing to have to do. Instead of going out on Friday to dinner, as we had planned, we spent the evening

home. Mom has probably told you all about this in her letters to you. I will say that the alarms have helped and given us some temporary peace of mind and have been the basis of several profitable discussions with Lenaya, I think....
Be happy and know that we all love you.

Love,
Dad

June 2, 1995

Dear Larissa,

....What I have been doing is organizing the fabric in my collection...I've needed something to keep me busy and occupied because we are going through another really hard time with Lenaya. I'm too discouraged to write more about it now. Besides, it would take hours. Please remember her and us in your prayers....

Mom

June 16, 1995

Dear Larissa,

What a jerk I am for not writing sooner. Sorry, I was hoping that if I waited long enough, I would eventually have something good to report. Should have known better, I guess. Also, it's harder to find a private time to write now that the computer is in the entryway.

Things are no better with Lenaya and we haven't really made a decision about what to do with her. She would be very surprised to know that we are thinking about putting her in some kind of a treatment program, because to keep her from running away again while we make up our minds and make arrangements, we are letting her pretty much do as she pleases. I'm afraid that your dad and I haven't agreed at all about what we should do. He was so glad to see her back safe and sound after her week away

that he didn't want to carry through with the plan of action we had decided on, i.e., taking her in immediately for a drug test, then having her taken to Whittenberg so she would have a hearing and (hopefully) be assigned a probation officer. But she was tired and wanted to sleep, and he thought that would be much too harsh. Obviously, I disagreed. We did take her to St. Mary's for a drug test the next day around noon and arranged for our psychologist to see us that day, which accomplished exactly nothing, if you ask me. She made me look like this raving crazy lady who was "out to get her"; no wonder the poor child keeps running away.
Apparently the world is just full of people who think it's normal for 15-year-olds to take off and spend a week with their friends camping out at the lake, doing drugs, sleeping with their 19-year-old lowlife boyfriend, going to a Grateful Dead concert in California than come home and act like life should go on as usual.

It took 9 days to get the results of the urine test and she did test positive for marijuana (no big surprise) and LSD (which definitely was)! They said it is very unusual to get a positive reading for LSD, because it only stays in the body for 24-48 hours and then in very minute concentrations. The amount in her body was not minute, however. They said she would have to still have been hallucinating at the time the test was taken! Moreover the marijuana level was very high, not a level you would find in the occasional recreational user. They think she must be smoking it every day. Which would explain a lot. Imagine what else we might have found in her system if we had had her tested right away.

But now even your dad agrees we need to do something. We did look into the program [you recommended]. It sounds like they run a very successful program and it's much less expensive than most of the places we have talked to. Unfortunately, the cost is still exorbitant, starting at $3100 a month at first, then gradually scaling down to about $2400. If we took out a second mortgage and tapped out all the equity we have in the house, we could keep her there for about a year. But should we be willing to do that? It seems to me that if she needed a bone marrow transplant or some medical treatment to save her life, we would somehow come up with the money, so why shouldn't we approach this the same way? Dad has been "too busy" this week at work to deal with this and he and Nicholas are leaving tomorrow for 5 days at Yosemite, so nothing is going to get done very soon. There are some shorter term drug treatment programs in our community that we are looking into, as well as a couple of promising-sounding programs in Utah. The problem with all of them is money....

For the time being, we are letting her do many of the things she wants to, like babysitting and going places with her lovely friends, and she still isn't a bit happy. She is once again making herself throw up after almost every meal, smoking heavily (and secretly, she thinks), staying in her room with the door shut all day, and wandering around the house all night when she should be sleeping. (All right, all right, I know I exhibit that last symptom myself, but I promise I'm not on drugs. Maybe I should be though. Tranquilizers for instance.) Summer school starts Monday and, while I'm pretty sure she won't really be going for very long, to not make her go would tip her off that we're up to something. I'm very sorry to burden you with this long discouraging letter, and now you know why it's taken me so long to write it....

In other news: this is youth conference weekend. Nicholas and [his friend] are having a contest to see who can get the most girl's phone numbers. Lenaya went, reluctantly. I just hope she doesn't disappear from there! Dad is busy with that, too, of course.

We hope you are having many joyous experiences there. I'm sure the days seem to fly by. Soon you will have served half of your mission ! We love you and miss you. Take good care of yourself. I will write sooner next time so the letter won't be so long. You'll probably have to wait for your P-day to have time to read all of this.

> Much love,
> Mom

6/17/95

Dear Larissa,

....I'm sorry this letter is short and boring. There really isn't much going on. I suppose mom wrote to you a watered down version of Lenaya's most recent runaway. I don't know what to think about her. We know for a fact that she uses drugs, everything is so out of control. As much as I love her I get so angry with her. She is so selfish and she kills Mom and Dad because of it. I can't help but feel helpless as there doesn't seem to be an end to what she will and will not do. I wonder sometimes if in five years we'll even know where she is. But this just comes from a bored, disillusioned, exhausted brain. Who knows what the future will hold? All we can do is pray for her and show her unconditional love and example. Maybe she'll catch on eventually....

> Lotsa Love,
> Cami

6-28-95

Dear Larissa,

....How is your family? I hope something gives and your parents find peace. Even the best parents can lose a child. I pray for them and for Lenaya. I think about you quite a bit....

> Love,
> Elder Nathan Cherpeski

July 3, 1995

Dear (Larissa) Sister Frey,

Events with Lenaya have taken much of our time and attention in the past couple weeks. I am sorry that kept us from writing much during this interval. Notwithstanding the pain attached to these events, I am very hopeful for Lenaya, perhaps moreso than for a long time. I think you will probably agree that choices we have made recently for her have the potential of working to her good. On the 14th, we received the report on the urinalysis for Lenaya. We were greatly troubled and shocked by the results. We began attempting to place her in a drug program. Largely upon the basis of the drug screen results, we decided she needed professional treatment. She appeared to be going downhill day by day. Ultimately, after we made inquiries and evaluated the whole matter, we decided to place her in your professor's program. We also had the daunting problem of finding some means to pay for the treatment, as we found pretty quickly that it was not covered by our insurance. In any event, we have gone forward for Lenaya's sake.

We drove to Spanish Fork on Tuesday, June 27th. She had awakened and showered and dressed for summer school. We told her after she had dressed to pack clothing for a week, and told her what we were going to do. We told her she needed help that we could not provide. She reacted very angrily at first, shouting about how stupid the idea was. During the morning, as we drove, she was very quiet and would not answer questions. By lunch time, she was more emotional and talked to us more candidly about her drug problems than she had before, partly in an effort to get us to purchase cigarettes for her. We got her a coke and gum and lunch at Burger King, and drove on. During the afternoon, she was more contrite. We stopped a few blocks from the place, at a K-mart, and purchased a few things that she needed, and then called him for directions. We met with him for some time, while Lenaya visited with a girl who is in the program and has been doing very well.... Mom got cold feet or, maybe more accurately, lost confidence in what we were doing and almost wanted to bring Lenaya back home, but finally acquiesced.

We drove afterwards to Clearfield and got a room. Mom went to bed pretty sick at heart. It is hard to describe the emotions of the day, for us and no doubt for Lenaya. I hope a day comes when we look back with joy to this day, and I have hope that it may be so....

Love you lots,
Dad

II. Refiner's Fire

Lenaya

Baby Girl

She gazes at her little baby,
rocking her to sleep,
with adoration in her eyes,
for this one she's got dreams.

As mommy rocks her little girl,
she plans her expectations,
her baby's look of innocence,
becomes one of accusation.

Mommy watched her baby grow,
the time went by so fast.
She went from being baby's first
to being baby's last.

She cries herself to sleep at night,
thinking what baby became.

What she never realized,
is baby did the same.

Baby changed to big girl,
rebellion in her eyes,
blood streaked face and shaking hands,
her mouth told mommy lies.

Baby was sent to rehab,
to face the problems that she must.
Mommy thinks of baby's face,
that always used to trust.

Mommy continues to cry at night,
four hundred miles away.
While weeping girl is once again,
doing just the same.

Baby sits in loneliness,
confused as she could be.
While mommy wonders to herself,
is this what she had dreamed?

-Lenaya Frey 1995 (15-yrs-old)-

The first week of detox was pretty much a blur. I remember a lot of physical pain; a lot of tears; a lot of confusion. The hours were endless. The minutes dragged into what felt like a lifetime. Where did all this time come from? What did the living do with all these seconds and minutes and hours and days? Most of my time had been spent high or seeking something to get me high. It was time consuming. I never considered what the rest of the world did in all that *time*. Every day dragged on like interminable waiting rooms. The crack above my bed became a study for determining countless stories of its origin. The four, white walls surrounding me became companions as I memorized every line in their texture. My body ached and shook with the pain of withdrawals. Often, I sat in the corner under a built-in desk screaming and crying, desperately trying to overcome the urgings for drugs… and the loneliness. I felt abandoned, weak, and friendless. And then, as if a fairy had hit my head with a magic wand, I began to feel physically better, though my heart remained sick. Adding insult to injury was the understanding that, in the midst of withdrawal and desertion, I was expected to clean in my new foster home. We were *all* expected to do chores. I came to understand that this location was one of many in the program. Typically considered the highest security and often the starting location, I lived there with others in and out of the program. Deborah had meticulous lists of cleaning jobs including the order we were to clean things like the bathroom. First, wash the sink, then the toilet (handle, toilet seat, under seat, floor of seat) in that order. Everything was inspected, and Deborah didn't hesitate to send you back to a job. She was powerful, fearless, and militant, but she had a softness discovered much later. Once, a boy who was living down the hall from me came home on acid and a couple of very large men came and handled it. I was intimidated. Deborah was married with three sons, though they seemed ambivalent about us: the kids in the program. Although we lived in their home, we scarcely interacted with them. Clearly this was Deborah's job. I can't even recall what her husband did, despite living there for over a year. Still, I do recall a mutual fondness between the two of us as well as a blossoming relationship with Deborah. She ran the household taking care of the discipline and all things domestic. When she went shopping, we usually went with her. It took several months before she would leave me home with her husband. Even then she took the phone cords with her. She was methodical, commanding pushups if you left the table without pushing in your chair. She didn't follow through as often with me as with the boys. It made her rule-following son mad. We didn't do much for entertainment; we cleaned, I wrote, occasionally we watched movies. The down-time starkly contrasted with constantly living on a mix of high intensity and speed. After the first couple weeks of sweeping detox, I began to feel tolerable. The fogginess in my mind drifted away like a distant dream, and I began to get a sense of clarity.

All along there were outings with the others in the program. There were four houses that I knew of sheltering youth in rehab. We all met regularly at "Joe's" house. I anxiously awaited his approach, conversation, counsel, concern. I was eager to be teacher's pet and show him what a wonderful job I was doing. Though the whisperings of my addictions were becoming quieter and less severe, I urgently wanted to get out of there. Desperate for praise, I even desired approval from a stranger I deemed responsible for robbing me of my freedom. I waited in vain, for apart from the interactions of acquaintances, he never approached me to talk. He was friendly with all of us and was a presence at our barbeques and game nights. Once, he took two of the borderline permanent boys to Wyoming to purchase fireworks. Upon their return we set them off at his ranch. Even now, decades later as I write this tears stream down my face. I felt such a mixture of emotions. The air outside was charged as fireworks lit up the star-kissed sky. I was developing friendships with the others there, but I failed to feel an intense connection I longed for. Goosebumps raised on my arms as I simultaneously relished the pleasure of this evening out of the house and longed for my old life; old friends; old me. I was relieved and disappointed. There was a beautiful patio with fountains and gorgeous flowers all around. My heart relished this newfound ability to appreciate the beauty, but my time with psychedelics had taught me I could have a heightened experience with the colorful lights flashing in the sky. I couldn't push down my desire to celebrate our freedom on acid. Such opposite emotions coursed through my body: exhilaration, dismay, fulfillment, desire. I studied the faces of the strangers around me; they seemed so content, thrilled even. Would I feel like them some day? Many had been in the program for years; even one year felt intolerable. They were excitedly talking about horseback riding and working on the ranch, but I never participated in any of that; I was never invited. I made a decision right then and there to do whatever it took to get out of this program as quickly as possible. I fretted about what it would take for me to prove my recovery. Who did I have to convince? My cravings for drugs were weaker every day; in an unreasonably short amount of time, I no longer yearned for them at all.

Deborah was considered the missionary mom. Men and women between the ages of nineteen and twenty-one often go on a volunteer mission for the LDS church in cities and countries away from their homes. One of the callings or jobs in the church is to organize their dinner calendar and be a liaison for them. As a result, we had elders over for dinner very regularly. At first I was annoyed thinking it was a set up brought on by my parents. It didn't take long for me to realize that all the elders had an amazing rapport with Deborah, and she was their mom away from home. She was a kind, service-minded woman. At the time, however, I perceived her as imposing and cold. June, the girl I met the first day became my best friend. She told me all the ins and outs of everything. She explained more to me about what I was supposed to be doing than all of the adults combined which left me confused. Was she the authority? As the summer came to a close, there was always the carrot dangling of working up enough steps to be allowed to go to school. I was beginning to feel confident and accomplished in my sobriety, but I was often perplexed that I had never received counseling. Joe only visited me one time, and my foster mom wasn't trained in therapy. He came several months after I arrived and sat outside of Deborah's house under a tree. I was all smiles. Here was my opportunity at last to wow him with my cooperation and success. He asked, "How do you feel you're doing?"

"Great!" I replied.

"I think so too," he said, "Would you like to go to school in the fall?"

"Sure," I coolly said, attempting to belie my eagerness.

"I think that would be good," he answered. And that was that. It was settled that I would go to school, and I had been counseled.

When I first arrived, I was homesick only for my friends. The deeper I got in sobriety, the more I recognized the absence of my family. It felt like a lifetime since I'd had any real relationships with anyone. I could scarcely remember the previous years and interactions, so the gnawing ache in my heart was unidentifiable. I couldn't comprehend or articulate missing a family I felt I hardly knew. I felt alienated from everyone. The strict rules dictating when and how long I could speak with my parents seemed insane. The lack of freedom for repairing our relationship left me feeling suspicious of everyone. June kept me in the loop and explained that good behavior equaled points and steps up in this program. She told me that eventually I would move to another house where I could talk to my parents whenever I wanted. "My parents agreed to this?" I asked incredulously. She shrugged, "My parents did. I wanted to talk to them a long time ago, but they aren't ready to talk to *me* yet." Once more I felt the familiar pangs of guilt. Why was I so ungrateful? Why wasn't my amazing family enough? Or more accurately, why wasn't I enough? For myself? I heard her same sentiment again and again over the next year. Often, the others in the program would insinuate that my parents were still too angry to talk to me too…but the idea never took flight. Despite my feelings of estrangement, I had unwavering belief that my parents had forgiven me; they'd never given me any reason to suspect they didn't have unconditional love for me. After all, I'd put them through hell and they still took the time, effort, and expense to bring me here! Having a sincere belief in their love powered me through many hard times. In my life I have been asked thousands of times what could have been done differently to help me make better choices. I'm not sure I can identify anything. However, not believing in their love for me could have prevented me from ever returning to the Lord, to the living, to my family. Feeling their love is likely the most essential element to my eventual recovery.

Months earlier, I'd done everything imaginable to avoid school, now; I was working the program to reap the *reward* of school attendance. The week before school started, I attended a beginning of the year dance. It was sensational! I was a celebrity in a town that hadn't changed much since the attendant high-schoolers were in diapers. I danced with countless guys and set my sights on one who would very quickly become my boyfriend. As the music vibrated the cement in the quad outside, I felt a little piece of me coming back to life.

My manic desire to break all the rules waned as I took each step, carefully treading through obstacles ahead. Attending school was a pleasure, particularly English where I regularly rehashed my very raw experience with drug addiction. I sat in the front row staring up at a poster which said: "naiveté is a virtue." I didn't agree. At all. The words were invasive and would enter my mind long after the final bell. Though I was inching further away from addiction, I little regretted my experience and refuted the notion that it was advantageous to be naïve. I began to seriously consider who I was while simultaneously attempting to be loved by all. I began to make friends, mostly respectable Mormon girls with high standards and clean entertainment. I didn't want to be in the popular crowd because they partied and I was terrified of relapse and being incarcerated in this program for life. But I wanted to be loved…or maybe envied. Because of long time ironclad friendships, it was hard to break into roped off relationships. It helped that I had already attracted the boy from the dance giving me instant notoriety. Still, it was wounding to ignore the whispers in the halls and the sudden hushed voices in classrooms when I entered. Never one to shy away from a challenge, I invariably walked right up to whomever had suddenly lost their voice and introduced myself. "Hi, I'm Lenaya. I am in Joe's program. Nice to meet you." This strategy was effective in making friends, and later, in assessing my competition with my boyfriend. He was kind, handsome, reputable, and preparing for a mission, but his parents had a strict "no dating only one person" policy which left me feeling vulnerable and jealous at times. The combination of upright peers and my new location seemed to immediately heal my addicted heart. I was happy to be a follower amongst a religious crowd, pretending dismay regarding some Mormon girls who pretended to be devout but partied on the weekends. Secretly, I was envious. I went to assemblies; I went to football games and dances; in short, I began to feel like a regular high school sophomore. I didn't completely attend class. Despite missing the last year, I was still ahead in most of my classes. A bright student, I had always completed school work long before anyone else and then reverted to either distracting my neighbor or sitting bored stiff. I instantly won the affection of all my teachers. I would do A work quickly and then make up any excuse to wander the hallways: "I need to finish up a project in—" or "I have to go chat with the guidance counselor about—" or "I have to go talk to Michelle about—" Michelle was another foster mom in the program. She was by far the coolest, most laid back, highest trust level house. She was also the detention teacher at my high school, and she and I hit it off as soon as one of the girls in the program who lived with her introduced us.

I would spend a lot of class time sitting in the detention room visiting with Michelle. We became very close; she counseled me in my love life, with my friends, with my monthly dates to all the formal school dances. I related well with adults. My computer teacher let me get out of countless class lectures in exchange for me reading, editing, and encouraging his true passion: poetry. Every day in his class, I would turn on the radio and read his poems while the rest of the class worked on computer units. I came to feel like an exception... the rules, assignments, the roles applied to everyone except me.

Gradually, I began attending church again; however, I did not attend young women so I must have done something else during the second and third hours. Maybe I went home, but it's more likely I hung out in the hallways visiting with people. I was moderately converted. One day, when I confided to the missionaries that I didn't feel worthy to pray, they explained that the Lord is our father and would never want us to stop speaking to Him because we had sinned. That opened the doors of communication for me, and I began praying again. I had never thought of God so familiarly. Their explanation resonated with me forever afterwards. God was my *father*; like my earthly father, He would want to hear from me.

There was this magical moment when I realized that all this time I had thought everyone around me was insane for not wanting to be happy when all along I had the wrong definition of happiness. It was refreshing. My parents, and siblings sent letters regularly; and I returned them often. Sister Seavey, from my ward back home, sent me letters every day with a thought or a scripture or a poem—every single day. I often wondered why she took the time to do it. More than a decade later, another woman serving in the church with me heard me tell of this kindness. Later, she asked Sister Seavey how she did that. Her response was that she knew the Lord needed me, so she was willing to do anything she could to help bring me back. I will always love her for her actions. Another sweet sister in my home ward, Sister Slater, wrote me an endearing letter about her own past, attempting to offer support, insights and help after seeing me smoking outside of the school. I've encountered numerous people fighting addiction without a support group. I had an unprecedented network. It felt as if the whole world was cheering me on. Later, too, I would hear from many friends and loved ones about all the times they put my name on the prayer roll at the temple. My name must have been on the altars of LDS temples for years. So much of my village believed in me and genuinely wanted me to be happy. I had vehemently rejected these kindnesses as judgmental invasions. How had I been so wrong? I took for granted the outpouring of love from the members in my church. Every person who falls astray doesn't have the cavalry going in after them. What I considered ordinary was in fact, extraordinary. Nevertheless it was still confusing to resolve these sentiments alongside the many drug addicts I had encountered and loved. They weren't sinister; they were rooting me on too. Like me, they understood happiness differently, but that didn't make them bad people. As a teenager, I struggled with the concept of loving the sinner, not the sin. My black and white spectacles had little room for shades of grey let alone vibrant colors. I would have greatly benefited from having more malleable definitions of good and bad, righteous and evil…they are incredibly fluid after all. Learning to avoid judging others also goes a long way in accepting people for their strengths and weaknesses.

I considered myself the therapist of my group of friends: the more experienced, wiser individual. I built confidence in the girls around me and tried to prevent them from going back to abusive or non-deserving boyfriends, becoming the door mat for their friends, or being manipulated by their families. I can't count the number of confidential, heartfelt therapy sessions I had in cars, bedrooms, and parks. I charged myself with the order of helping everyone through my mistakes. Ironically, despite outward appearance, I was nowhere near being emotionally healthy myself. True, I had abstained from mind-altering substances, but my eating disorder, secretive and shameful, raged on with intensity. And though I always pretended that my boyfriends were incapable of hurting me, I clung in desperation to my illusion of how all relationships should be. My good Mormon boyfriend was certainly the best guy I'd ever dated, but he was only moderately attentive, fueling my insecurity. I cherished my friends while I was there. They became my family just as I had made family of my drug-using friends at home. I was happy, but I was a little manic with my constant need for activity and stimulus. I never stopped moving; girl's nights often didn't end until the donut shop made fresh morning pastries. We would intentionally run out of gas in search of adventure; pulling over to shoot police officers with water guns because I, for once, had nothing to hide; hanging from chandelier at gas stations in the wee hours of the night. It was all good clean fun. I wasn't doing anything wrong, yet I had little to no "me" time, and I never dug deeper into my own psyche to uncover the source of my decisions. I was eagerly experiencing the sober life; every facet I felt I had somehow missed. But there was still something lurking in the shadows of my soul; ravenous; lonely; ready to reemerge.

Finding Me

Is it right to question who I am?
Right now?
Will I still be me tomorrow?
Why do I forgive so easily and look beyond people's faults?
How come I'm not quick to anger and easy to be around?
Positive attributes, people would say.
I wonder.
My happiness will shine to him, to her, to them.
Is it real?
I love to be the center, the spotlight shines on me.
Is it possible to be popular and well liked
but not have any friends?
I'm lonely!
I talk and laugh and play and brighten others days.
Who will calm my troubled heart?
Positive outlook, I go for my dreams.
If I want it, I'll stop at nothing. But...who am I?
My wild eyes and free spirit seem to be left in the past.
Are they really?
I want to be held, to be loved, to belong.
Does anybody know me?
I think I've grown above and beyond my years.
Is that just immaturity?
Speak your mind! People say. Tell how you feel!
I'd rather keep the peace.
What an act!
I think if life were a play.
I'd be the starring role because of how often
I pretend.
Steady as the sun, patient as a priest,
I'm always here for you. No matter who you are.
But I warn you.
It's usually a role critiqued to perfection.
Or maybe that's the act.
Maybe I really do care.
My mind says don't put your feelings in it.
Say that you care.

Act like you care.
But never actually care!
It keeps you safe from hurt.
Holds you at a distance.
I think it's impossible
Try as you might to avoid it...
You'll eventually care.
I will always be me.
And you will always be you.
Ten years from now I will still be me
And you will still be you.
Although I will be a different me,
And you a different you.
I think that's who I am.
Changing and growing, becoming happy with the person,
That is me.

-Lenaya Frey 1995 (15-yrs-old)-

Everyone in my life was good; so I was good. I was paralyzed at times with fear I'd be discovered as a fraud. I believed I was a fake on both ends. When I was around my new friends, I sometimes wanted to shout out that I was not like them. When a troubled new kid would enter the program, one who was abused and tortured, I'd think how ridiculous that I should live such a charmed life with loving parents and be here. I wasn't wholly good or bad. It was conflicting and confusing. Here I was; once again living a duplicitous life only without the extremes. I didn't have a clue who I was and began to be confused about who I was pretending to be. I continued to lie and scheme ways to have more freedom. I longed for a time when I could do whatever I wanted again. I pressured my boyfriend to be more intimate than he was comfortable with; I still used profane language; I bragged about my wild past every chance I got because I felt like it made me the cool girl, which it often did. And then, when I went home with one of my friends after school one day and she snorted a line of crank on her bathroom sink; I envied her with palpable jealousy. I didn't want to be good at that moment in time, but my freedom was so confined that I feared the consequence more than I could muster the rebellion. I bragged that I had quit smoking, but every time I inhaled the distant scent of tobacco and tar, my stomach twisted in knots and all I wanted was a cigarette. One night, while watching the news at home there was a segment on the lead Grateful Dead singer, Jerry Garcia who had just died. All the hippies were mourning in the streets. Whole cities had come to life; People everywhere were getting high while Tom Petty sang, *Let's get... to the point... let's hit.... Another joint...*My heart broke. I belonged with them. I should have been dancing in the streets too! I longed to celebrate his life, to give credence to his death. I felt robbed of my freedom, and also of my grief. I had committed to memory one of Jerry's quotes within the first few weeks of rehab: "Drug use is like a *cul de sac.* You turn to drugs to escape your problems, and then they in turn, become your problems." This was true, but I abstained. In my mind, because I declined to use when I was faced with drugs, I was stronger than drugs. I was fixed! I began to feel invincible. Believing I had arrived was a grave mistake.

I remember this period of life mostly with fondness. I lived the life of a normal teenage girl. Still, it was disheartening that many of my friends' parents and certainly my boyfriend's parents were wary of me. I charmed many of their fears, and the rest, I chose to ignore. In some households, I was a force for good in their teenager's life, in others, I was taboo. Though I began to get control of my substance abuse, I never stopped starving and throwing up. We had a lot of casseroles that I didn't love so that made the eating part relatively easy. At school I generally got a bag of pretzels from the vending machine, calling that lunch most days. There was a bathroom downstairs directly next to my room so I never felt like anyone could hear me. I wonder now, if the issue of my bulimia was brought up to the doctor or my foster mom. It seems like something that might have been important for my guardians to know. I weighed 145 prior to my love affair with ceramic toilet bowls and white powder. I never got above 115 pounds and loved buying a new wardrobe. My parents sent funds for me to get new school clothes. Since I'd been using drugs, I probably hadn't purchased a single article of clothing. This was my first time trying on clothes and thinking I looked fabulous. Of course I could still stand to lose a few pounds.

The instant gratification of short skirts and knee high socks didn't last. Instead of being consumed by euphoria, I became consumed by weight. I continued to attempt to starve myself. Every day I would convince myself that today I would do it. I was adamant that I would not consume anything with fat. Instead, I ate two airheads, some pretzels, and fountains of Mountain Dew. Every day I attempted to remind myself that I loved my new wardrobe enough to abstain from eating. Most days, however, by lunch time I would cave and have a bite of something on the forbidden list. Rather than accepting defeat and moving forward with my suppression, I would then make a mental list of everything I had wanted to eat for the day, or night, or week, and put into action consuming all of it: candy bars from the vending machines, nachos from the cafeteria, Glades fry sauce and Piccadilly chips. For the lunch hour I would eat everything. Then, once class started, I would get a hall pass and find an empty bathroom where I would throw up everything... trying always to keep the stomach bile off my face and out of my hair. I never could simply accept a bite of a forbidden food. If I ate even one cookie then it was the start of a binge. To this day it's hard for me not to consume everything I've ever craved when I cheat on a diet. I had rituals of wishing I was skinny every time I saw a shooting star or looked at a clock that showed symmetrical times like 11:11 or 12:12. I replaced my drug addiction with was no-less severe obsession with food.

As the semester continued, I began to build a close relationship with Michelle. I confided many things to her. My boyfriend did too which successfully made her my mediator. I loved how free she was, how open. I loved that she was so young. She understood. She was strict without being overbearing. I loved that she related to and was invested in students like me. Because I was disillusioned with the program and the lack of counseling (as well as the financial investment I was coming to understand), we began discussing other living situations. We schemed a plan that she and I would both leave the program. She would no longer provide housing for the program, and I would live with her, my parents paying a lesser fee than they currently were spending. It was a risk for her: this was a small town. I wasn't worried about it though. Partially I was trying to find more freedom, but also I genuinely loved and relied upon her. My only sorrow was leaving Deborah's house. We had grown so close, and I left without ever coming to her in search of a solution to my disenchantment. I sprung the news on her virtually while I was moving out. I went to live with Michelle and got a job working as a waitress at a local diner. From the moment I began waiting tables, I knew it was the job for me! I found all the grumpy old farmers and mechanics endearing. I made friends with everyone who walked in the front door. I made excellent money, but most importantly, I had a constant stage where I got to perform. I thrived in the fast paced environment. I felt like a star in a one-man show.

Larissa

"And if it so be that ye should labor all your days in crying repentance unto this people, and bring, save it be one soul unto me, how great shall be your joy with him in the kingdom of my Father!" (Doctrine & Covenants 18:15).

Though I knew my church culture was supportive of missionaries, I was still amazed at the sendoff I received and the remarkable outpouring of love. It was incredible. I was happily surprised that my relatives made the journey and so many friends showed up for my farewell. Three days later, I lay in the bottom bunk of a mission training center dorm, staring up at the mattress and wood above me wondering what I had gotten myself into. Upon any new responsibility in the church, Priesthood leaders place their hands on our head and issue a blessing from the Lord to help give insight and power to accomplish our assignment. I had to embrace the assurances pledged in my setting apart blessing for my mission. I was promised, "The Lord *personally* will watch over your family."

I thought college life was grueling, but the rigor of a mission was far tougher. Every minute of our day was scheduled. Practically the only time I had to myself and my thoughts were the 30 minutes to get showered and ready for the day. As part of an experimental tele-center group, I stayed six weeks in the mission training center. One of the highlights for me was to see the missionary who had knocked on my grandma's door, teaching and baptizing her. I can only imagine what it was like for him to see the fruit of his labors. It was a joyous reunion. My numerous instructors taught me the principles of teaching, and I delved into my scriptures with new vitality.

One of the best parts of serving a mission was the opportunity to focus completely on the Savior and not have to worry about finances, future or family. Sheltered in the work, I thought less about home. Later I discovered I was shielded from much of what was actually happening. I had opportunities to brush shoulders with General Authorities of the church and bask in the Holy Spirit that attended our numbers.

I arrived in Anchorage, Alaska, two days before Christmas during a winter that would prove to be the third largest snowfall on record. The trees sparkled with snow and frost. I became acquainted with moose crossing my path on a daily basis. Driving on snow-packed roads, I threw myself into missionary service.

All thoughts of my family were placed into the trust of the Lord, except when letters would push their way into my mind. Instead of obsessing about my own life, I became consumed with the lives of those I was serving. Though exhausting work, the days, weeks and months were so rewarding. My faith grew. I saw miracles on a daily basis and witnessed God's power. Occasionally a letter would arrive with vague allusions that things were going poorly. These pained me, but I continued on with my work. I did the only thing I could which was pray. Many times I thought my prayers went unanswered or that they might be answered in the future. Only later did I understand fully how God answered my prayers on a daily basis.

My first week, I thought I would freeze to death. After I traded in the wool coat and leather boots my parents had purchased for me for a down coat and Sorel boots, I thought that I just might survive. My companion and I tracted (knocked on doors) in the bitter cold, kicking clods of snow back and forth between each other, admiring the winter wonderland all around us. The responses to our door knocking were as varied as the people behind them. Some were kind but uninterested. Some were quite rude raining down hell and damnation upon us. Very occasionally, we met someone who wanted to learn more. Our real success came from member referrals or people who sought us out.

Lenaya and I are alike in many ways. We both possess all-or-nothing personalities. If I was going to serve a mission, I desired to serve with all the energy I had to muster and be the best missionary in Alaska. How could I measure that kind of success? The most obvious way was the number of baptisms I had, but I sensed that there was a danger in looking at those numbers and never dared to keep count. To this day, I have no idea how many people I taught were baptized. The only other easy measure I could see was obeying the mission rules and having the highest proselyting hours, so I pushed myself hard. Inspired by the stories of my grandma's missionary who knocked on her door during their preparation day, I pushed to work overtime, sometimes running faster than I had strength. I found myself frustrated if my companions weren't up to the same work ethic as me, and If I slacked I beat myself up. Those months were some of the most joy-filled in my life. Some days they were also the most discouraging.

On a typical day, I woke at 6 am, showered and got ready for the day, ate breakfast and then studied the scriptures individually and with my companion for two hours. We would head out at 9 am donning long johns, thick tights, a wool skirt, turtleneck, sweater, down coat, scarf, mittens and Sorel boots over wool socks. My companion and I packed a sack lunch and drove our car to the area we were working on that day and parked it. We broke up our time between tracting, calling on people who had taken copies of the *Book of Mormon*, visiting less active members, and teaching discussions to those currently interested. We also spent hours each week doing community service. I had a lot of practice teaching people and helping them change. I cheered at their successes and sorrowed when we watched them flounder. I learned to let go of the control and allow God to work in people's lives. I saw how crucial agency is for our choices to have any meaning.

We met Emily while she was living with her low-life boyfriend and raising her little daughter in a gray, cement apartment complex. We were instant friends. She loved each discussion we taught from the very start. She embraced the idea of modern prophets and came to church soon after. She was right at home in the ward. She embraced the Plan of Salvation and left her boyfriend when it became apparent that he didn't share her beliefs.

Every day my companion and I saw moose rambling through the bushes and marveled at the beauty of this amazing land. We helped people we were teaching to make commitments to quit smoking, start attending church, and read the scriptures. It was both exhilarating and exhausting.

I learned about communication and relationships with my various companions. I must have been hard to live with at times, because I was so exacting and driven. Slowly, I learned to love people unconditionally. Bonding with the other missionaries in my districts, I never felt a greater sense of camaraderie with a group of people before or since. Our common goals united us as we struggled through our individual challenges. Slowly the identity came to feel comfortable and that I truly was a missionary and not just pretending. The work was stressful as well as demanding, but I was happy to be doing the Lord's work and those times that I felt the Spirit so strong energized me.

We met a single mother and her large family who lived in a humble, welcoming house. They shared generous meals with us, and we talked and laughed and sometimes cried together. They deeply wanted to be baptized, but her ex-husband wouldn't allow it. After years of desiring to be baptized, their congregation held an entire ward fast for them specifically. Shortly after, her ex-husband finally consented for them to be baptized.

One warm June morning, fields of bright yellow dandelions blooming outside the apartment of my second Anchorage area, the phone rang. I ran from our bedroom to grab it and was shocked to hear my mom's voice on the phone. Missionaries are only allowed calls from home on Christmas and Mother's Day, and this was neither. She told me that Lenaya was much worse than they realized. She was phoning for information I had regarding a drug-treatment program. I gave her the information, chatted briefly and then she got off the phone. I simultaneously felt apprehension and relief.

Those first eight months in Anchorage formed me into a missionary. Not knowing what was in store, I was soon transferred to Fairbanks. Near the end of the summer, when golden days were starting to shorten and bright pink fireweed finished blooming, I headed north to my new area. This was the midpoint of my mission, August 9, 1995. Before I left I received a letter from Lenaya:

Dear Larissa,
      Hey there, How are you? I'm O.K. I just got your letter

yesterday. I liked the pictures. I was at Joe's when I got it and he mentioned that he thought very highly of you. I didn't realize that he knew you until just a little while ago. I've actually only met with him once since I got here. (In his office anyway) ....One of his students that I stayed with last weekend said that it's because he's been so busy. Things are all right here. I guess it just takes some getting used to. [Deborah's] house is not the easiest to deal with, but every foster kid has had to at some given point in the program. I like her and her family, but their tempers, rules, and ways teach you a lot of patience. I've gotten out and done some things that are fun. Joe tries to find activities for us to do. I get along good with all the other foster kids and am looking forward to the start of school as I will meet other kids my age. Although, I am also terrified because I've heard a lot of horror stories of the way the school I'll go to is. From what I hear it is very hard to get accepted, especially if you are pretty. Also, it's such a small town that everybody knows who the foster kids are and automatically assume things about them. I've seen that happen first hand already. I'm feeling kind of down today so it might not be the best time to write a letter, but I have my good days too. Some days I feel like I'm on the top of the world and realize how good this is for me and how miserable I was. Other days I'm totally homesick and miss drugs so much it's hard for me to see how this is helping me. All in all, though, I see how messed up I was and it's nice to not always be looking for the next line or what not. It's really hard though. I hope there comes a time when I don't feel so out of control of my emotions. As much as I've come to hate drugs, I miss them so much. I guess it just takes time. I love you and miss you. I run in the morning and go to aerobics in the night. It's awesome to feel so healthy and in control of my body. I look and feel good. I realized this is the best place for me. I'm working hard and doing my best.

Love ya,
Lenaya Frey

Lenaya seemed pretty candid on the outside, but I knew her feelings ran deep and that she had a long ways to go with Joe. I knew that he was a Behavioral Psychologist. I didn't realize just how much so until years later when I was working on my Master's degree in Counseling. His counseling philosophy was to change the person from the outside in. Change their situation, use positive and negative reinforcement or punishment and they will change. It worked to change her situation and get her a couple drug-free years, but I feel she could have benefitted tremendously from some counseling. I think it was her eating disorder that fueled her addiction for many years, and had she worked on the emotions that led to this disorder, she might have been spared some heartache.

It might not have made any difference. The what-ifs can drive a person mad if given free rein. My parents did the best they could in making these decisions. It isn't fair that parents have to make such tremendous choices when they are sleep-deprived and self-doubting. Still, it was comforting to hear from her and to know that she was safe.

Fairbanks was my refiner's fire. Right at the outset we started teaching a large number of people. We met Jillian in the Army barracks. She had requested a copy of the *Book of Mormon*, and we immediately started teaching her. Though she was surrounded by filthy language and worldliness, she embraced the Gospel and transformed before our eyes. She was soon baptized. We were tremendously busy, and I felt things more deeply. Soon after Jillian was baptized, a mother and son and a pair of sisters followed her lead. I felt on top of the world.

Living with a companion who is a complete stranger is an interesting prospect. It can teach us to love and serve someone and prepare us to work on more lasting relationships. I struggled with some of my companions. They were so different from me, even though we had the same purpose as missionaries. At times I felt very alone and misunderstood. I'm sure that I made mistakes and was too demanding of my companions. There were hard days and sometimes months when we weren't a great match. This was made more difficult as one by one, we watched all the people we had rejoiced with spiral into self-destruction and fall away from the commitments they had made at baptism. I questioned my purpose when everyone I taught turned their backs on our teachings.

As the fall colors fell from the trees and the first snow started to fall in Fairbanks I was at the lowest point in my mission. The days became progressively shorter. Cami announced her engagement. Nathan was home from his mission to Alabama and dating a little, much to my surprising dismay. We had been working with a couple who had AIDS, and she died. Soon after, her husband fell into despondency and tried to drink himself to death. It was heartbreaking to watch. Then Jillian stopped coming to church and never talked to us about what had changed. My heart was broken. I still feel pain all these years later when I think about her; she was my sister too.

There were jewels of joy along the way amid the dross of drudgery. My dad sent me a letter about my brother Nicholas. He had decided to try to follow every commandment, and he had never been happier in his life. I rejoiced to hear the changes he was making, and I sensed a difference in his letters. I witnessed firsthand that conversion is a personal matter. Even more, we all need to be converted over and over.

Through these struggles, I did all I knew how to do. I kept working. I kept going out day after day. I kept struggling to help people and teach people. I prayed more fervently and studied my scriptures with new intensity. Slowly, things became better. We taught new families who were also baptized. They made lasting changes in their lives and were so much happier. I grew in my communication skills and learned about compromise with my companions. I relaxed a little and eased up on my intense expectations. I was able to write in my journal after time, "Each night when I come home I feel so much joy from missionary work. The results of my efforts and the power of the Spirit are so rewarding!" Those times I felt isolated forced me to rely on the Lord, which is so much better anyway. Lenaya wrote me:

Dear Larissa,

Hey there, how are you? I'm great! I just got home and thought I should sit down and write you a quick note. It's 8:00 and I'm just getting ready for dinner. I had a terrible day today. I came home from school in tears. I decided to go down to the rest home and visit the ladies and sing for them. I talked with those who could talk and I fed those who couldn't eat and I comforted those in tears. I looked into their eyes and saw the Spirit shining bright and surprisingly enough, I forgot that I had had a bad day. They were such sweet souls and they made me feel so good. One of the staff members commented on how nice it was for me to do this for them and I was taken aback by this comment as I replied, "No, it's nice for them to do this for me." It's amazing what service can do for you. It makes you able to cope with anything that's sent your way. I find that if I go visit them before work, after school, their warmth and love lingers and prevents me from getting down when life isn't giving me lemonade. I just wanted to express my feelings real quick. I love you and I miss you so much. I'll write a longer letter soon.

> Love, always,
> Lenaya Frey

Fall slipped away, and winter hit with full force. Some new converts saved for two months to feed us a traditional Thanksgiving meal. It was a special night. I ached for their sacrifice and yet felt privileged to be so honored. I watched others who had so much potential let go of the rod of the word of God and fall into forgotten paths. I felt much like a counselor with so many of the people we were teaching. The temperatures plunged to -50, yet we found it exciting and didn't let it dampen our enthusiasm. We had angels watching over us at every corner and protecting us from the elements.

After years of letters from Nathan, I was coming to know that he was the one I wanted to marry. Knowing how important a decision marriage was, I had a hard time making up my mind. I finally wrote him my feelings and we were soon engaged, though I only told a handful of people. I was embarrassed that people might misunderstand, and I didn't want to be distracted from my missionary service. I stayed as focused as I could while he went back to college and we continued to write.

The days and weeks in Fairbanks stretched into months. One day, at a missionary conference while I was having an interview with my mission president, he informed me that I was being transferred to Juneau. I was ecstatic. I had always dreamed of going there but few sisters had the opportunity to be assigned to such a distant area. Most missionaries consider a few hours' drive quite a far transfer. My transfer was a five hour flight.

The view from my airplane was breathtaking. Snowcapped mountains and islands were wedged around the frigid ocean. Our landing was pretty tricky, navigating between the mountains, ocean and a glacier. Juneau, an extremely beautiful and lush city, is only accessible by airplane or ship. Bald eagles from the large evergreens swooped over our car as we drove and sang.

The remaining months of my mission were an absolute joy. I felt confident as a missionary, loved my companions, and loved the people we taught. I had grown to KNOW that God lives and that He has a plan for each of us. I also knew that we had the benefit of modern revelation through modern day prophets. I witnessed the *Book of Mormon* change lives again and again, including my own. I watched people overcome addictions and family problems through reading it and applying its principles to their lives. I believed in miracles, because I had seen them. My life was changed. I prayed to always be an instrument for the Master. Through my struggles I came to know that I truly was a daughter of God.

We were busier than I had ever been as a missionary, but it was a more joyful and less frantic type of busyness. We met a woman who had no hope and watched her life transform as she grasped hold of the gospel and was baptized. We worked with a wonderful woman, who had left the church, and saw the light of the gospel return to her when she was able to be re-baptized. These were people who I loved wholeheartedly and unconditionally. Someday we will have a joyful reunion.

When I thought back to receiving my mission call, it was amazing to think how the past 18 months molded and shaped my life. I would never trade this experience for anything. And then, as this beautiful experience was about to come to an end, I said my goodbyes. My last day in Juneau my companion surprised me with a going home "bridal shower." It was a sweet time with all the people we had taught. I flew to Anchorage and then the next day flew home on the red eye, full of anticipation over what the future held.

Lenaya

After the first year plus a few months, I went home for the summer. It was a struggle to leave behind my friends, my boyfriend, my foster family, my new life. Still, over the course of three months I managed to attend every church dance, go out with countless boys in our stake and have a wonderful albeit hectic summer. My parents were overjoyed at my return, easily mirroring my jubilance. Our relationship blossomed into a closeness I had not practiced with them before. I felt like I could talk to them about my friends and my life: something I had never felt comfortable doing. I had never so much as divulged my current crush, yet that summer I was able to share everything with them. It was eye-opening and peaceful. Nevertheless… we were changed. Jed sometimes seemed less than thrilled at my return; we were mostly strangers. Also, both he and Nicholas were asked to do dishes and help out in other ways while my parents walked on eggshells around me. They didn't demand as much from me as they certainly would have under different circumstances. At first it made me angry. I wanted to hold their faces between my palms and yell at them to be normal; treat me the same! I am not fragile! Other times, I characteristically took advantage and ran out to a party without worrying about any mess I left in my wake. Sometimes it made me feel anguish: that my parents had been so disrobed of their judicial authority that they didn't even ask me to fulfill normal familial responsibilities. Also, it seemed from my perspective that my dad spent much more time with my brothers than he had ever spent prior to my departure. It wasn't fair of me to hold a grudge against what I myself had prohibited, yet it still bothered me.

I felt like the sister/daughter/friend that they had never had. It made me a little gloomy about what I had missed out on in the past. Though my life was happy, my relationships under repair, and my sights set on the right path, I was still pretty self-interested. In my mind, I was the victim. *I* was the one struggling through a hard transition. It scarcely occurred to me that this might be hard for everybody else. Despite all I had been through, I mistakenly continued to believe that this was only *my* experience, *my* hardships, *my* journey, *my* feelings. A self-centered outlook is typical for most sixteen-year-olds; however, all teenagers don't leave such a deep chasm in their wake. Jed was probably more affected than we realized at the time. I'm sure it was hard for a child of nine to make sense of the situation. He once told his friends that he "used to have three sisters and a brother, but now only had a brother." I imagine he considered me a summer novelty, scarcely knowing life with me in it. Things with Nicholas were altered; I hoped not irreparably. He had been my best friend as far back as I could remember. As children we would knock codes on our adjoining walls to signal conversations until the wee hours of the morning. He knew all the details from before rehab and seemed resistant and apprehensive. Perhaps it was just too much to bear. Still, he kindly patched things up with me. We went to youth dances together. We talked and shared secrets and stayed up late like the old days. He, too, had to make sense of how my choices had impacted his life. We had gone from being best friends; allies in and out of our home; to something unknown. Despite his anger before I left, he shared his friends and activities, and outings with me. I have no complete understanding how I truly affected any of my family members. Some of the most eye-opening revelations have been discovered in the process of writing this book.

I stayed completely away from my old friends, feeling sick with discomfort the times I ran into one of them at the grocery store or at farmer's market. I didn't know how to love them and not be influenced, so instead, I avoided them like the plague. My fall-back plan had long been of running away from my problems. If I sincerely consider my motivations, there was an element of jealousy mixed with my anxiety regarding old friends. My entire transformation had occurred elsewhere. I didn't trust myself here. I didn't know if I wanted to be with them, or if I wanted to be this new person who would never fit in with my old friends again. But there was certainly a budding desire to be righteous. I was attending church; I was nourishing my testimony; I was trying to make good choices. It wasn't only out of fear that I avoided my friends; it was also out of a change of heart. This period in my life is, in many ways, the most confusing for me to deconstruct because, though I remember feeling like I was changing and growing and making the Lord happy, I also remember feeling completely and utterly unworthy; no matter what I did. Looking back, it's difficult to decipher how devoted to the Lord

I really was. My severe eating disorder contributed to my feelings of unworthiness. Everywhere I went people told me how amazing I looked. I had not regained my perceived chubbiness from years past and, because of my bulimia and anorexia, was slimmer than I had been growing up. Due to a limited understanding of the atonement, my eating disorder generated intense guilt.

Larissa returned home from her mission that summer which led to one of the most spiritual experiences of my life. When she first arrived home, Brother Stratton, a member of our Stake (a unit of community within the church typically including a dozen or so of the smaller units or wards), came to our home to set her apart via a blessing for her new church calling. I vividly remember standing on the stairwell, listening in as he placed his hands on Larissa's head and proceeded to give her the most beautiful blessing I had ever heard. I stood trembling on the third stair from the bottom, keeping my face on just the other side of the wall so that it was obvious I was there, but nobody could see my expression. As Brother Stratton blessed my sister, I remember thinking; *I wish that I could have a blessing like that. I wish that I was worthy to have a blessing so beautiful.* After he finished imparting the Lord's poetic words, he looked up at me and said, "Now it's your turn." Startled but pleased, I obediently if not apprehensively sat in the chair in the middle of the living room. Larissa, Nicholas, Mom, and I were all there as he laid his hands on my head and proceeded to pour blessings upon me. He told me about my experience in the pre-existence saying that my friends in the pre-mortal life were great women. He told me that I had felt the love of God. Then he uttered words which were sent from a loving father in heaven; a tender mercy, "Your slate is clean as if you had been baptized again. You have a true testimony of Jesus Christ that others can learn from." Every person in the room was sobbing by then. I was astonished. He said that I would publish works for the church because the way I phrase things would help many people. Then he said, "Now I'm going to answer the prayers of your heart." For several minutes, I would think questions or concerns in my mind, and he would specifically answer them. He told me many things about my talents and blessings. And finally, that I would help others through what I've experienced. After he finished, he sobbed as he gave me a hug, telling me, "You are a precious daughter of God. He loves you. I know because I just felt it." Most people will never have a blessing this detailed. The spirit was palpable in the living room that day. I thought my battles with Satan were done. My life would be easy from here on out.

Later that summer, I went to youth conference where I continued to be on a spiritual plane. We went out in the wilderness and participated in multiple faith-based activities, watched skits, and then were sent on a solo mission where we had to write in our journals following prompts.

Challenge one: Be as painfully honest as possible in identifying the three things you dislike about yourself.

1. *I have a weak will power and follow the crowd*
2. *I get jealous easily*
3. *I give in to temptations*

Challenge two: list specific things you intend to do to correct these perceived weaknesses.

1. *Pray and read EVERY day*
2. *Do not overeat*

Then they gave each of us a sealed envelope with a letter from our parents in it. We were to read the letters alone and then answer the following question.

Challenge 5: Open the sealed envelope and read its contents. Record your feelings and insights.

It is everything I have ever wanted to hear. I am filled with love and joy. I love my mom and dad so much and I am so very grateful to them for all that they have done. Words cannot express how happy it makes me to know that they recognize the accomplishments that were so hard for me. And it's wonderful to know that I have once again regained their trust (especially for mom to have reached that point). I love her so much, and her acceptance has always been something I've been insecure about. I no longer feel that way, and I look forward to more time spent with her and dad!

I was blessed with opportunities to feel the Spirit on countless occasions. The Lord truly showed His love for me constantly. But my distorted body image allowed Satan to whisper my inadequacies to my heart, and I continued to be consumed by my raging eating disorder. At Larissa's wedding, I was led to a new addition to my repertoire. It was at her home-town reception. I had eaten about a million mini quiches and countless tarts. I was so full I felt like I wanted to die, but I kept eating, binging in a way I had trained my body to accept when I went to events or parties. Typically, I would starve myself all day; thinking only of the food I would eat later that night. Once there, I would eat plateful after plateful regularly commenting on how I was one of those lucky types of people who can eat whatever they want. When I was overweight, I was far too humiliated to consume a lot of food in public. Now, filled with self-loathing, I pretended to be one of those illusions I had enviously spent my life hugging toilet bowls to be. After ridiculous absorption of food, I went to the mother's lounge where there was a private stall and locked the door. I stuck my finger down my throat and gagged a lifetime of insecurity. I heaved, careful to keep a tissue present to wipe the corners of my watering eyes to prevent the risk of mascara streaming down my face. We still had to take family pictures. I rejoined the party and continued to eat for the remainder of the evening, dealing with my discomfort until I could go home and safely purge with the shower running, free of the dark green bridesmaid dress my mother had made for me.

A guest inadvertently changed my life. Again. Eating a piece of wedding cake, she confided, "I might have two pieces of cake because I have to get testing done tomorrow and, doctor's orders, I have to take four laxatives before bed. Wink wink." I was certain that I had to discover what this magical thing called laxative was. I had honestly never heard the word. My eating disorder was the most secretive thing in my life. I always joked about what an open book I was, but I NEVER whispered in circles with others whom I suspected of playing the same malevolent game. Even jokes about bulimia or being fat made me squirm. It. Was. My. Secret. It was not something I could talk about for a long time. I was never even able to seek professional help for it. Fortunately, I finally opened up to Larissa who proved to be the help I needed.

So the day after my sister's wedding, I went to the Save On down the street from my house and hunted through the pharmaceuticals. When I found the magical laxative aisle, I was bewildered. There were dozens of options. The brand that targeted women and even came in a pink pill jumped out at me first. The bottle of 100 was half the price of other brands. I bought them, hoping, praying that nobody would recognize me. Despite being completely skinny, I waged war on the disgusting and fat image in the mirror. I imagined the cashier secretly laughing at me; deciding instantly that I was hopeless. I went home that night and read the directions. It said to take one to three, so I took three. The following day, I woke up and went to Costco with my mom—one of my favorite errands, the binger within has never been able to resist the abundance of free samples. It was 10:30 in the morning, and I was disappointed that my magical pill hadn't worked. I resolved to take twice as many that night. I was walking down the battery aisle when suddenly my stomach started rumbling. "I need to go to the bathroom," I blurted to my mom as I bolted to the nearest restroom. When I got there, there were a ton of women in the stalls, but it didn't matter. I was squeezing my cheeks together with a sobering knowledge that at any moment the dam was going to break. I ran into a stall and exploded for what felt like an eternity. Everything I had eaten the day before seemed to pour out of me. The feeling was indescribable. Like every other drug I had been addicted to, the euphoria was instant. I felt at least five pounds. lighter, and when I got home the scale confirmed just that. I had read that you shouldn't use laxatives as a way to lose weight because it was only water weight, and you would gain it right back as soon as you rehydrated. Standing on the scale that read 115, I vowed never to drink a glass of water again.

That summer, I starved myself until I couldn't. Then, when the cravings for food got too great; I gave in and ate something fat free (typically a bagel or rice), threw it up, and then followed it with a handful of laxatives that night. By the time I returned to Utah, I was 100 pounds taking upwards of fifty laxatives per night. I did the same thing with laxatives as with all drugs. I started small, built up a tolerance, and failed to ever consider my health or future. My stomach hurt every second of every day. There was blood in my stool every time I used the bathroom, which was all day. I never told a soul. I suffered in silence simultaneously relishing all the cute outfits my bony legs fit into while agonizing over what a lonely life I had, once again, chosen.

I went back to Utah to live with a very concerned Michelle. My significant weight loss didn't go unnoticed. I disregarded her concerns and simply went along as usual. When it grew more challenging to throw up and starve due to shared bathrooms and dinner times, I began to put on a few more pounds. It wasn't a lot, but it was enough to cause me alarm. Michelle had these expensive drops she put in her drinks to control her appetite. I began stealing them and making myself disgusting but effective cocktails every morning. She repeatedly asked me if I'd seen her drops which I regularly lied about. She thought she was losing her mind. Eventually she found my stash, but by then I already had one foot out the door. She explained how it made her feel to be lied to, and I genuinely felt bad, but my eating disorder had far more control than anyone I loved, or didn't love, including myself.

That was my junior year of high school. I continued to be semi-active in church mostly considering myself to have a testimony. Returning to school life, I struggled with the lack of communication with my boyfriend. It hurt that his parents insisted that he date other girls. I took it as rejection and cheating, and felt that they were judging my past. In retrospect I realize they were simply trying to obey the guidance of the prophet and not let their teenage son date exclusively or seriously until after his mission. I believed he liked me best, but I was too insecure and jealous to let him date other girls even if it was simply platonic. I confided my misgivings to Michelle, and she agreed that I should break up with him. I got asked out by another guy at the time, which made it much easier to end things with my first sober boyfriend.

I dated this new guy for the remainder of the year. We were a terrible couple. We fought incessantly and were extremely mismatched, but we couldn't stay away from each other. There was a pattern in this type of relationship throughout the next decade. I knew early on that we wouldn't work, but that never made me leave. I grew to love his family like my own which was part of the problem. I craved a replacement family and found it in them. My attendance in church started to dwindle as we began to be more and more intimate. He was the only active member of the church in his family, so there was little pressure on him to attend, and I conveniently worked many Sundays. His parents partied and laughed making me feel, once again, like I was missing out on something; like their lives were more fun than the couples their age in my church. I groped for understanding of the varying shades of grey in religion. I still knew the teachings of the gospel were true, but I was beginning to wonder if that mattered to me, or if excitement was more important.

Almost at the end of the school year, one of Michelle's former detention kids met me and persistently pursued me. He had been in and out of rehab and jail his whole life. I immediately felt more comfortable with him, even sober, than I had with my last two LDS boyfriends. Something in me said, *he is your people. You are him. He is you.* It stuck. Though he smoked and drank, I didn't feel tempted by that. However, it wasn't long before we began having sex. Once I let down my guard, I was no longer very sensitive to the Spirit. His substance abuse began to seem less and less important, and my comfort with him felt telling of where I fit in this world.

At the end of the year, Michelle and I had a passive aggressive falling out. We never outright argued, but I began to feel like a pawn in her money game once I discovered my parents had taken out a second mortgage on their house and were still behind on what they owed. She came to me demanding that I get in touch with my dad so that he could catch up. I felt used. I'm sure she did too. I had lied to her, disappeared at my boyfriend's house, and ultimately stopped confiding in her. We were both heartbroken. I can't recollect exactly how everything went, but I know that I trusted her less as soon as I came to understand the significant financial burden placed on my parents. Meanwhile, I worked five days a week at the diner, paid for all my own toiletries, cosmetics, entertainment, and clothes. Also, I ate every night at work and on nights off at my boyfriend's house. I felt like I was not a financial burden in the least, leaving me feeling resentful and injured. I imagine Michelle felt wounded as well, but I had lost trust. When I left that summer, I brought all of my belongings with me for the first time since I'd moved to Utah. I also took many of the clothes that I had borrowed from her daughters. I justified this to myself, arguing that they had commandeered many of my outfits, but now I see I was simply a thief. The lines of integrity were beginning to blur.

Just before I left, I had a profound spiritual experience where a friend of mine received a blessing. As she was blessed, I stood in a different room, tears pouring down my face. It felt as if my heart and soul might burst with the power of love I felt through me. I kept thinking that this was only a small portion of God's love. I was overcome with the Spirit. Afterwards, the stranger who had given the blessing came to me in the other room, put his arms around me and whispered in my ear, "The Lord loves you, and you know it. You have felt His love." I was left, once again, with the complex feelings of closeness to God and complete unworthiness. I wondered why and how God could love me. I certainly didn't. I often wonder why I had these little moments throughout my life. Why did God find it necessary to sustain me at times when I was either unwilling or incapable of sustaining myself? Why didn't God just leave me? I have come to understand the answer is in the parable of the lost sheep. God will do anything to save even one in His flock. At the time, I couldn't understand and wouldn't until many more hardships, obstacles, and trials. Eventually though, I came to know that God never left me... I left Him.

My second summer home intermingled moments of clarity and truth, with flirtation with relapse and sin. I went to church every Sunday. I participated in church activities. I went to Girl's Camp where the spirit was strong and beautiful. I felt purposeful, like God intended for me to be an example and to teach those who were like me. I felt compelled to love everyone around me and to help them have greater eyes to see. I had the opportunity to participate in a reenactment of Pioneer trek where I felt God's love. I regularly felt the Spirit. But, as summer drew on, I also began being promiscuous—sleeping with multiple men. I stayed out late every night. I went places where I knew the Spirit wouldn't join me, and I began inching further and further away from the gospel. I worked at a doctor's office and continued to abuse laxatives. I passed out multiple times that summer from extreme dehydration. I was consumed by thoughts of being fat, and only felt confident between the sheets with men. My eating disorder and promiscuity, completely related to one another, led me to let my guard down. My feelings of unworthiness and poor self-image encouraged the promiscuity. I was searching for anyone to make me feel sexy, beautiful. The attention and the desire helped to combat my body-image, but the sex led to intense feelings of guilt. It became a vicious cycle. I was selfish and insecure. I got a tattoo that summer—a new form of rebellion. I knew that my parents wouldn't approve so I lied and went with my boss. I kept my tattoo hidden from my parents and friends for a long time. My clothes got more and more revealing, and I was courting sin by the time the summer came to a close. It was time to determine where I would live the following year. My parents were so kind and generous to offer me the choice of staying in Nevada or going back to Utah. I'm sure it was discouraging to pay a fortune for their daughter to grow up without them. What a sacrifice it was. It's challenging for me, especially now that I'm a parent, to comprehend what that feels or looks like. I struggled with the decision. In some respects it would have made perfect sense for me to stay. I was already heading down a dangerous road so what difference did it make? In hindsight, I think I craved the complete freedom that Utah brought. I had no plans for relapse. Though I was on a downward trend, I genuinely believed my sobriety was safe.

III. Hope

Larissa

"I bear testimony that you cannot sink farther than the light and sweeping intelligence of Jesus Christ can reach. I bear testimony that as long as there is one spark of the will to repent and to reach, he is there. He did not just descend *to your condition; he descended* below *it, 'that he might be in all and through all things, the light of truth'"* (Tad R. Callister, *The infinite Atonement* 101).

It was so hard to balance hope for Lenaya with my five senses. I tended to grab onto hope for her future and dismiss little warning signs as flukes. My boundless hope was dashed to pieces each time she relapsed, and I learned to have a more tempered hope, to protect my heart from shattering. Loving and supporting an addict can be a fine balance. Too far on one side of the fence and we can plunge into forgetting to love, a few inches to the other side turns into enabling. I get nervous when I start to think of prayer as a type of childish begging for what we want, but true faith requires us to have hope for a different outcome, "if ye have faith ye hope for things which are not seen, which are true" (Alma 32:21). Also, "A lack of faith leads one to despair…" (*Bible Dictionary*, Faith).

Home from my mission, engaged and full of anticipation over my upcoming marriage, I quickly found a summer job and spent the rest of my spare time with Nathan. Being with Nathan reassured me of my decision and swept away my doubts and concerns. I don't remember seeing much of any of my family members, but I did have a chronic nagging apprehension for my siblings.

One sunny Sunday afternoon, I received a call from a High Councilman, one of twelve assistants to the President of the Sparks Stake, Brother Stratton. He wanted to meet with me and asked if he could come over. Half an hour later we were sitting in my living room, where he extended a call to teach the Stake Mission preparation class. He then proceeded to use his Priesthood to set me apart, giving me a blessing. Placing his hands on my head and before even setting me apart, he mouthed the words that soothed my deepest secret fears, "The Lord knows of your great fear in raising your children in righteous paths. Be courageous in teaching your children from the very start and all of them will be kept safe from the turmoil of the world. You will see terrible things all around you, but if you teach your children from the very start, it will keep them out of harm's way."

After issuing this magnificent promise, Brother Stratton continued to pronounce other amazing blessings upon me. For a moment, I caught a glimpse of my eternal nature. When he finished, we looked up and noticed my sister sitting on the stairs. Without pausing, he said, "Your turn." She came down and replaced me in the chair. I still remember the power and majesty I felt in her presence. I also had a feeling that she was not done with her path of temptation. With a sinking heart I knew that there would still be poor choices in store for her, yet I remained hopeful.

Next, Brother Stratton called Nicholas out of the periphery and gave him a powerful blessing. He proclaimed that Nicholas had turned the corner. He was a powerful noble and great one and was blessed with peace such that others would want to come to it. We were all three changed that day and bonded by the experience of glimpsing our own greatness and the true nature of our eternal identities. None of us forgot what we learned that Sunday afternoon.

In the heat of that July, Georgia hosted the summer Olympics, and focus was placed upon the notorious Olympic Park Bombing. Despite the chaos that was in the world around me, I turned away from my fears and proceeded in faith, embarking on the next season in my life.

Only two weeks later, Nathan and I were married on August 9, 1996. After a short honeymoon to Bryce Canyon and a reception, we arrived back at BYU, with enough money to pay one semester of tuition, our apartment deposit, and first month's rent.

Though we were happy, the first year of our marriage was difficult for me. There was not enough money for both of us to go to school and pay our living expenses, so we agreed that I would work and later try to go back to school. I tried not to be resentful that I couldn't start working on my Master's degree. It was a year of adjustment, because though we knew each other on a deeper level through our years of writing letters, we weren't used to living with each other in the day to day monotony of life. To make matters worse, I hated my first two jobs and felt a huge letdown after the thrill of my mission. I wasn't using my degree in Psychology and I felt very unfulfilled and unhappy. I slowly adjusted to married life. I was grateful to be married to such a good man and after a year of adjustment I grew much happier.

My job continued to be a source of unhappiness for me, and one night I came home overwhelmed and cried on Nathan's shoulder for a long time. He gave me a blessing which comforted me and then we walked together to the corner newsstand and bought a paper. I hoped to find something better that I could apply for. Upon arriving home, I scanned through the job listings when my eye caught an ad for The Center For Change, an eating disorder treatment facility looking for Psych Techs. I applied the next day and was interviewed and hired soon after. Life became much better after I had a job that I loved.

Around that time Nicholas sent in his missionary application and received a mission call to the Dominican Republic. Cami and her husband Cory were living in Provo, and before Nicholas left we brought Lenaya up to their house to spend some time with him. I wrote letters full of unsolicited advice to him every week. It was wonderful to hear of his ups and downs and remember my own experiences. A month after he left, Nathan finally chose a major in Public Policy, and Cami and Cory had their first son. Life seemed to be speeding up.

My new job gave me much more access to the mind of someone struggling with an eating disorder. During group therapy I detected traits of my mother in a woman across the circle from me, Lenaya in the girls two seats to the right, myself staring me in the face. An intensity and vulnerability grew out of these daily groups. Upon listening to a resident read her autobiography to the group, I grew to both recognize the hell of living with an eating disorder but understand the compulsion to keep coming back to it. So many of these women had suffered the damage of past abuse that I started to hypothesize all the possible abuses Lenaya might have suffered that led her to drugs and an eating disorder. That she even had an eating disorder was still unconfirmed by her, but I had strong suspicions.

It wasn't until Lenaya came to live with us briefly that I had more understanding of how bad things were. What we thought would be a long-term situation ended up a long line of her couch-surfing stops. She was meticulous about cleaning up after herself in the bathroom and even carried the trash out to the dumpster for me. That offer raised red flags and after she was gone for the day, putting my private-detective inclinations to work, I ransacked the dumpster to retrieve her trash. Luckily, it was nearly full and I didn't have to dig far. I tore the discarded bags open, finding evidence that was far worse than I had expected. Multiple empty boxes of Dulcolax and other empty pill containers confirmed my fears and piled on new ones. I had worked with many girls who used laxatives ritually. They tended to be farther down the slope of addiction and despair. This was no minor eating disorder, and while I knew her pain, I was unable to do anything for her.

Lenaya

I convinced my parents that a much better solution to their financial burden was to let me move into an apartment in Provo. I was completely over high school; feeling condescendingly older than my peers. I was on a dangerous road already with the promiscuity and intensity of my eating disorder, but as far as substance abuse went, I continued to feel bullet proof. At the time I thought my motives were altruistic; subconsciously though, freedom was calling my name in the form of parentless apartments and no curfew. I enrolled at UVSC to finish my last year of high school. Majoring in Early Childhood Education, the cost of books was my first financial slap in the face. The second blow was my daunting course-load of twenty-four credit hours which would prove to nearly break me. I embraced the BYU culture and started dating Mormon students. I also met and started dating Brad, who, despite being raised in the church, was rebellious against the standards and defiant towards his parents. Naturally, I was most drawn to him. He quickly became my soft place to land with his gentle and unassuming ways. He was noncommittal and didn't require any obligation from me, often pretending to be my cousin when other guys would come pick me up for dates. Markedly intelligent, we argued philosophies and ideologies with zero vulnerability. We became intimate straightaway with the understanding that there were no strings attached for either of us. I also dated several returned missionaries who were charming and handsome, but I already felt like I was not like them. The old instincts of rebellion and freedom began kicking me from the depths of where I thought I'd abandoned them for good. My sleazy attire included bare midriffs, halter tops, miniskirts, and plenty of shirts that would expose my new tattoo. I didn't exactly scream model Mormon wife to the guys I dated. Many of them stuck around much longer than they should have.

Elise and I went to dances and parties and then back to Spanish Fork to hang out with our high school friends, many of whom were now drinking. I was having sex and abusing my body in multiple ways; it was the obvious next step to go ahead and begin drinking with them. In moments of insecurity or solitude, I had what I called "drugmares" waking up in a cold sweat either desperately wishing I hadn't done what my dreams whispered to me, or worse, wishing that I had. Many of my summer hook-ups drank and smoked weed often leaving me feeling envious. My persona over the summer was "girl next door," and I clung to it, never giving in to the urgings to indulge in the mind altering substances around me. But I opened the door and invited that environment into my life again. It was one more pebble on the cobblestone path I was creating.

It's indescribable what it means for an addict to relapse after abstaining for months and almost years. It took one Everclear Mountain Dew popper to make me wonder why on earth I ever thought it was better or more fun to be sober. I reveled in the yellowish substance muttering, "where have you been old friend?" As I sat in a circle with my friends and dumped the liquid down my throat, the burn flared my nostrils and warmed me from my mouth to my stomach. The fluttering wings of a buzz emerging from my stomach to my soul felt like magic. I always thought old adage, "once you're an addict, you're always an addict," was ridiculous never thinking *I* was one drink away from the brink. In that instant I discovered the cliché is painfully and irrevocably true. I got drunk *one* time, and I was smoking cigarettes and weed by the end of the night. *The end of the night.* My year and a half of sobriety, vanished with one disgusting glass of booze. By week's end drinking and smoking had become habitual… once again.

Elise and I began smuggling alcohol and boys into our BYU approved bedrooms. This was a violation of the rules on multiple levels, but who cared? We were having a ridiculously good time and were, as usual, invincible. We had a bottle of sickeningly sweet peach schnapps which we decided to drink straight up. I got hammered, laughing, spilling, sploshing peach liquor down the sides of our bookshelves while belting Faith Hill at the top of my lungs into my makeshift brush/microphone. Brad was there with us, probably laughing more *at* us than with us, but still having as much riotous fun as we were. We decided to go bowling and, for perhaps the only time in my life, did the sensible thing and *walked* there. We continued our serenading as we stumbled down the street, puffing on long overdue Camel Lights. Elise was being silly and kept saying, "Watch out for camels, they spit!" while she left her saliva mark on the sidewalk. We got to the bowling alley and it was black light bowling! We couldn't contain our excitement at the happy coincidence and rushed to get our lane. Our white hot pants glowed purple hues while we threw twelve pound balls down the lane and praised the glorious sport of bowling where, win or lose, you get to take a ball and knock things over! Even while walking home, shoes in our hands and "ciggies" between our fingers, joyous songs belted from our bellies and our lips. By the time we walked in the front door, the combo of sweat, smoke, and sugared liquor got the best of me as I rushed to the toilet to puke. It was one of the few times I ever threw up from drinking and has forever tainted the scent and taste of peach flavoring. Instead of dampening the mood, this only provided us more hilarious material for our stand-up comedy—the funniest show on earth.

Another night, on a quest to pounce hot guys, we decided to go to a dance at UVSC. We took shots of tequila and chased them with beer and then, feeling excited and playful, we began wrestling with each other in our living room. I must have lost as only moments later we were in the emergency room where a doctor stitched me up. As he did so, I joked about how he'd better get a move on because there were fine men ready to meet us. All of us laughed and joked and had a regular party in the hospital room. The doctor at one point said, "Don't you know it isn't smart to harass the guy that has a needle in your eye?" This was the running joke of the night. We ran from the hospital, stitches and bandage no hindrance and fulfilled our goal of meeting stunning men desperate to know us. We went from dance to party to houses to late night stupors smoking cigarettes and forging bonds with so many people; some would leave lasting impressions, others would fade with distant memory as the moon disappeared and the sun took its place in the day sky.

I was extremely thin, but Totinos pizza, munchies, and late drunken Taco Bell runs slowly added a few pounds to my physique. Elise and I shared an apartment with four other girls: three rooms, one bathroom. One bathroom for six girls wasn't sufficient for my toilet needs. Suffocating with the fear of those extra pounds continuing to multiply, I pretended to find out about a new way to lose weight. I told Elise that I'd heard laxatives make you lose pounds overnight. I semi-confided in her to get her to join me and share my secret. Like most adolescent girls, she was willing to try anything for a quick body makeover. We took laxatives that night. The next day, she was doubled over in cramping pain complaining about the stupid plan. Pretending I was miserable too, I privately conceded she wouldn't be my co-conspirator. I would have to find another way to get around the ten watchful eyes in my dorm. I went back to throwing up in the shower and trying to make it in and out of the bathroom five times before anyone else woke up. I was drinking, smoking, and getting high with reckless abandon. I no longer cared what I did because I was already doing so many things I knew didn't lead to happiness. The life I'd worked so hard to find seemed overwhelmingly over.

Relapse was different than experimentation. When I began exploring drugs, I was certain that I was the happy one. Everybody else was wrong about what happiness meant. This time I knew better. Considering myself a failure, feelings of intense depression and guilt tried to raise red flags, but I numbed my emotions in the only ways I knew how. Once high, feelings of invincibility, excitement, and pleasure successfully replaced my insecurities and gloom. The desired effects of drug use might not have been substantial or lasting, but they were riddled with instant gratification and fleeting laughter that I sought to keep indefinitely. I'd do anything to not feel guilty... anything to not feel sorrow... anything to escape responsibility. Sobriety crushed me with unresolved emotions, so I tried desperately to avoid it. However, I vehemently believed that my substance abuse was a choice; I was still in control and could quit at any time... I just didn't want to. Many people never choose to do drugs because they "hate the feeling of being out of control." I *loved* it. Sometimes those demons still threaten to make me dissatisfied with my life: the yearning for no boundaries, nobody to care for. And yet, in real life... in real, *sober* life, I desire control and order. It's hard for me not to be a micromanager. Part of my motivation to be high was connected to how high-strung I have the capacity to be. I always considered myself to be utterly carefree and spontaneous, but perhaps that's another thing I was hunting at the bottom of beer bottles and ceramic pipes.

Desperate to keep the pounds off and feeling defeated, I started to plant the seeds of meth. I explained to Elise how you lose so much weight in a matter of days when you're on it. I tantalized the gift of skinniness over her hoping that she knew somebody that could connect us to some crystal meth. My sensationalizing worked, and she was able to find people in Spanish Fork with contacts. Upon meeting them, I manipulated them by purchasing *some* meth, but conveniently being with them when they sampled their supply. I never traded sex for drugs in the way of, "I'll sleep with you if you give me drugs," but that doesn't mean that I wasn't calculating. I always knew who the right people to hook up with were. I always found a way to either date or befriend the person most readily able to supply me with drugs. And so, in a few short months I'd gone from eighteen months sober, to back on crystal meth. In some ways, it was a drastic leap from sobriety to strung-out. In others, it was a gradual and almost imperceptible process. Every time I read the *Book of Mormon*, when I get to the parts where the Nephites begin being wicked again I want to yell at them, tell them how ridiculous they are. Don't they know that when they're righteous they are blessed, and when they're wicked, they are punished? It seems to happen so gradually that I want to shake them and tell them, "You know better! You've experienced this too many times not to know!" I was incapable of seeing this in my own life. I'm sure my family and loved ones felt overwhelmingly the same: like they could shake me and point out the obvious connections between righteous living/ happiness, complete debauchery/ misery. For a time, I failed to see anything.

In the world of methamphetamines, it doesn't take long to spiral out of control; one breath to permanently be out of touch with reality losing all hope and humanity. Instantaneously nothing and no one matter anymore. My original goal of weight loss lost its significance in the euphoria of being on speed again. Brad expressed grave concern for me, trying to intervene and help. It was too late before it began. I was completely incapable of understanding why anyone wanted me off drugs. Why couldn't the whole world go ahead and mind their own business? My life was, as usual, just fine!

I don't think we were in our BYU approved housing for more than two months before we were evicted for having boys in our bedrooms. Ironically, that was probably the very *least* of our offenses. I went to live with one of my friends and her family in Spanish Fork, and Elise went home. Her home was her haven, and it only took a moment for her to see the absurdity of the path I'd pulled her towards. She'd never asked for any of this, and it was a great blessing that she could live apart from me to regain her vision.

My mind had no off button. I've scarcely if ever encountered anybody else who will continue on the path of destruction long after everyone else has bailed. I had no interest in quitting, but once again found myself in a situation where I would have to hide my drug use from my friends and score meth on my own. Part of me dreaded the prospect, another part reveled in the fact that I didn't have to share or justify my extensive use. In some ways lying really is easier than telling the truth. This concealment went on for about a year before I quit trying and just gave my life to drugs.

Larissa

"...I raise my voice with others throughout the world who warn against abuse of drugs beyond prescribed limits....From an initial experiment thought to be trivial, a vicious cycle may follow. From trial comes habit. From habit comes dependence. From dependence comes addiction. Its grasp is so gradual. Enslaving shackles of habit are too small to be sensed until they are too strong to be broken. Indeed, drugs are the modern 'mess of pottage' for which souls are sold. No families are free from risk" (Russell M. Nelson).

Although I had no context for it at the time, the first drug treatment program that my parents sent Lenaya to was founded on a Behavioral theoretical viewpoint. Nearly 20 years later, as I was studying for my Master's Degree in Counseling, I understood that Behavioralism in the Psychology world was still vogue during her stay there and was based on the theories of classical and operant conditioning. Basically, the idea is to use reinforcement and punishment to change behavior. There is very little, if any attention paid to thinking or emotions and the focus is solely on actions. As long as patients were enrolled in the program, they found success and were able to stay off drugs. Learning to jump through the hoops to earn more freedom was enough for many to make a permanent change.

Since then, research has shown the power of changing our thinking as well as behavior. I wonder if Lenaya would have benefitted from addressing some of her deep-seated insecurities and not turned back to drug addiction. Maybe it wouldn't have made any difference. When we love and worry about addicts, we often second guess our attempts to help.

Rehabilitation programs then and now have mixed results. Relapse is considered the rule rather than the exception. Longer term programs seem to have better results than short term, but few people carry health insurance that will pay the prohibitive costs and many lack the resources to pay for the costly programs. Often, as in my parent's case, people resort to mortgaging their homes or taking out loans in hopes of rescuing their loved ones only to have the money squandered when they are unsuccessful. We wondered many times, if the sacrifice was worth it.

Even though addiction may look the same between individuals, the cause and motivation for use differ widely. Some cite genetic predisposition or point to psychological problems and social influence. Trauma can lead to addiction or for others addiction simply is a way to escape life. Many believe in a multi-causal model that integrates many varied causes for addiction (Capuzzi and Stauffer 12).

With such a complexity of possible causes for addiction, treatment becomes even more complicated. Very few people are lucky enough to only have a single addiction. Our brains are the center of addictions. The connections that we have in our certain parts of our brain are hijacked by euphoria producing chemicals (Capuzzi and Stauffer 17). Substance addictions including illicit drugs, prescription drugs, tobacco, caffeine and alcohol all make very significant changes to the brain chemistry, called neurotransmitters. Our brains are actually changed through the use of substances and it becomes not a matter of wanting to stop, but healing the brain. In 2009, 10.1% of youth from ages 12-17 were using illicit drugs ("Behavioral Health").

Process addictions include behaviors such as gambling, sexual addiction, compulsive spending, food addiction or eating disorders, and even internet or work addiction. Research has found that approximately 40-50% of sexual addicts are women. Many family members of addicts are found to have their own relationship addiction that is dubbed codependency. People often replace or trade addictions. "Denial is the undertone of all addictions" (Capuzzi and Stauffer 43). There are many different approaches to addiction counseling and often overcoming addiction requires medical and professional help.

Addiction in adolescents is made more complicated in the fact that their pre-frontal cortex or thinking part of the brain is not finished developing until around age 27, so their judgment, decision making, and emotional control is compromised before beginning risky behaviors and do not develop while they are using (Capuzzi and Stauffer 322).

Even though it was a huge financial sacrifice and burden for our family, those years that Lenaya was in the treatment program were crucial for her to allow her brain to develop and heal so that she could grow emotionally, intellectually, and spiritually. Though we questioned as a family later if it was worth it, I emphatically believe that it was worth every penny and every sacrifice.

Lenaya

I was living with my friend, Kylene and her family who were kind to take me in. I reverted to my perfect daughter role and flattered every member of the family. I got along with her parents far better than my friend did, which is typical for teenage girls. The medicine cabinets in this living arrangement opened new doors for my experimentation. They had prescriptions for anti-anxiety meds, anti-psychotics, pain pills, mood stabilizers, ADD meds, you name it. Every day we began popping copious amounts of prescription drugs, sometimes snorting them before she headed off to high school and I went to the community college.

School was a blur. I barely remember attending although I know I did. I worked at the pre-school on campus to earn credit towards my early childhood education degree. I cringe to think what would have happened had those precious four-year-olds been left to my sole care. I did observations, wrote papers, and participated in class, all while wasted. A twenty-four credit course load reinforced my reckless behaviors. Here I was trying to escape the burdens of a life of accountability while piling giant lists of dreary chores on my schedule. During finals I stared at my blue computer screen, completely high, for hours. Kylene had recently jumped out of a driving car while we were wasted and being ridiculous. As a result, she had a never ending prescription for the Percocet we were snorting morning, noon and night. I was attempting to write twenty-five pages worth of case studies, essays, and journals I had procrastinated to the last minute. I remember staring zombie-like at the blue screen as if in an out of body experience. I don't know why I didn't just drop out, but for some reason, not passing my classes was not an option. After staring blankly for hours, I decided to go for a drive and smoke some weed. I got in my car and drove along icy roads. I saw a brick wall at a turn notorious for car accidents because people regularly lost control around the bend. I wasn't suicidal, but I remember thinking that if I got into a wreck and ended up in the hospital, then I would have an excuse for not finishing my finals. I didn't want to die; I wanted a way out. I sat in front of that brick wall for only God knows how long. I listened to Wynona Judd's "Is it Over Yet?" on my tape player rewinding it over and over again. I sat there in my car: high, alone, overwhelmed, lost, empty. I finally got the nerve to hit the gas. I came screeching around the corner at full speed assuming that when I hit the brakes on ice, I'd take off like a turbo jet. Except. I didn't. Angels continued watching over me that day. I was simultaneously relieved and irritated. I'd love to be able to say that this was my low point; my rock bottom. It wasn't. I went back to the house and wrote papers until the sun came up. Miraculously, I managed to pass all my classes, getting A's in most by manipulating kind-hearted instructors. Those credits were not easily won, and the losses were far greater than an F on my transcript.

Right around this time I went to Planned Parenthood to get my Depo shot. I'd been on the shot since I was thirteen, but this time they refused to give it to me unless I got an annual checkup. A few days later, I got a call from the nurse saying that I had abnormal results and would need to come in to talk to the doctor. She couldn't release any information over the phone and, of course, it was Friday. I had to wait a long, agonizing weekend to find out what was wrong. I instantly felt certain that I had AIDS. I had been promiscuous without using protection, and it was finally catching up with me. I was only scared momentarily because I got annihilated and was numb to anything. Still, in the wee hours Saturday night, I sat high with a paper and pen and wrote. I tried to express my fear and anxiety; I thought I was free-writing stream of consciousness. When I looked at the page, I discovered that it was just scribbles slanting down the page at an angle like a toddler's proud page of "cursive." It didn't say anything. I was appalled and flabbergasted. For the first time I vaguely understood that I might not be in control of my drug use anymore. Panic stricken, I began to acknowledge on some level that I might be addicted to drugs. Dawning comprehension revealed that all of my incredible insights and feelings of invincibility might very well turn out to be a toddler scribbling messages in script nobody could decipher.

I realized then that I needed to stop using. That was the first time I ever made a conscious decision to abstain from drugs. Rehab had been my parents' doing. This time, I chose to stop of my own volition. When I took a pill the next morning, I had already changed my mind. I justified I had been overly hasty; over-dramatizing my writing *faux pas* through delirium and stress about AIDS. Days later, I lost my meth connection to a drug bust which forced me to dry up.

I was convinced there really was no need for me to abstain from other things. Instead I drank heavily and took diet pills and mini thins in amounts that would probably kill others. I rationalized that without the meth, I no longer had a problem. After the weekend was over, I went to the doctor resolute in my ability to live life to the fullest until it ended prematurely. I was told I had pre-cancerous cells in my uterus that they wanted to look at more closely. I gave an audible shout for joy which was met with perplexed and concerned stares. I didn't even bother to explain that cancer was nothing compared to AIDS. Miraculously, I never contracted an STD. I believe a huge portion of my protection came through the Lord answering my faithful parents' yearning prayers. My death sentence and resolve to live a worthy life flitted out the window faster than the wings of a hummingbird. Once again, I was in control of my own life; except that I wasn't.

I continued to live with Kylene and her family for a few more months before she gave me the ultimatum: no more smoking weed. The irony of the pill-popping friend setting this boundary wasn't lost on me then or now. Like always, I hid it until one evening I ran into her at a gas station with a notorious pothead, and she raced me home to tell her parents. By the time I got there, they were already on the phone with my parents arranging to take me to the mental division of the hospital. I pled with my parents over the phone begging them to believe that I didn't have a problem. I was certain a rehab wouldn't even take me. Apart from the pills which had substantially slowed down, all I'd done for weeks was smoke weed and drink. My parents ultimately told me to prove it by going to the hospital, but not before asking me about the ridiculous amount of laxative boxes in their garbage from my most recent visit. I insisted that they were from a lifetime ago and I was finally getting around to cleaning them out. They weren't convinced. Kylene's parents took me to the psych ward where they drug tested and interviewed me and refused to admit me because I was nowhere near hazardous enough for their facility. I felt jubilant and victorious. However, once again, I had nowhere to live. The last thing I ever wrote at their house was a letter to myself.

Dear Lenaya,
I'm writing to you today in hopes that the next time you read this, you'll be

at a much better place in life. I'm writing this as a reminder to you, so that you never forget again what life is about. You see, you aren't happy right now. You know you're not. Before, when you were messing up, you had an excuse because you really thought that you were happy. But it will never be the same because you've experienced happiness; you know the real definition. Just always know, please always remember, the gospel is happiness. It is the only pure form of it. And until you give in and live your life accordingly, you won't be happy. And I know it's hard. Life is. That's all life is, just one big decision. You take different paths all the time. Sometimes you take the right one, and sometimes the wrong. And that's okay, that's how you learn. But there comes a time, when you've learned it all, and you just need to live what you've learned. You're lying to yourself and everyone in your life. And until you face the truth, you'll continue to be miserable. And I believe you'll make it. I believe that the morals instilled in you will ring true and get you out of the frame of mind you're in. I really want you to get there. And I also hope that someday you'll realize your potential because even though you feel worthless as if your existence doesn't matter, someday you'll know that you are a marvelous creation of God and that you have such a special purpose. And I know I'm not in a sober state of mind right now, but I also know that everything I'm writing is true. One more tip: your family loves you more than words could ever express. Please stop hurting them. You've hurt them enough in your life. I love you. Even if it appears as if I don't. I do. Good luck, and I hope someday I disappear and you take over again. That's all, take care of yourself,

Lenaya Rachel Frey 10-02-1997

I don't remember writing this. I do remember one night long ago while attempting to write a paper for school, a house full of people doped up on meth, I began typing every word that came out of people's mouths. Not thinking, not doing my homework, just typing. I remember reading it back to my audience to great surprise. At first we laughed until our bellies hurt and we had to scrape the dried saliva from the corners of our mouths and eyes. And when we had exhausted all of our pleasure, we sat, mouths and eyes gaping open as we came to an understanding that we couldn't articulate something only our hearts could understand. There was nothing funny about it at all.

Larissa

"And [Moses] saw God face to face, and he talked with him, and the glory of God was upon Moses; therefore Moses could endure his presence. And God spake unto Moses, saying: Behold I am the Lord God Almighty, and Endless is my name....And, behold, thou art my son; wherefore look, and I will show thee the workmanship of mine hands....And I have a work for thee Moses, my son; and thou art in the similitude of mine Only Begotten; and mine Only Begotten is and shall be the Savior....and I beheld his face, for I was transfigured before him" (Moses 1:2-4, 6, 11, Pearl of Great Price).

The first few years of our marriage were times of simplicity and growth. Because we were always saving up for the next semester of tuition and staying on top of our bills, there wasn't much else left for fun. We found enjoyment out of the simple things of life. A walk to the park, reading a book together, going to campus, cooking dinner in the evenings, watching movies with friends were what we were able to do, and it was wonderful. Lots of times we felt the urge to buy football tickets or go out to dinner, but realized it simply wasn't possible.

Nathan worked cleaning carpets and later laying carpet. Once I had my job at the Center For Change I felt much more fulfilled, as I was growing and learning in my field. We moved into student married housing, enjoying the company of wonderful people. Along with keeping busy with our church callings, we volunteered at the local suicide hotline. Together Nathan and I celebrated holidays, starting our own traditions. We were industrious and found ways to pick fruit locally to can and shopped at the grocery discount stores. At the time I felt very limited, but as I look back I can see that it was a wonderful time for us to bond together and work as a unified couple.

Officially called a Psychological Technician or Psych Tech, I worked at a residential unit for people who had severe eating disorders. Each morning, we woke the girls up and weighed them and then monitored them while they got ready. We always had to flush their toilets, so we could make sure they weren't abusing laxatives or throwing up. We ate meals with the residents, enforcing strict rules. After eating, we waited in the living area for 30 minutes talking with them and helping them through their anxiety.

My favorite times were attending all the therapies with them during the course of the day. I was personally impacted from attending daily education class and group therapy as well as music, art, recreation and movement therapies. I realized all people have some dysfunction, and I started to see the dysfunction of own my life. I attempted to break cycles and increase communication personally.

One lesson in an education class that changed my life significantly was about communication. Nathan and I didn't fight a lot, but there were times that my feelings were hurt and I clammed up. He asked me what was wrong and as is so common I always answered, "Nothing." Not knowing any better, he accepted my answer, shrugged his shoulders and went on his merry way. I would be seething by his response. What I learned in class was that when I told him nothing was wrong, I was in reality testing him to see how much he cared. I became so upset because my feelings didn't seem to matter to him, and I was also more distraught because rather than share my feelings, I was stuffing them inside which is another dysfunctional behavior.

The instructor taught us to respond when someone asked what the matter was and to be honest about our feelings. They also taught us to phrase them in "I feel..." statements rather than accusing statements that might put the other person on the defensive. I found it incredibly difficult to take this advice, but I practiced and started to get better at expressing my feelings. Surprisingly, I discovered that the very experience of saying how I felt, actually worked to lessen and dissipate the negative emotion. After a while, despite the challenge for me, I even learned to express how I felt before Nathan had to ask what was wrong. Our relationship improved and our communication grew healthier.

Though my parents were loving and nurturing, I started to understand that they had not been raised to express their feelings. I think they were terrified by emotion and didn't know what to do

130

with it, so they avoided it. Whenever we run away from our emotions and avoid them, they will still impact us and often the intensity is heightened. We all had different ways of dealing with these whether healthy or unhealthy. Lenaya turned to drugs and her eating disorder.

One of the practices at the CFC was for the girls to be open and honest with the other residents about their eating disorder. Usually around their first week there, they had to write and read their life story to the group. Always intensely emotional sessions, hearing story upon story, I recognized themes and heartbreaking patterns of lives destroyed and health wrecked. I learned their secrets and understood how differently their outward appearance was portrayed compared to their inner self-contempt and shame. I discovered that the eating disorder was not really about the food, but more about the feelings and often struggle for control.

We were encouraged as employees to read the literature in the field, so I pored over books and articles that also expanded my understanding. I was able to use this knowledge to confront Lenaya about her eating disorder. Though she was in complete denial, I made it very clear to her that I knew that she had an eating disorder and that when she was ready to talk about it with me; I would be there for her. My compassion grew while my judgment shrank.

I practically received free therapy for the nearly three years that I worked there and really admired all the doctors. Group was a powerful processing and normalizing experience. It was a place to go and feel a sense of connection and learn to communicate safely. The residents also had individual therapy nearly every day, and as I saw them come and go I wondered what it was like in those closed rooms. I wanted to be the therapist who would bring back the girls to start their journey through self-discovery and healing.

Still young and naive, I tended to polarize my thinking. I didn't see all the different shades of grey that accompany most situations, and believed that there had to be some cause of Lenaya's addictions. Sure that some trauma much have started all of her behaviors, I searched for a cause. One discussion around that idea with a Psychologist at work was eye-opening. While I was wondering out loud with him what must be the cause of my sister's problems, he looked me in the eye and asked why I thought there was a cause. I sputtered out my belief that something had to have caused it, and he challenged my belief saying simply that people do drugs because it feels good and they want to keep feeling that way. He dispelled my erroneous belief that something outside had to have caused it. It was an important shift in my understanding.

During these years Lenaya sometimes called for help or made attempts to keep in touch. She called me from the emergency room on a Friday night when she was getting stitches, creating an elaborate story and downplaying the seriousness. She called to talk at times when she felt down. She came over to visit occasionally, going on about the dates she was on or what was happening at work. As her life became more and more out of control she started going from job to job always having a reason for leaving that made perfect sense to her but was harder for me to pin down. She was very superficial for all those years, saying what she assumed I wanted her to say, throwing in religious lingo that seemed phony. I caught her in lies constantly and learned not to believe a word that came out of her mouth. Relationships built on lies can never be genuine.

My parents started to worry about the safety of leaving their car in her care. Acting in the role of detective, I scouted out her car for them and took it to a hiding place with a key they had sent me. My dad planned to come out and confront her in an upcoming visit. Nathan and I visited her in various homes and I felt despair when I was faced with the harsh realities of her lifestyle.

My family still seemed to be in some turmoil, mixed with an intensely busy schedule. My dad had challenges at work and switched law firms. Jed became a teenager, and I can only imagine how lonely it was for him at home as an only child with an absent father and a mother who had spiraled into a terrible depression. With my dad's calling in the Stake Presidency my family felt constantly in the fishbowl, magnifying their apparent failings for all to see. Even when he was released from his stake calling, my dad was called as a Bishop of their ward three weeks later, so there was no letup. My mom always tried to be open and honest with people about what was going on, yet at times it was almost more than she could bear to go to church facing unsolicited advice and smug sympathy. Still, church was a rock to her that kept her from floundering and most people were truly supportive to my family in myriad ways.

Lenaya

Even finding myself homeless yet again, I was unwilling to go home. I'm still surprised that my parents didn't insist that I return to Reno. Of course, they'd seen how effective their demands in the past had been. I'm sure they felt pretty helpless. My role as a parent is still fairly amateur, but even when my two-year-old defies me and I feel like there's nothing I can do about it I'm left with intense feelings of inadequacy, guilt, sorrow, and frustration. I imagine those feelings were intensified in my parents' situation. I bounced around from house to house, staying with a variety of people, moving upwards of fourteen times that year. I lived with Larissa at some point, though I don't remember if it was after this eviction or a later one. Moving was exhausting. Eventually, I landed in what I dubbed "crack house" number one based on the appearance, and later, because it had lived up to its title. Amy and I set out to find an apartment and ended up in a little house with separate entrances. In one half of the house lived an overweight slightly mentally disabled woman. She lived alone though I think somebody brought her groceries and help fairly regularly. In the other half lived two girls a little older than my seventeen years. They agreed to let us move in. There was one bedroom, so we had bunk beds in it, a queen on one side of the living room, and a couch on the other side. We had make-shift closets all over the place and one bathroom and kitchen. The back was a dirt lot perfect for when we began having massive parties. Our closest neighbor was far enough to be fairly immune to our noise. One of my new roommates moved out weeks after my arrival because she was not impressed with my moral standards. The other stayed and we became close friends.

The house quickly became a monstrous party house. We'd have raucous parties without any planning. Suddenly there would be fifty people pounding beer, smoking joints, and snorting lines all over the place. Because of our relative isolation, the police were never called. It was ideal. Apart from having to regularly clean up blood and vomit, the situation couldn't have been better. We partied morning, noon and night. We had pounds of weed in boxes on the floor. We drank 40's from sun up to sun down. I took whole bottles of mini thins during meth dry spells. We forged a group of friends we took to calling the Spice Girls due to our diverse appearance and general affinity for one another. We dressed in a way to get the most possible attention. It felt so powerful to cause a room to hush when we walked in. We went to house parties where guys waited in line to talk to us. We heard cat calls everywhere we went. We got pulled over by guys on the freeway trying to get our numbers. We gave numbers out like we were networking for careers. Between us all, there was never a shortage of awesome places to be, or alluring strangers to invite to my pad.

Our days ranged from driving around blasting Sublime or Tupac, to hiking around nature trails while smoking weed and cigarettes, to getting tattoos and piercings. Some teenage girls get matching necklaces or friendship bracelets. At the time, tongue rings were a new, inventive, crazy hard-core thing. Our friendship token was to all go get our tongues pierced together. As we drove there, the nerves set in. I couldn't believe we were going to go through with this. The idea of holding my tongue out while someone jammed a needle through it was both barbaric and tantalizing. We blasted Blink 182 as we rode in Amy's red Jetta to our future glory. We'd been told not to take pain pills because they thin your blood, but we gave the warnings no heed. At the shop, we each took our turn in what looked like a dentist's chair. I'll never forget what it felt like as we exited that building, walking together in a group, crossing the street. I felt so big... so alive... so free. I felt so bonded to my friends... like we were part of a club of unrestricted revolutionaries and no one else could join us, with or without tongue rings. I felt exclusive and prevailing and rebellious.

My blue Geo Prism was a tool for risky behavior including jumping it over railroad tracks, driving it off road, piling people into it like a clown car, and all other types of truck-like stunts. One day, Amy and I were tripping on acid, laughing hysterically at our distorted perceptions when we decided to look at the beautiful earth up close. We took my car to the base of the Wasatch Mountains and discovered a road leading all the way up. There was a torrential downpour. The air smelled fresh and invigorating. The trees were emerald green with a shiny coat of high gloss accentuating their glimmer. Though the sky was dark and foreboding, its invitation for adventure wasn't lost on us. As I drove up the mountain, we philosophically took apart every world-notion familiar to us. The farther up the hill we climbed, the closer the leaves were, kissing the roof of my Geo. We giggled tremulously while we listened intently to the sounds of the forest coming to, and sustaining life. The birds seemed to be speaking to us. We kept driving, around every extreme turn, up the cutbacks until the road got more and more narrow. We thought it strange that the road was all but disappearing in front of us, but chalked it up to the dense forest ahead. Finally, it occurred to me that this was, in fact, not a road but a hiking trail. I said this out loud which began another round of hysterical laughter. I had driven my car all the way to the top of the mountain on a bike trail! It was awesome. We were so thrilled with our adventure and drove until my car could no longer make it through the narrow gaps between trees. We dubbed this the best weed-smoking spot on earth and, in the pouring rain, sat on the hood of my car, covering the pipe as we passed it back and forth relishing the fresh air as much as the THC entering our lungs. Sopping wet, I was electrified in that moment. On acid I experienced earth's beauty in a more physical manner. I felt the green leaves and orange blooms and rough bark within myself. I felt my outside surroundings on my inside. I didn't buy the notion that acid was bad for me giving little credence to damaged brain cells. I added this to my list of things the world swears are harmful just so there isn't anarchy in the streets despite having seen its horrendous effects first-hand with my caveman boyfriend. Unlike meth, acid brought with it a tranquility…this time. It was tricky getting my car out of there, but we reversed for a significant portion until we reached a place wide enough to turn around Austin Power's style.

When I was on a meth dry spell, things were better, and I had human connections and interactions. When there was plenty of meth, I smoked it out of all the light bulbs (a fairly common technique) on our property until we had only one left which we moved from room to room. In the midst of a strung-out adventure, darkness is frightening. My mind played tricks on me that brought the air to life in a more sinister way than the acid. In time, our solitary bulb got used, and we lived with candles from then on. At that point, or perhaps before, we shoplifted food, toiletries, light bulbs. We all stole toilet paper from our various jobs. I was still waiting tables though I never had any money to show for it. I was a clean freak while strung out and more than once cleaned up someone's bleeding head before it stopped gushing. I was known for picking up limbs of passed out party-goers to vacuum underneath them while they slept. It didn't take long for our toilet to get plugged up and overflow. We tried everything without success to fix it and, in the end, just made everybody use the backyard as a toilet. This was especially putrid due to the vomit, the large number of people who were in and out to party, and the laxative abuse. Every morning, I would run outside and explode from the night's laxatives in between the bushes. For some, that might have been a deterrent, but it didn't and couldn't stop me. At times, when I had plenty of meth for weeks at a time, I wouldn't eat and therefore didn't need to take laxatives. But when I ate, I braved the bushes early in the morning praying that nobody spotted me.

Our living arrangement changed frequently. At one point two friends from high school named Matt and Corbin got kicked out of their houses for partying and disobeying their parent's rules. We were all too happy to take them in. I immediately started a relationship with Matt. We had long been friends with them, but our bonds were forged deeper through the constant companionship. It made it seem even more of a party house with our co-ed additions. Corbin was hilarious and became our constant entertainment. He was a ham to begin with, but liquid courage often made him a one-man show. With them, there was also more food suddenly in our fridge. Corbin once decided that he was too hungry to wait for the steaks to marinate. We found him at the kitchen table with a steak in one hand and blood dripping down the sides of his mouth. We joked about that for months! Matt, crazier of the two, supplied a never-ending supply of drugs. Parties abounded, recklessness ensued, and we carried on in our complete debauchery. If those walls could talk, they'd disdainfully disclose stories of broken noses, busted heads, weapons, drug abuse beyond measure, more casual sex than some brothels, alcohol, alcohol, alcohol, and eventually, the smell of death that permeated the air. Of all its residents, there are two of us still alive. The light bulb scarcity was never resolved, and hollowed out pens and straws littered every surface. People scrambled for tiny pills and miniature plastic bags. No one left that house unscathed. And yet, despite the wretchedness we were a bonded, dedicated group of friends capable of laughter, tears, excitement, and plenty of fun.

It's hard to describe how horrific and wonderful the same

experience can be. It wasn't only the addictions that kept us there. It was the freedom, the exhilaration, the constant flying with no regard for a future because we felt invincible. It makes me think often of Dickens' words, "It was the best of times, it was the worst of times."

Perhaps part of my recovery is mounted on remembering how horrendous life was. But I need to acknowledge that we were still people forming bonds and loving each other in our distorted and limited capacities. We shared many drunken nights where we solved all of life's problems with our "philosophical" discussions. I find it challenging to properly explain how much of an escape it is to be high. Any uncomfortable or vulnerable, or unpleasant feeling can temporarily be replaced with feelings beyond anything the sober world has to offer. We chain smoked our cigarettes, went to concerts, zoned out to amazing music, met people everywhere we went. We loved each other. We had inside jokes, funny sayings, hilarious anecdotes, in short, friendship. We experienced life in a way few people describe. We lived on the exhilarating edge of something dangerous but enticing. We were anti-establishment; anti-rules; anti-sobriety; anti-boredom. We lived and breathed escape, thrill, ecstasy, pleasure, and instant gratification. Regardless of our losses, at the time, I never thought I was missing out on anything. Even now, with so many years of sobriety under my belt, the desire for escape can be so compelling at times that it tries to lure me back in. Fortunately, hindsight is clairvoyant; I know how that story ends. But at the time—defying reason, control, and logic—messed up on drugs was where I wanted to be. It's like coasting over the waves of the ocean, the feeling in your lungs just as you sharply inhale with a physical response to something immaterial. In essence, it is dangerous because it is excruciatingly gratifying.

Shortly after moving into the "crack house," my mom came to visit and check up on me. She insisted that I take a drug test which I agreed to. I chugged some drug test elixir from the nearest head shop. The results were inconclusive although showed I was a walking pharmacy of over-the-counter drugs. I honestly don't recall much of our agreement or conversation. I remember her being helpful and kind to my friends and me. I also remember tearing through the house like crazy attempting to hide or get rid of any paraphernalia. In the end, there was too much so the beer bottles and pipes just stayed where they were and I kept my fingers crossed that she had suddenly become Helen Keller. Before she left she purchased and helped us wallpaper the house. We only got half-way done and promised her we'd finish it. Once she was gone, more pressing things like snorting lines had to be taken care of, so we left the house half old-fashioned mustard floral, half new-age neon abstract brush strokes. It added to the unlivable quality of the house as well as the psychedelic charm. Every time we had acid or mushroom parties, we'd trip out on the time warp. We'd start in the 50's and evolve to modern time. Drug-enhanced conversations centered on the bizarre wallpaper my mom was able to start in a few hours, but we were too drug-induced to complete in several months.

Larissa

"Can a woman forget her sucking child, that she should not have compassion on the son of her womb? Yea, they may forget yet will I not forget thee. Behold, I have graven thee upon the palms of my hands; thy walls are continually before me" (Isaiah 49:15-16).

I only had post-partum blues with my first child and my last, but both experiences completely overwhelmed me. My first case revolved around the loss of my independence which then carried with it a leash of unending guilt. My last, ironically, centered around the knowledge that I would never have another baby, even though the waves of sorrow were brimmed with a bit of relief. I enjoyed my first pregnancy and as many first mothers do, I recorded every feeling, impression and physical experience of pregnancy. Brandon was born in the spring of 1998, the first day of Nathan's summer semester. It was a textbook delivery and he was a perfect baby in every way.

I felt tremendous love for my baby, having only a narrow understanding of what a monumental change had come into my life. I worried less about Lenaya and became more preoccupied with my own little bundle of perfection. Brandon really was a beautiful little baby. His sweet little toes and fingers enthralled me. His pure dependence upon me filled me with a sense of purpose.

When Brandon was only six weeks old, I had to go back to work, demanding every ounce of my strength physically and mentally. Nathan was still going to school, so I switched to a night schedule to keep from getting a babysitter, both for financial and protective purposes. Working while breastfeeding on a 5 pm to 5 am shift was challenging. I knew from my time as a missionary, that I wanted my main focus to be on my children and intended to be a stay-at-home mom as soon as possible. My greatest desire was to shield my children from the evils of the world I was witness to, while preparing them for what they would inevitably face. Though challenging, my work arrangement allowed me to be home with Brandon most of the days and

Nathan scheduled his classes and work around my schedule. We managed to balance with occasional help from a neighbor or Nathan's sister.

I grew up hearing that the Latin meaning of my first name, Larissa, means cheerful or joyful, and my middle name, Marta, means bitterness. As I both marveled at the precious new life in my protection and feared for my sister's trajectory, the dialectics of my name came to make perfect sense. As human beings, we are capable of feeling pure bliss and penetrating sorrow at the same moment. As an adult, I discovered the Russian meaning of my name is Citadel or Protection. I do feel looking back that I was placed in the same family with Lenaya to be a protector and I felt deeply my new role as protector of my children.

Ever the good PI, I called my parents routinely with reports of Lenaya's whereabouts and her plight. I kept her tethered to the family as much as I could, which wasn't much at all. Weeks would go by without any sighting, yet I saw her every weekend in the eyes of the girls I worked with. Mingling with the residents, I talked them through their pain, distracting them from what I knew must also be Lenaya's very same cries of hopelessness. I patiently unlocked bathrooms at bedtime and waited as they got ready, flushing their toilet after them as a policing policy to keep them honest.

Once the residents were settled, Nathan brought Brandon to me for his nighttime nursing on my break. This time was my light in the long dark nights and always went too quickly. Those were marathon nights. After they left, the evenings dragged on, sometimes with little worry just checking the sleeping residents, others on high alert when we kept one on one contact with a suicidal girl.

I sped home before the sun rose in hopes of grabbing a few hours of sleep before Nathan went to class. The next night would be harder in my zombie-ish state, but week by week, I somehow trudged through that year. The first couple of days after my weekend shift I felt less than human, but by Wednesday I was feeling great again. Then, I hit the rewind button and started it all over again the next night. The human body is an amazing creation. Somehow I survived this year, and have since felt an immense compassion for people who work the graveyard shift.

Soon after Brandon was born, Nathan and I felt a strong impression that we should have another child soon. Though I worried about how this would work financially, I trod with careful faith on the trail I had committed to. When Brandon was just a few months old, Nathan and I celebrated our second anniversary. He let me sleep in after working the night before and surprised me with a dozen red roses when I woke up and a nice breakfast. We had my cousin and his wife watch Brandon while we went out to dinner. Times like that were nice, helping us get through the nights of a relentlessly screaming baby or pacing the floor when he was sick or fussy.

Lenaya came over to visit us from time to time. She loved Brandon instantly and was always so good with him and all children in general, absolutely loving them. I drove her to work from time to time and did what I could for her. I would often receive random calls from police officers, and I knew that she was not doing well, but I had no power to do anything but pray and love her, so I did that.

My goal as a mother was to be happy raising my children. I knew many unhappy and bitter mothers who resented their children. I wanted to deliberately make my children a top priority out of desire rather than obligation. As is typical of young mothers, self-doubts and wearying exhaustion overcame me at times.

Nathan was blessed with a scholarship that took care of tuition for a year. I started to get into a routine and experienced the normal ups and downs of life. We still had time for fun in life. We got to travel home for Christmas break and I spent time with Cami and my cousin who also had little ones. I found time to do family history research, joined a book club and made it to several play groups where I could commiserate with other moms about daily life. I started putting together a book of family stories going back four generations and went on several trips to record and gather up all the memories we could. Each trip we came home loaded down with pictures of family, and stories that we would remember and cherish.

A little after Brandon's birthday, I started feeling extremely tired and soon discovered my hopes to become pregnant were realized. Nathan and I rejoiced to learn that another boy was on the way. Excited, but also very aware of the toll this would take on my body, I experienced a new level of exhaustion. Nathan and I took a vacation to Twin falls, Idaho, my birthplace and that of my father and his mother as well. We had been working on a project to gather and compile stories for four generations on all sides of our family. This led to numerous trips, tape-recorder in hand, digging out our heritage to pass down to our children.

My dad's parents had divorced when he was young and he grew up with his mother and two younger brothers, knowing very little about his own father's family. We visited my paternal grandfather's extended family and my step-grandmother Teddy. She shared some stories that gave me insight into the Frey past. Mental illness had plagued my paternal grandma's life and I believe that it directly resulted in my grandparents' divorce. Teddy told how Grandpa Frey faithfully paid his child support, but that as the children grew older, they started missing their visitation appointments, until they saw their father very little.

Years later, when my father was in his first year of law school with two young children and a wife to support, Grandpa Frey called my dad to see if he could spare a week to go help his younger brother. He agonized over the sacrifice of an entire week missing classes and work, but ultimately made up his mind to go. Bonding, understanding, and forgiveness bloomed out of this week, made even more precious when my Grandpa fell dead of a brain aneurism only two months later. During our visit to reclaim memories, Grandma Teddy showed me a picture Grandpa Frey carried in his wallet to the day of his death--it was of his three young boys.

Though I never knew about my Grandpa Frey until hearing these stories as a young adult, I was raised on the stories of my father's maternal line. My favorite was always the story of Great Grandpa Hartley. A wealthy plantation owner in North Carolina, who regretted his bad habits of drinking and gambling. John Hartley went into the woods one day on a personal wrestle with God. He prayed all day telling God that he knew it was possible to take away his natural desires in order to be the man he longed to be. At the end of the day, he reported that he saw a light and from then on never went back to his old habits.

After this experience, John Hartley had a dream in which he was in a cabin with the devil. He was chased round and round the room. Noticing an opening near the corner of the room, Grandpa Hartley, sought escape, plunging into a new landscape he had never seen before. Later, he and his wife sold their land and possessions to travel west and ended up in Idaho which was the very landscape he had witnessed in his dream.

After our trip to Idaho in search of our heritage, Nathan and I felt a change in our priorities, and with the mounting pressure of work and a changing schedule, I left the workforce for what would prove to be a 20 year break in order to be a full-time stay-at-home mom.

At the time, more of our family was living in Utah County than in Nevada. Nathan was still at school when Cami's husband was in Law School and Nicholas, home from his mission returned to BYU. Lenaya was somewhere on the fringes, popping in once in a while for family gatherings. We kept in pretty close touch, getting together for movies or game nights and later when we started having kids getting the cousins together.

Cami's husband finished law school, and after a clerkship for the Utah Supreme Court, started his career in Arizona with their two boys. Nicholas was left behind to finish his schooling. Nathan was nearing the end of his Master's program in Public Policy and began sending out resumes across the country. We crossed our fingers and waited for some sort of response.

Lenaya

Corbin died shortly after he moved in. We were on our way home from Warped Tour in separate cars. There was some kind of an accident on the freeway, and we were stuck at a complete stop for hours. We had a bottle of Malibu rum, which is sickeningly sweet by itself, but what did we care? We were stuck for hours, so we laughed and drank and smoked weed and got smashed figuring stuck in traffic could be just as fun as sitting in our living room. When we got back to our house, the messages began pouring in. Corbin and Jacob were in critical condition. Every time I hear a siren since that day I can't help but think, *people's lives are being unalterably changed right now while we carry on in our normal fashion.* We booked it to the hospital, but by then, Corbin had already passed. We begged to be let in to see Jacob but to no avail. Corbin's parent's hearts must have shattered when they got the call. I knew it was heart wrenching then; now that I have children I can hardly consider how a parent moves forward after hearing those crushing words. Corbin had always wanted to serve a mission though been unable to curb the addictions and dedicate himself. His obituary aptly read, "Corbin began serving his mission on July 11th." About a year later, I wrote to his mother. I'm not sure what prompted the letter, only that I felt I needed to tell her that I made it; I was doing well, and that his life *and* death hadn't gone unnoticed. Her reply was comforting to me:

"Life isn't easy, but it is good. I miss[Corbin]. I always will. But I thank my Heavenly Father and Savior, Jesus Christ for watching over our family and blessing us with so much. I pray that you will always feel their guiding hands in your life also. You will never go wrong if you allow them to be a part of your life."

Corbin's death changed everything. Everyone moved out of the house except for Matt and me. We talked of a future; of marriage and babies all the while doing drugs and partying. Then, without any indication, Matt came home from work and told me he was moving out. I had no dignity as I sobbed, begging him to stay, trying to make sense of his departure. His lips were sealed. He had no explanation. He had his share of heartaches burying a fiancé and an unborn child.

Still, I sat on the front porch drenched in tears while he packed up his belongings into his white tracker and left. The song I had listened to the night I sat before the brick wall made more sense to me in that moment than it ever had before or since. *Tell me when, I can open my eyes. I don't wanna watch you walk out that door. There's no easy way to get through goodbyes, I'd probably try and talk you into staying once more. Should I lie and say it's all for the best? Wish you luck and say I have no regrets? Smile and say goodbye, so you don't see me die inside. Is it over yet? Is it over yet?*

Left as the last standing resident, I too decided to split. For some reason, I attempted to shampoo the carpets and clean the house even though we all left like thieves in the night. We gave no notice, and hid from our landlord. Elise and Jacob came to check on me the day I left. Jacob would continue to look out for me in the coming years. I took twenty-seven mini thins that day in memory of Corbin. He claimed everything good and bad happened with the number twenty-seven. My heart felt broken. I was abandoned and my future looked solitary. Death was the beginning of a separation for our crew. When I vacated, the toilet was still broken, the wallpaper still unfinished, and the backyard was a veritable dump of blood, vomit, and feces. To my knowledge, no one ever lived there again. It was condemned and, within the year, demolished.

There are only two remaining survivors of people who lived in that house. Like me, Amy has been in and out of rehab many times over the years. Last I heard, she was working hard to get her children back; a fate I hope never to experience. There was a time when I thought I could definitively say that would never happen to me. But an addict understands the first time you utter those confident words, you may just find yourself right back in the clutches of addiction. From what I can tell, she seems to be doing well. She looks happy. I hope she will be out of treatment for good this time. I hope she will get custody of her children again. There is no shortage of losses to tally when you are an addict. No shortage.

Larissa

Though we both lived in the same city, we might as well have inhabited separate planets. Most of the time I was left in the dark as to Lenaya's real life and the few glimpses I had into her world were grim. The same day I heard about Corbin's car accident, I was picking cherries to can with Nathan at an orchard. I felt sad about the accident, but it was the first time I'd ever even heard of a boy named Corbin, so I didn't recognize the significance. We had no context for what she was experiencing and no way of knowing the extent of her addiction, she hid it so well. I played the private detective for a long time, checking alibis, catching her in lies, tracing her whereabouts, or carefully interrogating her. I could only guess at the seriousness of her addictions.

Soon after Corbin's death we had a Frey Family reunion, giving me a chance to talk to Lenaya when I picked her up. She had decided to move out of her place because she was sick of the constant party and was starting to realize that her life had no purpose and was going nowhere. She was a little tearful and said that she hit bottom when she realized that she had lost control of her life and had no way to stop people from going and coming in her house. It was a party every single night that she lived there. She told me that at first she loved having so much control and freedom, but she was starting to see that in reality, she had lost every ounce of control.

She told me that she was moving in with a friend and was going to try to finish her independent study classes. She explained that she had offered a prayer the previous week and received two phone calls from friends right after who were doing well and were concerned about her. I encouraged her to go get counseling at a drug counseling center I had found. Very confused about her future, she seemed afraid of even voicing the desire to change for fear that she would relapse and become a failure in our eyes. I didn't want to push her, because I felt it needed to be her choice to change, but I definitely wanted to be there for her to give her encouragement and hope.

Her change was, as usual, short-lived.

A few weeks later I rapidly discovered that nothing had changed, and she just wanted our help to get out of her living situation. She had seemed sincere, but her motivation to work lasted about a week. She lied incessantly to me. The lies ranged from blaming counselors for not being there at her scheduled appointments, to excuses for why she missed work or lost a long stream of jobs that turned out to have been invented more often than not. Even when I confronted her on lying she refused to admit it. Such a clever liar, I often believed her stories, though in time I became more wary of what she told me. Knowing that her bulimia was raging, that she was drinking and using drugs, all I could do many times was pray for her.

Sometimes it bothered me that Lenaya appeared to have no consequences or repercussions to her actions. She seemed to always skirt by without any troubles. The first real negative interaction was her misdemeanor charge, but she even seemed to slide out of that one. Life appeared to bail her out of every trouble. What I didn't realize was that much of her life was actually quite miserable, and she experienced plenty of consequences. I wouldn't wish some of her experiences upon my worst enemies. With only a narrow vision of what I thought her life was, I missed the broad panorama of the self-inflicted misery she experienced.

The more our two worlds clashed, something inside of me broke and shifted. I let go of my former role, recognizing that she would not be controlled. Part of overcoming codependency involves detachment: giving up trying to control the addicts that you love. I vowed internally to never play the private investigator role again. This departure from my familiar path ultimately paved the way for us to have either no relationship or a true relationship. Anyway, I was moving on with my own life, and I didn't really have time to follow her around anymore. It was agonizing to not know where she was and to be kept guessing about her safety. Even twenty years later it is hard to talk or think too much about. Once during a conversation with my parents, my father became choked up uttering, "It's wrenching even now."

I learned to simply live my own life. Enjoying patio gardening, I transplanted my peas and tomatoes. I cooked simple meals each day. Occasionally I splurged and bought the ingredients for lasagna. Every morning I took Brandon on a walk in the beautiful sunshine and played in the park. Life went on. Our car broke down, we read books, we went to work, we attended church, Brandon learned to crawl, I went to doctor's appointments, we celebrated holidays; yet I was helpless to save my sister.

Lenaya

Again without a place to live, I bounced around all over for a bit before one of my friends who lived alone with her dad offered to let me live with them. I feel greatly indebted to a myriad of people in my life who I thanklessly took advantage of. I'm fairly certain I never properly thanked any of my kind benefactors for offering me a home. Instead, the greedy eyes of the monster within hunted for and used drugs. I remember hiding my meth use from both my friend and her dad... turning on the shower and opening the window so that I could smoke the rocks rather than snort them. They lasted longer that way, and I could spread them out more evenly. My greatest fear was running out of my reserve, especially since I had to be so sneaky in acquiring my fix. While living there, I continued to work at the diner until the umpteenth time I was too hung over to show up. My boss of four years told me over the phone not to bother ever coming back. I thought he was just angry, and I showed up again pleading for my job. This time, I was unsuccessful. I can only imagine how many shifts I'd missed. I attempted to work at a call center where I lasted one day—my last real regular paycheck job for a long time. I also managed to find another meth dealer and became fast friends to take advantage of supply as was my way. I lived off the grid for the next year or so. I shoplifted more than ever and eventually got caught. Ironically, it was ten days after my eighteenth birthday. As a result, I was arrested, booked, and then released. The police officer clearly felt sorry for me. I was stealing laxatives. I sobbed as I explained that I didn't want my friends to know. It was true, but it was also about time I got caught. I had stolen thousands of dollars of merchandise. That became my new job. I would go into Victoria's Secret, pile on twenty-five $50 bras and then return them to another location for cash money. I did the same at Mervyns, Smiths, and Walmart. Eventually stores began implementing programs where you had to either show a receipt or id or only gave customers in-store credit. I couldn't buy drugs with in-store credit, so the jig was up. Still, thievery kept me in drugs for a long time. I continued to be reckless playing games like speeding up at four way stops... testing fate... feeling invincible. I terrorized people and burned bridges because I felt brave and cocky and didn't care who was injured from my peacocking power. I stole gas virtually daily. In those days you didn't have to pre-pay so we'd cover the license plate with snow or mud, fill up the tank and take off. We did the same at restaurants. We'd eat three course meals, then order dessert and before the waiter made it back to the table, run!

I mostly reconciled with my friends and though I was heavily partying still, I went weeks, sometimes months in meth dry spells. I'd think that life could go back to normal and be fine, but then it would creep back into my life in a variety of ways. Meanwhile, I'd encountered a guy named Anthony multiple times. The first time we met, he introduced himself and told me how cute I looked with my pony tail. I invited him to a party, but he declined. He explained to me that he had recently gotten out of jail and had almost a year of sobriety. I was disappointed because I had no business dating someone who desired sobriety. Months later, I ran into him, the only sober person at a party, and I thought it was fate! Excited feelings bubbled up in my belly as we flirted and talked through the night. I thought he was gorgeous and charming and, maybe just the distraction I needed to stay off of meth indefinitely. His group of bachelor roommates and my crew of single girls began a new inseparable group. I grew more infatuated with Anthony, but it seemed he was only interested in me platonically. I eagerly anticipated any indication that he was interested in me as more than just a friend. Somehow, he managed to live with and spend his time with alcoholics and drug addicts while staying sober. It couldn't have lasted for long.

After what felt like eternity, he invited me into his bedroom alone one night. We immediately started breathlessly and passionately kissing and had sex for the first time. I left on cloud nine so enthusiastic about his newly discovered romantic feelings for me. I didn't know it at the time, but he had relapsed that night and was on meth. I thought he was spectacular and began spending all the time I could with him. It never occurred to me to be concerned about his jail time. It seemed everyone I knew had done a stint here or there. It was just part of this life. In fact, one of his best friends eventually went to prison for bank robbery and told us that he was happy to go because at least he could see his family again as his parents and most of his siblings were already locked up. When we started hooking up and spending time together, he told me he was thirty-years-old. I took it as a joke since I was barely eighteen and everyone he lived with and partied with were in their early twenties. Even after I looked at his license I didn't believe he was that *old*. On my thirtieth birthday, more than a decade later, I couldn't help but imagine being where he was on *his* thirtieth. In the beginning we talked and laughed and enjoyed one another's company. For his birthday I made him a creative card with all kinds of things on it, and he got teary-eyed saying it was the most thoughtful thing anyone had ever done for him. His response meant far more to me than it should have. There were tiny moments throughout our eighteen months together that were tender; tiny moments of bliss in a world of pain. His smile; his approval; his desire; could make me forget any ill will I'd ever had for him. He was adamant all along that we weren't a couple. He had no interest in becoming emotionally invested in anyone or anything. But I believed we *were* a couple minus the semantics. I didn't demand his dedication on paper, but in more subtle ways, I thought I had it. Later I'd come to understand that I'd never had a glimmer of his loyalty. I used to wonder if he loved me in his own twisted way. He said it only once. Two beings as damaged as us were utterly incapable of an emotion as pure as uncomplicated love. Like me, his drug of choice was meth. A practicing Mormon all of his life, he got mixed up in drugs in his late twenties when his father had what should have been a minor heart attack. Anthony had an inhaler at the time and gave it to his dad thinking it would help him. Instead, it was determined that the inhaler somehow exacerbated the predicament and was the cause of his father's death. Guilt-ridden and hopeless, he began partying with reckless abandon. Getting to know him taught me you might be better off being an addict when you're young. At least I'd had people trying to correct my destructive behaviors all along the way... even to the very end. Developing addiction far from the grasp of authority or concerned parents can be much more devastating; it's less likely someone will offer a way out.

Meth turns everyone who uses it into monsters, but Anthony was particularly altered by the substance. He became one of the hermit types: paranoid, sex freak who stapled blankets over the windows, put boxes over lights, and ultimately hid out in a cave, climbing in and out of windows, and disappearing from society. In the beginning, he was charming. Even when we used together, he was outgoing and fun, and we were never strung out for more than a night; a day here and there interspersed with boisterous parties and drunken undertakings. Still, our relationship was nothing short of tragic. It started our fun-loving and adventurous; it ended in a black abyss, void of all natural affection.

My recklessness increased in the following months. I felt starved of attention with Anthony. I would do anything to get him to notice how crazy I was. Anthony and I spent more time together which left less time for my friends. Eventually Anthony's house was raided so he and a few others moved into a little house divided into two rentals by a wall. I followed shortly after to live in "crack house" number two. Once I moved in with him, I saw less and less of my friends. The house turned abominable at a rapid pace. Anthony and I, and anyone else who spent any length of time in that house were constantly strung out. If you weren't a methed-out zombie, you likely wouldn't stay long. We had run-ins with the police resulting in misdemeanors like possession charges but never jail time. Typically, we threw the tickets away and forgot about them entirely. Later, when I would appear in court for charges, I'd be shocked to discover I had bench warrants for tickets I couldn't recall. The house was filled almost entirely with meth dealers and ex-cons. There was no such thing as loyalty left in our hearts. Friends stole from each other, from family members, from lovers. We ceased to be human and were replaced with demons. I would do anything to fuel my addictions. We stole identities, check books, credit cards; whatever we could get our hands on. We knew the employees at the nearest pawn shop by first name.

As deep in drugs as I was, there was one more first left for me. I did something I had never even considered before. My life, my health, my relationships were all in shambles. I was so wrecked; such a heap of human waste, so ridiculously and unapologetically debilitated it's hard to even comprehend. I continued to use anything and everything. One night, my last friend and codependent drug hunter Jessica and I had taken several hits of acid. We went far away; it felt like we drove for hours. We arrived at a pristine, beautiful house that belonged to strangers where we met her pseudo boyfriend. I was giddy, and happy, and numb. I was laughingly catching the air around me and marveling at the beautiful colors everywhere. There was a long, white stairwell leading to the basement. There was a dark hallway with a crumpled towel at the end on the floor. It stood out to me because it seemed, like me, to be out of place. We went into what I assume was her boyfriend's bedroom. He had an outdated water bed which we mocked good-naturedly. I sat on a chair, next to the bed while I watched him shoot Jessica up with meth and a touch of heroin. Sweat instantly beaded on her upper lip. She moaned with desire. Her breath got fast and perspiration on her lip seemed to be contagious as tiny, glistening beads popped up all over her face. She writhed with what I could only describe as intense pleasure. Through my clouded judgment, my inability to make choices, my confusion about what was reality or a distant dream; I determined I would also like to shoot up. Anthony and others of my clan had been doing it for months. I had no interest. I still got high. Yeah, my nose hurt and bled like crazy frequently, and my lungs were likely taking a beating, but as long as I got high I didn't need to go psycho like I had seen so many do. Except in that moment, I wanted to feel like *she* did. So I asked if he would shoot me up. He hesitated; maybe sensing that this was larger than all of us; larger than any teenage boy and teenage girl should ever be faced with; larger than a simple needle prick and some chemicals. He only hesitated for a moment; then he filled a syringe, using a spoon but not cooking it like I'd seen in movies. Instead he broke a tiny piece off of the filter of a camel light and put it in the spoon and inserted the needle filling the chamber of the syringe. Much later it would occur to me how easily I could have died; one little drop of air; one little drop too much. In this moment, I was already high high high high high. And then suddenly, I was much higher. I didn't feel a thing when the needle went into my vein. He pulled the syringe back until a tiny drop of crimson blood filled the tube. Then he pushed the tube forward. The drugs went into my veins. I coughed. I could taste the meth in my throat. I felt out of breath, and dizzy. Then the world stopped; just stopped. I sat there, on that water bed, floating, falling, the world gone, nothing else existed except the beating of my own heart; the breath that I only knew I was breathing because I could see the silent rise and fall of my chest. The beads of sweat now on my face went unnoticed, unfelt. A little tickle traveled my body; a strange unexplainable feeling invading my form from my head to my toes. It was poetic and beautiful. It was haunting and tragic. It was exciting and freeing. It was repugnant and nauseating. It was everything and nothing. *Everything* and nothing. Everything and *nothing*. In the distance I heard waves unfurl like the echoes of the steps in a deserted ballroom. Where were the waves coming from? The pin drop? The footsteps? The air? Where did it all come from? Where? Where? Where? I have no idea what the rest of that evening held. I was up, high, awake, for a long time. Typically my high didn't last so long, nor was it ever so intense as that night. I haven't a clue where we went or how we got there, but I remember coming down. I was sitting in my living room, the sun shining in from all directions. It was a Sunday. I have no idea why I remember that, but I am certain it was a Sunday. I sprawled on our dirty couch, trying to find something, anything to ease the pain. I needed sleep, but I felt as capable of that as of walking out the front door singing to the neighbors. I sat there and sobbed deep-gulping-breath-convulsing sobs. Anthony walked into the room. Anthony, who by this point was nothing more than a glorified roommate whom I loathed... and wanted. He walked over to me and put his arms around me in an unprecedented gesture of kindness. "What's the matter?" he asked, "What's so terrible?" I was touched by what appeared to be concern. I thought he was past all feeling, and yet he seemed to be genuinely worried. But I couldn't tell him; I couldn't say what I knew; what I had absolutely found out in that moment; that my life was over. It would never-ever-no-matter-what-ever be the same. And I cried. I mourned the loss of my life. I was resigned to the fact that this was it for me. This would be my demise. I knew I would never stop using and never stop shooting up and that from this moment forward every waking moment I had would be in locating, attaining, and shooting meth and heroin through my veins. It was a mournful and awful experience and I wept. It was such exquisite pain, this suffering brought on by my own clouded judgment. This moment that would define my very person; this choice that would steal all I loved and rob me from myself under my own watch. The blackness was the darkest chamber in the lining of my heart. I shed bitter tears; wholly, unceasingly, resulting from unimaginable grief and loss. I had chosen to embrace the walking dead; for I was dead already. This was the first moment in all of my delusion that I *understood* it was no longer a choice...any control I felt I had was gone.

Me and My Shadow

He always reminds me that he knows. He knows the pain—
of a thousand lifetimes lived in one year.
He knows the disgust—
of the feeble minded bottom dwellers that know my name by heart.
He knows everything.
He has a habit of allowing
me to discard the painful memories, like
the time my delusional and delirious lover ran out of dope and
I had to hide in the closet all night long,
petrified of what he might do
if he found me.
The memories
I can't take. He hides them within
so that I always know...
he knows.
He likes to sneak up on me,
Like scorpions in darkened hallways, to remind me.
So that when I'm free,
all I see
is the grotesque bloody scene in a deserted hotel room,
where all the junkies meet
blocking my vision.
So that I can't see
the beauty that lies
within me.

-Lenaya Frey 1998 (18-yr- old)-

Because we went so long without sleep, we truly were zombies. Nothing was real. We lived with literal ghosts who haunted us whether the sun or moon shone in the sky. They knocked on windows, turned on or off our power, sang haunting arias from other rooms, closed kittens in our heater vents, and did other unspeakable things.

It's remarkable how far a person can go before reaching rock bottom. I know it looks different for everyone, but for me, I'm astonished at the depths I had to drop to before I determined it was time to start climbing. Things spiraled downward for what felt like an eternal term. I eventually severed all contact with family and friends. It was a complete process to return a call from my pager. We had to use a payphone across the street, but a lot could happen to derail me from the time I thought about returning a page to the time I made it to a pay phone. Typically the process took at least twenty-four hours if it was accomplished at all. I would usually have one task on my mental to-do list, and it would hover over me all day. I would always come back to this urgent need to finish some arbitrary task I rarely saw to completion. My brain was in a perpetual fog. Nothing was clear. I felt like I was sitting under a rear view mirror. Everyone could see me behind them, but I was incapable of making anything out except for the occasional eyeball reflecting in the mirror at exactly the right angle. Eventually, everyone I knew stopped paging. Some of my friends would pop their heads in to check on me from time to time. Daylight became my enemy. If I had to be outside in broad daylight for any reason, I found myself crossing my arms over my chest, my hands linking around my neck. It was a subconscious gesture probably to avoid anyone seeing the growing wreckage of my veins. It was imperceptible to me until much later when I realized it was habitual. I self-consciously stood like that long after I got out of that life. I was listening to The Doors and playing solitaire at Jessica's house when her roommate, John, tried to convince us that we'd checked out of society, of life. I explained to him that it wasn't a big deal; nobody had noticed us check out; it was under control. Sure, we were wrecked, but it wasn't affecting anybody but us. Jaw dropped and eyebrows lifted, he incredulously asked, "You mean to tell me that you really think it's completely normal that nobody has heard from you in months? You think your family hasn't noticed your disappearance? You don't think anybody saw you slip out the back door of reality? Really? You really think that?" I did. But as soon as I saw his face, I partially realized through the fog the horror that quite possibly my parents faced. In seconds I went from thinking they were clueless and innocently oblivious, to realizing that might have been the most ludicrous belief I'd ever had.

John didn't use meth at all. He was very anti-tweaker. A few weeks later, I went with him to a Reggae concert after drinking psychedelic mushroom tea. The concert was an absolute thrill; hands in the air, eyes closed, feeling unity and a divergence from societal norms. We sang, yelled, smoked weed, and listened with baited breath as the band went into another anti-slavery crescendo with tremolo guitars playing in the background. John was utterly wasted and kept drinking from the flask of whiskey he'd brought in his pocket. After the concert, we went to his brother's house where there was a party. I was pretty wasted myself and needed to sober up a bit. I went upstairs to the filthy bachelor pad bathroom and chopped a line of meth with my license. I quickly snorted it feeling much more on point when someone began banging on the door. I hurried and stuffed my little baggie behind my license and emerged from the bathroom. Only moments later, John and his brother got into a fight. From what I could tell it was about nothing more than John being too loaded to not be aggressive. He said we were leaving so I grabbed my purse and jumped in the car. I put on my seatbelt. He did not. He started driving faster and faster. I begged him to slow down. He kept telling me it was fine. I pleaded with him to please slow down, that I was scared. Finally, the fear from my voice must have registered because he turned his head from the road and looked at me saying, "You really are scared huh?"

"AHHHHHH!" I heard a scream. I didn't know it was mine. I saw that the road curved directly ahead of us. In my memory, we rolled a half turn landing upside down in the ditch. In reality, we rolled four and a half turns. I was hanging upside down from my seat belt. Josh's head was gushing blood, and he was semi-conscious. Pieces of glass protruded from our blood soaked skin all over our bodies, although my injuries paled in comparison to his. Unbuckling my seatbelt, I came crashing to the ceiling. The doors wouldn't open, so I climbed out my window. The ditch was steep enough that I had to dig with my hands and fingers to get out. I desperately searched for my drug-laden purse in vain. Giving up, we started walking back to his brother's house, wasted, adrenaline rushing through us, and a little hazy on directions. We walked for what felt like a marathon under the starlit skies swiftly approaching dawn. When we finally arrived at his brother's house, a group dispatched to tow his car out of the ditch before the cops arrived. I was given strict instruction that I was to bail solo if the police showed up because I was underage. I explained to them the seriousness of my lost purse and everyone was on a mission to find it and get the car out. Though it took several hours for the police to be alerted, we were unsuccessful in both of our tasks. The guys, though strong, couldn't get the car on four wheels because to do so meant to flip it over while simultaneously lifting it up the ditch walls. The ringing sirens alerted us to incoming company, and I quietly disappeared down a back street, attempting to cover up the blood from the top of my head. It took me a long time to get my bearings straight, but by early light, I had walked home. I walked in the door, expecting Anthony to be concerned both for my appearance and absence. He was on a bender and didn't recognize the shards of glass in my hair and the blood on my head, arms and legs. Instead, he was freaking out about where I had been all night. It was too much. A major brawl ensued resulting with the people across the street threatening to call the cops. I got in the shower and Anthony left so I took my time taking the glass shards out of my body and rinsing them down the drain. I was anxious, but more than anything, I felt severely and irreversibly alone. I didn't know what was going to happen with my purse or wallet. I had to wait until John got out of jail. Who knew how long that would be?

Several days later, the constable knocked on my door. It was slightly ajar and there was about a pound of weed sitting on my coffee table. I jumped to my feet and out the door slamming it behind me. The constable said, "You may as well open the door; we already saw the drugs." A verbal battle of rights ensued while I exclaimed that they didn't have any right to enter, and that they must be confused because there was nothing on the table except for some magazines. Eventually, they opened the door. It was inevitable. By then, others in the house had hidden any incriminating evidence. The constable certainly could have pursued it, but he must not have cared about marijuana since he was there to serve me papers for a felony charge of possession of methamphetamines in a controlled zone (there was a school around the block). Apparently, they found my purse. It was over 100 yards from the wreckage. I could have made John go down for it, denied being there, denied the drugs. Somewhere inside I still had a tiny shred of decency because the thought of anti-meth John doing jail time for my drugs wouldn't let me. At the time, somebody had to take the fall. I didn't have the heart to not take responsibility. Later, John told me that the police informed him that he was incredibly lucky not to have had a passenger. They said that a passenger wouldn't have lived. I was incredulous. I lived. In fact, at the time I didn't think I had any long term damage. Months later I would discover that my sciatic nerve was pinched. Years of physical therapy helped, but it was ironic to have a long term injury from an accident I couldn't even claim.

Despite having serious charges against me, I partied harder and harder shooting up more ccs every time, making worse choices daily. More than once I heard that little voice inside my head, pleading, crying, begging, urgently whispering, "pieces of you are dying right now." I brushed those words aside, knowing they were true. I told the voice to silence itself. I rationalized that those pieces would come back to life someday. Someday those pieces would breathe oxygen and smile and nod and live vibrantly again. Except that some of them didn't. Russel Brand wrote, "I cannot accurately convey the efficiency of heroin in neutralizing pain. It transforms a tight white fist into a gentle brown wave, and from my first inhalation 15 years ago it fumigated my private hell. A bathroom floor in Hackney embraced me like a womb, and now whenever I am dislodged from comfort my focus falls there."

I look into the mirror and recognize the damage I've done. Though nothing sheds more light than the dismal looks around me. Energetic and upbeat for only an instant then the cravings hit. No longer a person, just a bottle of rage and hate and fear and sorrow. Then, happy and loving again. A fatal circle, a process of death. I watch myself fade more each day, yet I succumb to the evil; it outweighs my life so that I let everything go and give in... every time.
Lenaya Frey 1998

I did careless things to the people I loved too. Only years later would I learn a fraction of the damage I'd done. I must have owed money to everyone I knew though I have no recollection of ever borrowing it. I always had an emergency explanation for the money I essentially stole. I called friends on the phone saying incredible things. I picked my face more and more until I legitimately looked like the meth head that I was. I stopped feeling much of anything. Things were at an all-time low with Anthony. I regularly walked in on him having sex with strangers not caring enough to fight. I was beyond all feeling.

Larissa

"Hope has the power to fill our lives with happiness. Its absence—when this desire of our heart is delayed—can make 'the heart sick.'....Hope is a gift of the Spirit. It is a hope that through the Atonement of Jesus Christ the power of His Resurrection, we shall be raised unto life eternal and this because of our faith in the Savior. This kind of hope is both a principle of promise as well as a commandment, and, as with all commandments, we have the responsibility to make it an active part of our lives and overcome the temptation to lose hope. Hope in our Heavenly Father's merciful plan of happiness leads to peace, mercy, rejoicing, and gladness. The hope of salvation is like a protective helmet; it is the foundation of our faith and an anchor to our souls. There may be times when we must make a courageous decision to hope even when everything around us contradicts this hope. Like Father Abraham, we will 'against hope [believe] in hope.'....Hope sustains us through despair. Hope teaches that there is reason to rejoice even when all seems dark around us" (President Uchtdorf).

Nathan was nearing the end of his schooling. We faced greater financial strain as I was working fewer hours. We no longer had my good health insurance and planned on using our school loan to help pay for our next baby. Nathan was starting to apply for jobs all over the country which resulted in a long stream of rejection letters. It was a challenging transition for me being home without the positive accolades that come from a work environment. Our car finally died, and we had to take on a car payment. I felt discouraged by Lenaya's self-destruction and pondered giving up on her. It was painful to have my hope squashed over and over again.

Fall arrived with a chill in the air that brought with it mixed feelings. I was excited for a new season, but I missed trips to the pool and playing at the park. Worried about feeling housebound, I still tried to get out with Brandon who was now a toddler. On my birthday, waddling upstairs from my pregnant belly, I spotted a gift bag sitting on my front porch. Pulling out the delicate tissue paper I drew out a little dollar store trinket. Plastic and gaudy, it was the ugliest present I had ever received, but the card indicating that Lenaya had remembered my birthday and had brought it over to me with love was a treasure. I felt a surge of the Spirit in that moment on my doorstep to the depth of my soul letting me know that however discouraged I felt, I was to never give up on Lenaya. I still have that trinket sitting on a shelf in my bedroom. I consider it a sacred gift.

Soon after that we moved into a new apartment because our student housing was being remodeled. We found a nice apartment in a family neighborhood suited to the city's name, Pleasant Grove. I stopped working full-time when I was a few months pregnant, and while I was so happy to not be working nights any longer, I had to take some time to reinvent myself. Endless hours of time somehow needed to be filled each week, and I went to work creating a routine to fill them up.

Every day we walked to the Lindon Park which was a mile away and played on the playground for at least an hour. The hills at the back of the park were great for exploring and in the fall provided piles of acorns and leaves in which to crunch. During each walk I surveyed the different neighborhoods, scoping out each of the houses and daydreaming about the day when we would be able to buy our own house. I critiqued the different lawns and color schemes finding different aspects that I preferred of each.

We took trips to the nearby Deseret Industries Thrift Store, the only place that I could afford to window shop. I savored the great bargains I could find, like a toddler bed for Brandon for only $5. He and I perused the toy and book section and occasionally came home with our little treasures.

We took trips to the Pleasant Grove library and checked out a stack of books to read together. Craving intellectual stimulation, I spent the afternoon on our front porch, perusing borrowed newspapers while Brandon played around in our front yard with his rescue rider. I chased him around in his wanderings. Sometimes we would sit in the car, and I would let him drive the steering wheel just to get through a long day.

Never will I forget the overwhelming feeling of making it through each day until Nathan arrived from work. Partly, we had absolutely no money then, so I had few options, but partly it was just the season that I was in at the time. There was a wonderful simplicity in those days. I was focused on one task at a time, whether it was changing a diaper, or reading a story, or breathing in the fresh air around me. Fall became chiller and soon turned into winter, but we still bundled up for our daily walk and played in the sparse snow.

Our second son, Andrew was due to be born on Christmas Eve, but to my relief he came two weeks early. Close to the shortest day of the year, we bundled our precious new son and took him home amid the frigid weather. A sacred feeling abounded in home with a new baby at the height of Christmas, and I felt closer to our Savior and His birth with my own precious little child. Brandon loved his younger brother, despite normal bouts of jealousy and was very protective of him. Our own little family was growing. The future was very uncertain as Nathan started to fly out for interviews between Arizona and Oregon, but it was full of hope.

Lenaya

I think my dad's arrival coincided with the phone calls he'd likely received from police regarding my most recent offense. I imagine their hearts stopped when they heard of an accident... and a purse... without a person; *without* their daughter. I wouldn't give him my real address for fear he'd walk in on something he shouldn't... or worse, tell the police where I lived. I sent him on what must have been an incredibly frustrating wild goose chase. It's hard to imagine how disconcerting it would be to be unable to trust a simple reply like an address. He was concerned about me, of course, but he was also worried about me driving around under his insurance always inebriated. My parents were concerned about the liability as they should have been. Any one of the thousands of stupid choices I made daily could have robbed them both financially and emotionally. He was coming to take me home, though he probably already knew that I wouldn't willingly leave with him. His secondary purpose was to take my car. However, shortly after arriving, he had the prompting not to take my car, but rather to take me off of his insurance. Later, he'd explain how the prompting was indisputable. He knew with certainty that the Lord was telling him to let me keep the vehicle. He didn't know why, and he likely received protests from my mom about it. By the time he tracked me down to have a conversation, his words were unprecedented: "I was going to take your car away, but now I feel like I shouldn't. Instead, I want you to know that I love you, and you will always have a place at home with us should you choose." He gravely and lovingly expressed, "I'm not going to play Sherlock Holmes anymore. I'm not going to be a private investigator. I'm going to let you live your life while hopefully always retaining the knowledge that your mom and dad love you."

At first I was ecstatic. After almost a decade of hiding from my parents and the great efforts they put towards controlling and fixing me, I was relieved. Nobody checking in on me! I only had to worry about the police! The elation stuck with me for several days. But slowly, and at first imperceptibly, I started to be afraid. This experience would prove to be the pivotal moment in my recovery. My dad was truly inspired by the Lord. Once the daunting realization that no one was going to fix me set in, I started to be terrified. Who was going to save me? Who was going to pull me out? Who was going to catch me and put me back together again? For the first time, I felt in charge of my recovery, not just my rebellion. For the first time, it was up to me to get out of this life. I felt incapable, inadequate, and nowhere near strong enough for the task. Somewhere in the back of my hopeless thoughts, I'd always had this hope for salvation, that eventually my parents would win. I realize no one gets away with their addictions, and there is never a winner. Not long after this conversation I took the reins in my recovery and meekly took baby steps towards help.

In his journal, Dad wrote: *We learned of new problems plaguing Lenaya and eventually I felt I needed to require her to hand the Geo. She is so talented, so lovely, so bright, so articulate, so compassionate if she will, and yet she is now lost on her way. I don't know what to do. I hope she will be able to change her life. I hope we may be able to help her. I talked with Lenaya on Monday and again on Friday. I grieve for her. I have hope...*

We learned today, much to our sorrow, that Lenaya has actually not been employed since August 28. I may fly to Utah on Wednesday to ask her to return the car to me and to see if I can get her to come home. I did not feel like working today, after we learned this news, so I came home early and have worked on the picnic table...

Today, we have attended conference sessions and plan to speak with Lenaya shortly. We are going to let her have the car. It may not help her, but she needs to know we love her and have hopes for her even if she has shown she continues to make mistakes.

In the following weeks, devastation after devastation occurred. Anthony was holed up in a mangy hotel room, but I didn't have the heart to go drag him out. Most of me wanted him to stay there. As the sun went down, my compassion took a hold and I realized that nobody else was going to get him. I went to the hotel where the manager eagerly gave me a key as he didn't want to call the cops, but he wanted Anthony out. I opened the door to his room. What I saw there was indescribable, though even if I could, I'd never paint that picture of horror. I should have taken Anthony to the hospital, but I didn't. I should have asked for help, but I didn't. Instead, I spent hours prepping and returning him home, mostly against his will. Once there we both slept for what felt like the first time in all of life. When we awakened, the fog had barely lifted, but the repulsion crushed down upon our hearts. We spoke of a new life; a different life; a better life. We determined that together, this was the end of our drug use. We *had* to break away. We *had* to make it out alive. Less than half a day later, one of our dealers showed up with a fresh batch of glass (a high-quality mixture of meth and heroine). I knew that if I used, Anthony would use. I was fairly certain that if Anthony used, he would die. I would die too, though my death didn't feel as imminent.

Together, we sentenced each other to death.

It got so that nothing could erase my fear, my hurt, my horror. I couldn't get high enough to eliminate the anxiety and dismay I experienced around the clock.

I ran to Vegas with two friends. Just as we pulled up to the strip, we got into a fight with the driver about who got how much of the last shot we'd done. Jessica and I jumped out, and the driver left us there. We walked up and down the strip for two days in a zombie state before somebody came and picked us up. We dined and dashed for food. We met some old guys, snorted their cocaine, gambled their money, and then ran. But everything felt different. Though we experienced rush after rush, it wasn't fun. I continued to feel anxious and afraid but resigned. I knew that my parents weren't going to save me, and I felt incapable of saving myself. I forfeited my life before it was even over.

We got home, and Anthony was as angry as I'd ever seen him. I didn't really care. He was desperate for drugs… too far gone to be in contact with any of his usual dealers. Also, he'd lost a quarter of meth, he was certain. He spent days meticulously scouring the house inch by inch. Every single strand of carpet was searched. I was certain he was delusional until Jessica spotted the quarter. She quietly put her foot over it and picked it up when he had his back turned. We left and laughed hysterically while we shot up. He would continue to look for it for days. I wish I could fully describe how completely devoid of humanity we were. On paper, I realize that I come across as callous and mean, but it was more than that. I was not human. None of us were. When the neighbor's kids were born with deformities due to her constant meth use while pregnant, it didn't even jar us. I've seen the demons of this earth. They are people, like you and me, real humans that slowly, sometimes silently, disappear.

I got pulled over while smoking glass out of a light bulb. When one person tried to hide it, he shattered it under my seat. I knew we were all going to jail. Because two of the passengers in my car were wanted, the focus immediately shifted to them, and the police let me go. I felt like it was another sign urging me home. Later that night, I was laying in my bed, considering what to do, where to go. I know it was just a delusion, a sleep deprivation hallucination, but I saw a little girl as clear as day walk into my room. She didn't say a word, but she lifted the sleeve of a jacket in my closet. She looked at me with an expression of such sorrow, and then she walked out of my empty house. I had forgotten, but in our most recent raid, I'd shoved a syringe in the pocket of that jacket in an effort to hide it from the cops. I took this ghost girl's visit as another sign that I needed to leave. I tried to convince Anthony to run away with me, make a new start somewhere else. I wanted to get out of this life, but I wasn't ready to go back home. His refusal left me feeling rejected. I longed for a change, needed a change. I went to the cemetery where I always felt close to Corbin and, instead, felt uneasy and vacant. I felt like he, too, was urging me home. Jessica signed away the rights to her daughter. We sat in her truck, watching her little girl play in the yard. High. Numb. She insisted that she was doing her daughter a favor. She was. But it was still all too heart wrenching and devastating. The losses were piling up. The forces were pointing me in a new direction.

The crack-heads were fighting in my house when we returned. The emotional toll of the day was more than I could stand. I had to get out of the house. I left just as I saw strangers with baseball bats emerging. I walked up the street to John's house. He was about to drink some mushroom tea. I welcomed the calming, happy, hallucinogenic state. I giddily drank the tea, grateful to have escaped the monsters in my house. The escape was short-lived. I instantly started the worst trip of my entire life. I couldn't shake the feelings of the day, the urgings of the week, the demons of my heart and surroundings. As I walked up and down the streets with what used to be friendly trees and whispering grass, instead, I saw a sea of desperate, sobbing faces. I couldn't escape—everywhere I turned there were people. Their sadness was sucking my very soul from my body. I went back to John's who was dancing, feeling the upbeat reggae he listened to, incapable of speech, just feeling good. I climbed into the dark closet in his bedroom and tried to ride out the terrible high. It was the final straw. When I woke up the following day, still curled up on the floor of the closet, I called my parents. My only memory of the conversation was four words: "Can I come home?" My parents, led by the spirit, purchased a ticketless flight for the following day. They didn't waste a moment.

I walked home to talk to Anthony. He flipped out. He was crazy with rage and confusion. I don't know what had become of the baseball bats and angry strangers from the night before. We yelled bitterly, angrily, devoid of any affection, his face burning with rage while he accused me of an assortment of malicious indiscretions. But then, just as suddenly as the anger emerged, he softened. The urgency and intensity of coming down must have been subsiding. His entire countenance changed, and we spoke softly, in a kinder manner than we ever had. We agreed to get better...again. I would seek help in Reno while he found a program there in Provo. We promised we would get help, sober up, and then be together forever. I packed up a bag with just a few things vowing to return for all of my belongings soon.

I will never know how many sleepless nights my parents lay awake wondering if their little girl was alive. I can't imagine the heartache they felt at this time. And as I write this, I find it comforting to put my own suffering in context of the suffering I have caused others. It humbles me to think of the exquisite pain they endured after doing nothing wrong. The Savior too did NOTHING wrong, yet He knows my pain and suffering because He is the one who paid for my sins. I am convinced that the Lord plucked me up and walked my feet to the phone to call my parents. I will never know the amount of time my parents spent kneeling in prayer on my behalf. I hope to never experience the sorrow and pain I caused them in those years. Though I was ill equipped and scarcely able to pursue a change in my life, my parent's and loved one's prayers were surely answered as my world continued unraveling all around me. Their prayers would continue to be answered in miraculous ways.

I continued throughout the night to use drugs because I was an addict. I hardly had a choice. As nightfall came and friends dropped in and out of the house, I began to panic. *I was a drug addict.* The literal meaning of what I'd planned began to sink in. *I will not be able to shoot up tomorrow if I get on that plane. What will my parents think of the shell of a human I've become? How can I possibly go through with this?* Satan gripped my heart and filled me with such terror that I made up my mind not to go. I couldn't believe I'd ever come to such a preposterous decision. Once again, the Lord intervened. He knew me, and He knew my parents. He had heard their pleas. He would answer them. As the time arrived for me to depart to the airport, Jacob was driving down the freeway and followed a prompting to show up on my doorstep. It only took seconds for him to assess the situation, seeing my suitcase packed and then shuffled away into a corner. He said, with tears in his eyes, "I'm supposed to put you on a plane today." He drove me to the airport, tears running down his face much of the hour drive to Salt Lake City. We didn't speak much, but, in that moment, he was an angel sent to minister to me in one of my greatest times of need. He later wrote me:

"I hated every moment that you lived in that house. That house was such a terrible place, it had a negative aura. I remember feeling that you were trapped by whatever was in charge of that house. I knew that if you didn't get out of that house, you were going to die. I remember one day just knowing that I had to come over and send you home. I don't remember if we talked about it before that day. But I had thought about it for a while before then, and it had to be the day you left. The timing was perfect, the guy that you were living with was not there, or he would have lost his mind and probably killed me. But I remember coming there and calling your dad who was so excited and accepting, and I recall he set up the plane ticket to get you to Reno. We were scrambling around your house when you finally decided to go; gathering up all that we could that was yours. I'm willing to bet you left things behind. You had to go home that day, and that was the way it needed to be."

Indeed, I too felt that I would not be alive had I stayed in that house. I was too reckless. I was too addicted. I had lost all hope. That is one of the most dangerous places a person can be: the quintessential rock bottom. Later though, I'd discover the power of hope. Even when it feels like all is lost, because of the atonement, hope *always* exists. Sometimes, the things that are invisible are far more real than the things that can be seen.

IV. **Light**

Lenaya

The plane ride was dark, and I kept my light on over my head. I had an envelope and a pen. I remember jotting down notes, certain that I'd have to write a book about this someday. I instinctively knew that this was a momentous occasion, even if I was cognitively unaware. The lists I made and notes I took are completely nonsensical to me now. I held on to them for a long time, but everything on them is lost to me. I don't even recognize the names and places that I painstakingly wrote. I vaguely remember getting off the plane. It seemed like a lifetime since I'd seen my parents. They were careful. I was careful too. It resembled a first date; awkward and cautious. We tangoed around each other making small-talk never speaking of anything impactful or serious. When we got home, Mom had saved me beef stroganoff, one of my favorites. I ate for what could have been the first time in days. It felt so strange to chew, to move my jaw up and down and feel the texture of the noodles give way beneath my teeth. Is this what eating always felt like? Quickly I felt full. I went to bed shortly after and slept for what felt like days, but they were likely figurative. When I awoke, pain overtook me. It felt like I woke up in a completely different body than I fell asleep in. It was like a toddler, falling asleep in the car only to be moved to their crib; confusing and complex. I hurt physically, like my body had been in a plane wreck, but more than that, my brain hurt; everything was so hazy. My chest felt as if my heart might pump right out of it due to anxiety and terror. I didn't know exactly how to proceed. I stepped out my bedroom doorway and into the hallway and sat on the top step to the staircase. My mom was immediately by my side asking what I wanted to do. She said she wasn't going to force treatment on me again and needed me to take the lead. I imagine she'd looked into programs because when I said, "I think I need to go to the hospital," she promptly drove me to a brand new treatment facility, the McClean Center. The people there questioned me but didn't seem to understand that I was dying. They were calm and collected, like they saw people like me every day. In fact, they did, but that concept was too foreign for me to be able to digest.

The following weeks were a blur. I know that I ate, and spent time with my family. I know that each hour of sobriety made me feel more and more human. I know that the fogginess in my brain began to clear and my surroundings began to make sense. I chain smoked, crazily reliant on it. I went to the treatment center every day, my mom chauffeuring me to and from. My program this time included counseling, primarily group therapy. I thrived on it. It was one of the most instrumental things in my recovery. At first, we discussed our history, but we didn't dwell on it. It was important for each of us to assess what our drug of choice was, why we were in the program, and where it all began. It was disconcerting to look at the questionnaires and discover the degree of my abuse beginning almost a decade earlier. I was the youngest in the program at only nineteen! Over the months we went over various packets about powerlessness, unmanageability, and the twelve step program. I learned about triggers and dependencies in ways I'd never heard before. But the most helpful thing to me was group. The seven or eight of us who participated grew very close over the treatment time. Some memories I shared were tragic: "*When I was 12 I remember counting pennies out of the vase my parents have because I didn't want to come down off of crank and I was broke. Days later, when I came down I was disgusted with myself. Counting pennies seemed so desperate.*" I recognized the advantage my faith had in my recovery. Perhaps because I had felt the spirit so often in my life, or because of the foundation instilled in me by my parents, I instinctively knew that it was a blessing to have a belief in and relationship with God. Even if I felt too guilty to approach Him.

I recognize how helpful AA is to people around the world, but it was not helpful for me. I've seen miracles wrought from twelve steps, but it was not the right fit for me. I attended a few meetings where members said, "Hi, I'm Al, and I'm an alcoholic." The room would echo, "Hi Al." Then he would proceed to say, "I've been sober now for twenty years," followed by an explanation of his rock bottom, or experience, or what he does to remember that he's one drink from the edge. The entire time I sat there, I was uneasy. It hurt my stomach to imagine myself twenty years down the road, still here in this room, smoking cigarettes and rehashing the past. I determined quickly that I'd rather spend twenty years as an addict than in this room. Every addict has to find what works for them. For me, group therapy was incredibly helpful because we almost never talked about yesterday. We didn't share our stories of how we got where we were. We focused always on today and tomorrow. What might I have to deal with? How will I handle that? This spoke to me. I needed to focus on my future; I couldn't stay in my past. One thing I'm grateful AA taught me was that I was actually fortunate to hit rock bottom with relatively little collateral damage. Many people talked about their own horrific treks down to mangled babies, dead wives, and best friends wrapped around trees. Also, I understood for the first time that I could probably have been a functional alcoholic for the rest of my life. If I hadn't experienced terrible things, I likely would not have sought help. I could have circled the drain for the rest of my life. Taking one day at a time was crucial. It was too overwhelming to imagine never using again. It was debilitating to consider making it to the following Monday. I had to think in days, sometimes in hours.

My relationship with my parents continued to heal. We slowly made progress. I enjoyed being around them so much that it was disheartening to begin to understand how much I'd lost; how much they'd sacrificed for the sake of *my* addictions and choices. We watched TV together and went out to eat. I relished my ability to be frank with them. We got along well and I, again, began to understand what it was to be a family. It's unfortunate that the family attachment so many people crave, I rejected and ran away from. One evening, I was lying on my bed reading a book when my dad popped his head in my door and, with tears glistening in his eyes said, "You'll never know what it does to my heart to know my little girl is safe in bed tonight." I cringe when I recall my sharp tongue and insolent attitude for so many years. After having children of my own, I had a better idea about what that must have meant. I hope to never understand fully the depth of their despair. And yet, they never lost hope. They remained steadfast, loving, and faithful when they very easily could have decided that all was lost.

Still, it wasn't all breezy. Recovery was harder this time. I had to relearn many things that people take for granted. I had to decipher my emotions when I was ill-equipped to understand or articulate them due to my stunted emotional development. The world of feeling was poignant and confusing and powerful. Sometimes it's too hard; too much. Even now, it cuts too deep: the combination of exhilaration and love and loyalty with tragedy and despair and betrayal. It feels giant; too big to hold or wrap my arms or heart or head around.

About a month after returning home, I had to go back to Utah to appear in court for a possession charge. I also wanted to retrieve my belongings from my old house and see Anthony. We hadn't talked often, but I was under the impression that he, too, was getting sober. I was excited to see him and all my friends. My court hearing went well. Because I was facing felony charges, a conviction would mean jail time and a mandate to remain in Utah. It was in my best interest to show the progress I'd made in Nevada. Up to this point, I had always believed the judicial system cared only about making money and making my life miserable. I felt justified in my belief that they cared nothing for my well-being. This hearing proved otherwise to me. It was the first time I could see that the judge was genuinely interested in my success. He didn't want my money, he wanted my freedom. He lowered my charge to a misdemeanor and mandated rehab (which I was already attending) and three years of probation. I also was required to pay a hefty fine, but it was a victory regardless.

My family went somewhere, and I determined to ride my sister's bike to my old house. When I got there, the place was unlocked, deserted, and barren. All of my things were gone. Most everything in the house was gone. After a few minutes of solitude, neighbors and friends crowded into the living room exclaiming how happy they were to see me. They explained that the house had been raided shortly after I left and Anthony was still in jail. One of the guys said that Anthony was due to get out that day, and they'd all come over to welcome him home. When he arrived, he looked weak and tired. His face showed visible relief at my being there. It only took moments; however, for the crew to offer him a vial of meth. The whole room sat down to shoot up. I thought it would be too much for me. I thought I'd be jealous or tempted or something. I was shocked and relieved to discover that it was repulsive to watch. It was like an out of body experience as I looked on in horror at what only a few weeks earlier had been me. And then, I needed to get out. I wasn't tempted by the drugs, but I was feeling ill at the monsters around me, *inside* me. It was too revealing too soon. I wasn't ready yet to explore what my addiction really looked like. I was an infant on the path to recovery. I explained that I wasn't comfortable there. Anthony panicked and got up to wrap his arms around me, only he clumsily faltered and was unable to make it to me. I quickly walked to the door where he stumbled, pleading with me to give him another chance and come back tomorrow. "I promise," he said with perspiration on his upper lip, "I'll be sober tomorrow. Please come back. I love you!" My lips said okay because they couldn't mutter what my heart already whispered to my soul. I would never be back. Not tomorrow. Not ever. I left feeling elated. Free. Complete. Fixed. I knew that I would never be back. More importantly, I knew that I didn't want to. My heart was not broken because I had changed enough in those weeks to discover that I had no use for a man like him in my life.

That elation was short-lived because the following day I did return. I didn't return for him, but I didn't have the will power to stay away. I hung out with the old crew; so confused about who I was. I knew I was happier in my new life, but I felt like something was missing. Glennon Melton said it best: "We love our sensitivities our lava our addiction it's who we are." We ended up driving to the city, hanging out at one of our old pads. I didn't do drugs, but I drank a beer which was certainly risky enough for less than thirty days of sobriety. By the time I got back to my family, they were furious. Mom was angry, and dad tried to soothe things over via the phone. I understand now that I was selfish. At the time, I felt justified and offended that after accomplishing the impossible feat of not using drugs despite having access for twelve hours, I should be celebrated, not condemned. We drove home the next day. I'm sure the combination of beer, dehydration, and malnutrition led to me getting a severe kidney infection. My mom drove all the way from Utah while I burned with a fever in the backseat. We went straight to the hospital upon entering Reno. They rushed me in, ran some tests, did an ultrasound, and then went to give me an IV and antibiotics. When the needle came close to my arm, I thought I was okay. In my mind I thought, 'I can do this, I am strong,' but I started shaking and sweating, and otherwise looking pretty wrecked. I explained to the nurse that I was a recovering drug addict. Visibly alarmed, he explained that it was dangerous to inject a patient with an IV when their body was anticipating drugs. He first injected me with some sort of pain medication that knocked me out before I could count to ten. When I awoke later, I remember being sobered by the notion of a physical response to what I always deemed a mental addiction. It was shocking to understand how invasive the chemicals I'd been abusing actually were.

Return

She came
Back for him today. Through tears and screams, she had promised
that she would. The house—HER house—no longer familiar:
the same old carpet with beer and blood stains!
The bathroom and kitchen still giving off the same
rank smell, like the toilets at Dennys. The same
mess that she had left behind several months ago...
or was it several years?
She couldn't remember: not time, not him, not even herself.
She was in a freshly pressed suit looking
like a marble chess piece to a set belonging only
in the game room of a house with pillars. She was afraid
to brush against the walls, of HER house, afraid
of contamination.
She looked around bewildered; had she really lived here,
once upon a time?
She missed him.

She crept down the blackened hallway, the distinct scent of crack cocaine floating
through the air.
She opened the bedroom door, HER bedroom door. And there he was,
crouched in a corner—afraid and frail.
Dark circles left
where his head should have been. Bruises and tattered clothes left
for his body. Had she forgotten so easily?
She had changed, why hadn't he?
Didn't the world stop when she shut her eyes?
And didn't he revolve around her?

He looked up;
He saw her;
He smelled her;
He missed her.
And then…he turned away.
He did not know her.

-Lenaya Frey 1999 (19-yrs-old)-

That was the last time I saw Anthony. He called collect a few
times over the years. I never accepted charges. He called directly a
year after we had last spoken and asked if he could borrow money. I
simply laughed and hung up the phone. The rest of my friends from
that era slowly disappeared. When they were in town, I'd invariably
meet up with them always leaving feeling disgusted. I recoiled at the
fact that I was like them once. The longer I was sober, the safer I
felt. I received letters from Jessica addressed to my misspelled name.
She wrote:

"I knew that myself, my soul, everything that created me wasn't worthless,
however living my life as a junkie, I am worthless and I finally looked at that and
cared enough to do something different. I remember when I saw you for the first
time after you had moved. Your smile was real and oh how it was so big and
true. You were so full of life, glowing and shining so bright. Knowing and
thoughts of your strength and courage has helped me. All I have to do is
remember and hold the thoughts of seeing you for that first time to help motivate
and inspire me."

And in another letter, she chronicled the heavy losses stacking up among my friends in my old life including jail and death. It wasn't enough to say I'd changed; I was a different species.

I've spent a lot of time trying to figure out why I got so many chances at sobriety. Like others, I was certainly in and out of rehab, but my stints at sobriety lasted exponentially longer than those of my peers. Why was I the lucky one? I believe I owe my success to my family, my faith, and my support network. I was blessed with a net, a trampoline, a bounce pad, and a mat. Being raised in a devout Mormon home, I was given the foundation of a testimony and faith. I learned to rely on the Lord from a very young age. I saw miracles and successes and had answers to prayers that were undeniable. I had a loving family who supported me, and most importantly loved me despite all my terrible choices. I understood more than many of my peers that I was a daughter of God. Those elements were crucial to my success. I wish that I could have offered the same support to everyone I knew who was struggling, but I was barely keeping my own mouth above water at the time. I often felt guilty that I got to go to rehab and church and get clean when I'd been far more fortunate from the start than so many others. It was a naïve way to see things. There are so many different ways people overcome addictions. I was lucky, yes, but that doesn't mean that others who weren't as blessed were incapable of reaching sobriety too. Plenty of individuals have overcome far more than me with far less resources. Also, I've learned that it doesn't serve anyone for me to feel guilty about success. Something that I've continually worked on learning is that my success doesn't diminish others and vice versa.

In addition to the after care and group therapy I attended, my parents paid for me to go see a psychologist. They'd tried when I was a rebellious teenager to get me to see a beloved family friend, but I'd refused. Now I asked them if I could go see him. He helped me in ways that I can scarcely articulate. Our first session together he said, "we have a major advantage here and that is that we already love and trust each other." It was true. He's an incredible person. He and his wife both enthusiastically root people on and build them up. One of the main dilemmas he promptly addressed was that, due to being in a mind-altered state for a decade, my emotional maturity had been stagnant. Though I was nineteen, I may as well have been twelve. My nineteen-year-old self had to learn how to feel—something I had never experienced without relying on mind-numbing agents. More than anything, he helped me to better understand who I was. No matter what I did, I felt like an actress. He helped me to resolve my fraudulent feelings.

Her laughter sounds so real.
Now she is back on the stage. It's another scene she stars in. How wet her tears are, how she makes you feel what she is feeling. Except, she isn't feeling anything. She's an actress. The tears are fake, the laughter her own façade
-Lenaya Frey 1997 (17-yrs-old)-

I'd explain my thoughts and feelings to him, and then he would articulate for me the feelings that I couldn't put into words. It was incredibly helpful to be able to name what I felt. Every time I left his office I felt lighter, more healed. He helped me learn how to forgive myself, and he helped me to understand that, "if you can't be alone, it typically means you don't like the company you're with." I didn't understand how much my self-destructive tendencies stemmed from my own self-loathing. He helped me to slowly start seeing myself in brighter lights. He also helped me decipher what actions were pretend, and what feelings were real. The irony is that most of what I categorized as fake was actually authentic. I'd been duplicitous for so long that I couldn't remember which side of the coin was me anymore. I thought that I was always happy because I was so good at pasting a smile on my face and offering a maniacal laugh. The deeper we delved, and the more we analyzed, the more I understood that I *was* happy. It *was* my nature, not my act. I had a cheerful disposition inherited from my dad. I got so good at deceiving that I couldn't help but lie to myself. I continued to attend after-care and therapy and slowly started a lifelong process to feel safe in my own skin.

I began attending church again in the singles ward (a congregation organized specifically for eighteen to thirty-year-old single adults). I was apprehensive at first. I still smoked cigarettes. I'd spent so much of my life running away from church that it felt foreign to attend willingly. Shortly after, I determined that it was time to quit smoking and start the repentance process with my Father in Heaven. I was making amends on the earth in a variety of ways, paying fines, making retribution to several stores I'd stolen thousands of dollars from. I wrote monthly checks accompanied by a letter stating that this was the first of x amount of checks I would be sending in order to reimburse them for what I claimed. I could only manage to pay a couple thousand dollars, but it felt healing to do so nevertheless. I met with my bishop, and he was loving and kind. He counseled me and helped me to see how I could repent; what I could do to be forgiven and, harder still, forgive myself. I felt so close to the Lord. There's something about being in the repentance process that forces you to put God front and center. Over the years I've struggled to duplicate those feelings of closeness I had with my Heavenly Father at this time. I prayed continuously. I felt like He was my best friend. I relied on Him for all things. I pondered over the scriptures and truly studied them rather than just reading them. I went to Institute classes where I met others my age and learned more doctrine. Although I had been raised in the church, I had a major absence of knowledge. My LDS peers had learned doctrine and theology for the decade that I'd hardly been able to stand. I had a doctrinal deficit that was compensated for with my spiritual aptitude. I attended activities and events with church members, constantly marveling at how much fun they were able to have being sober. I made good friends, and we did diverse things like riding ice blocks down hills, going to dances, playing games till wee hours of the morning, going on hikes, swinging in parks in the middle of the night. My life before had been so grueling and morbid that this was a welcome relief.

Unlike my first taste of sobriety, I didn't long for the drug-induced state. I didn't envy people at parties, and I didn't want to use. The very prospect of it frightened me. I felt certain that, like the people at AA, I was one puff away from ruin. It ended up being easier to quit smoking than I thought it would be. I went to my family doctor and visited with him about what I could do to quit. He prescribed a mild antidepressant. I'm not sure how much it helped, but it wasn't as emotional as I anticipated. Driving was the hardest because it was so habitual for me to smoke while doing so. It didn't take long before the cravings dissipated. I continued to take the antidepressant for a few months. Then, not seeing any difference with or without it, talked to my doctor about eliminating it. Within four months I was completely sober. I didn't smoke; I didn't drink; I didn't take any prescriptions; I didn't even drink caffeine. I also, for the first time since I began, was not taking diet pills or laxatives or throwing up. I had gotten so emaciated, that in the four months of eating normally, I'd gotten back to my ideal weight of 120 where I stayed for about a year. I exercised, but I wasn't consumed by the scale or how my clothes fit. I began to feel like I always imagined the rest of the normal world felt. I rejoined the living and felt amazing.

Larissa

Nathan graduated with his Master's degree one month after Lenaya came home, and two weeks after Andrew was born. We still didn't know where we would end up and were hopeful that one of his interviews would lead to permanent employment. We woke up Christmas morning to an anonymous call instructing us to check on our front porch. I was overcome at the sight of bags of groceries, wrapped presents and basic household needs piled up. We never discovered who the generous donors were, but my heart still swells with love at the memory of the Christ-like charity given us from members of our Pleasant Grove ward family.

Brandon had a little cold, which I proceeded to catch in my sleep-deprived state. Andrew had his days and nights mixed up for a while, so subsequent to being up with him until three in the morning, I would have to drag myself out of bed to help Brandon just a few hours later. My mom came out to help after a few days, which was a relief since Nathan had to leave to go to a job interview in Redding, California for several days. We merely survived those days. We were financially at an all-time low, because I couldn't work and Nathan's internship ended when he graduated.

In January, Nathan had four more job interviews in California, Arizona and Oregon. We had no idea about where we would end up. Out of money, we had to put all the airline tickets and hotel rooms on our credit card and knew that the baby hospital bills would start pouring in soon. On top of everything, Nathan tore a hole in his only suit pants. I just had to laugh, or I wouldn't be able to stop crying. Despite all these challenges, blessings still flowed into our lives. I won a $100 gift certificate from a drawing at the mall which was just enough to help buy Nathan a new suit for his job interviews. We were blessed with a greater patience. Eventually, Nathan was offered a job in Redding, and after praying about it, we felt like that was where the Lord wanted us.

A week before our move, newborn Andrew caught my cold. He became very lethargic. After not being able to wake him for eight hours, I took him to the hospital. He was admitted for RSV, which was very traumatic for me. My worst fear had come to pass, and I stayed with him all week, while we found help for Brandon at home. Nathan did his best to pack and get ready for the move, but without the help of our ward Relief Society women, he would never have gotten the packing done let alone cleaned our place. I was so relieved when we were released from the hospital and got the okay to move to California at the end of the week. I got Andrew secured in the car, drove to our house, met Nathan with the moving van rental and headed to our new home and our new life.

Moving to California marked a new chapter in our lives. We arrived at his new job with few ambitions or expectations other than being happy to have a job. Nathan worked in the finance department in charge of applying for and managing grants. A year into the job he felt discouraged and unhappy and wondered whether he should go back to law school. I discouraged it, feeling it didn't fit his temperament. Eventually, he was promoted within the city and became more content.

Situated only four hours from the Reno area, family was close enough to visit but far enough to have comfortable boundaries. Our first winter in Redding marked a record rainfall. This rain was different from anything I had before encountered. Every day I took the boys for walks in the warm drizzle, taking in the fresh smells of growth and soil.

Redding was a refreshing change for us. I had never lived anywhere with palm trees, and all the bushes flowered and were beautiful. It felt like our Garden of Eden. We finally earned a consistent paycheck and started to make a dent in our credit card and hospital bills. Nathan was called to be the Young Men's President soon after our move. We were the cute young couple in our ward, with everyone competing to hold our baby. Several months later, Nathan was called to be a counselor in the Bishopric. It was difficult to have him be gone more, but I was stretched through the experience.

We spent the first year living in a comfortable apartment paying off our hospital bills and then a house practically fell into our laps. A family in our ward was upgrading and needed to sell their house. Our first home was only 1300 square feet, but it was in a nice neighborhood, and we were ecstatic to have a big yard to let our boys explore and to grow a garden. My days were filled with reading books, playing trucks and trains, making meals, changing diapers, doing laundry and all the other tasks of a young mother. This was an exhausting, yet incredibly rewarding time in my life. I was finally doing what I had set out so long ago to do.

Around that time, I attended a General Women's Conference where our prophet, President Hinckley gave an excellent talk directed toward the mothers of the church. It spoke to me. Looking back, this talk marked a turning point in my life. Seared into my memory were three challenges presented to mothers: 1. Make sure your children stay away from alcohol and drugs, for some who encounter these substances there may be no hope, 2. Be careful in who your children are friends with, and 3. Make sure your children get a good education. I drank in this counsel, setting out to fulfil these admonitions.

I started to think ahead to when Brandon would start school. After scouting out our elementary school, my heart sank and I felt uneasy. The playground felt more like a dark, dreary battlefield. I knew instantly that I could never send my kids to this school. I researched local private schools only to find them far out of our price range. One evening when Nathan and I managed to find a babysitter to look after our brood, we went out to dinner and to browse a local bookstore. I happened upon a homeschooling section and picked up a few books. I had always held a very negative view of homeschooling, seeing homeschoolers as either lazy or religious fanatics, but what I read offered a new look at this education option. Pursuing interests at individual paces and bonding more as a family appealed to what I wanted for my family. The more I read, the greater I was convinced that this was the solution for my family. Nathan was a bit slower to coming to this idea, but he gradually started to join me in my sentiments.

As we started to broadcast our plan to family and friends, I was shocked by the forceful discouragement. Fortunately, my personality generally becomes more strong-willed in the face of obstacles or peer pressure, and I forged ahead in preparation for the plans I had made. This was *my* path. While, I had an overall positive experience with public school and feel that many people have good experiences, I felt that I needed to do things differently. I often think of Robert Frost's poem, "The Road Not Taken." This was a point that I took a different path, and it indeed has made all the difference.

That next winter, Andrew ended up back in the hospital, his health proving to be his constant challenge, but we got through it with the help of supportive friends. My boys were growing up and loved each other. I was vulnerable, due to constant sleep deprivation making parenting a challenge but also a joy.

Lenaya

Jacob and I began talking on the phone daily. We determined to pursue a romantic relationship as he prepared for his mission. Life was looking bright. I flew out to Utah and sang at his farewell. It had to be quite a shock for plenty of the people in the congregation to see Elise and me singing at Jacob's mission farewell. It is likely that much of the congregation in this tiny town was acutely aware of my past. I hope and imagine that it was met with more confidence than disdain. Jacob left and we wrote each other regularly. I felt certain we would get married in two years. I felt safer and safer in my new life.

My brain started to work properly again. I began to feel like I could contribute something to society and enrolled in classes at the community college where I took a placement test and scored high enough to register for classes that were probably beyond me. I never had finished high school or gotten my GED, but I managed to sneak in the back door to higher education and no one ever questioned me. When I first set foot back in the classroom, my heart soared. I felt a desire and love for learning that I never knew I had. It was exquisite so sit in a room with like-minded people discussing literature and psychology. I thrived surrounded by white walls and sitting in narrow desks. Within the first week I knew that I wanted to major in Secondary education and teach high school English. By the second week, I realized that I wanted to *be* my English 101 teacher. Whenever she stood in front of us talking about literature and symbols and meaning, I felt my heart pounding and the hairs on my arms stand up. It was intensely exciting and gratifying to be able to understand complex ideas and participate in the discussion. My goals and path began to take shape, and I pushed onward towards the things I wanted out of life.

I worked as a hostess at a family-owned restaurant. I enjoyed working there, but I missed the hustle and bustle of serving tables. I wasn't twenty-one yet, and it proved to be more difficult to get a serving job underage in Nevada than it ever had been in Utah. Still, I loved the restaurant environment. I met a lot of people, most of whom partied, but that didn't bother me. I didn't feel left-out or envious. I had my own social circle which was sufficient for my needs. I was never going to use again. I was certain. I was indestructible. I was sober for life.

To: Methamphetamines

With a distorted view of a hollow world,
Your emptiness can grip my soul
You bury emotions in the dark abyss,
Your enticing, cold black hole.
But today you touched a piece of me,
You weren't supposed to touch.
Your addictive arms still clutched me tight,
But I hated you enough.
For today I gained the courage,
To break your awful chain.
With familiar eyes and senses,
I'm resurrected from the rain.
So farewell to you my nothingness,
Goodbye to lonely hate.
Hello to the world I used to see,
Welcome the golden gate.
For I no more shall be enslaved,
No binds can hold me down.
Through this life I'll vibrantly tread,
With feelings I've refound.
So long, you beast, you dragon's scent,
Goodbye you mournful pain.
Hello freedom and, once again,
Hello to being sane!

-Lenaya Frey 1999 (19-yrs-old)-

I thrived during this year although I continued to recognize the losses. I understood more acutely than I had before the multitude of things I'd sacrificed. I dreamt of summers bathing in the sun; carefree and with only the normal responsibilities of young teenagers. I forced myself to grow up way too fast, losing out on childhood. I forced my parents to suffer the loss of their child at a very young age. I missed out on friendships, spiritual growth, emotional maturity, and academic success. I retrieved some of those things, but the bulk of

186

the losses of an addict are irreversible. So many things die by the wayside, never to be revived. Of course, I gained other things that I wouldn't have otherwise too. I understood the Atonement in profound ways. I learned of strength unforeseen in my idyllic youth. I grappled with demons and ended up in the arms of angels. There is value in trials. We could not progress in this life if we didn't have to overcome obstacles.

It was a pleasant year; a year of peace and growth and love. I progressed rapidly, excelling in school, nurturing my relationship with God, and making amends in my familial roles. I was happy; the kind of happy that has substance and doesn't disappear with the chemical high.

I met Forrest in one of my classes, and we started dating. We had an exhilarating romance, though I was still certain I'd wait for Jacob. Forrest was very religious and active in a local Christian church. I naively mistook that for meaning he was open to *my* religion, *my* spirituality. We discussed religion a lot. We certainly disagreed on many points, but because this was only a temporary relationship, I didn't get alarmed about major perspective differences. He was a great person, an attentive boyfriend. We traveled; we explored; we talked for hours; we studied; we spent all of our time together. And then, without warning; we fell in love. My letters to Jacob waned until they ceased entirely. His returns stopped too. Later I would learn that he had other battles he was engaged in, but at the time, I felt guilty. I was confused. It was challenging to compare feelings for someone tangible right in front of me to someone almost fictitious in letters. It wasn't long before we found intimacy in our relationship which further complicated things: first, it was a commitment that we weren't equipped to make. Second, it was a trigger for me... next to my eating disorder; sex was my biggest trigger for relapse. The guilt almost immediately began consuming us both. I went and talked with my bishop who cautioned me to get out of the relationship. I agreed that was the safest decision to make, but every time I tried, my arms almost involuntarily found their way back to him. We determined to eliminate the intimacy and return to our previous relationship. That was only successful for a short time. We broke up repeatedly through tear-soaked eyes begging the other to stop being who they were. We were compatible in every way as twenty-year-olds. The problem was that our futures were completely and permanently different. He could not, would not raise children in the Mormon faith. I could not, would not conceive of making it this far and sacrificing a temple marriage. Had we never had children, maybe we could have been happy. We toyed with the notion. But, we both knew that a life for us without children would be unfulfilled. At one point, he agreed to raise our children Mormon, anything to avoid having to walk away from one another. I couldn't stomach the prospect of marrying a man that believed his wife and children were going to a hell I didn't even believe in. I stopped going to church mainly because I felt guilty which did not convey to him the importance of my faith. Eventually, we decided to be complacent; to continue to be together knowing that we would not end up together. We always had a plan, after our next big trip, or the next celebration, or the next wedding of friends that we'd end things. But after the next big event always came another. And so we stayed in a terminal relationship. It was really no different than being delusional with drugs; this desperate attempt to pretend like we were going to come out unscathed. This silent knowing while we both smiled and nodded. It was heart wrenching; devastating. We had incredible times, scaled walls and climbed water towers; went wake boarding, and walked on ice; jumped in ponds, and rivers, and oceans blissfully unaware that anyone else existed on the earth. It would be too much for anyone. And for me, it was more pretense than I was capable of with barely a year of sobriety under my belt. I yearned to not feel. I had to find an escape. And just like that, I ended what would have been my second sober relationship; only I didn't leave.

V. Roots

Larissa

"When you feel there is only a thin thread of hope, it is not really a thread but a massive connecting link, like a life preserver to strengthen and lift you. It will provide comfort so you can cease to fear. Strive to live worthily and place your trust in the Lord" (Richard G. Scott).

In the front of our Redding house was a grand old Pine about 5 feet in diameter, housing birds and squirrels who would contentiously pelt us with pine cones if we paid them too much attention. The roots from this old tree spread out throughout our yard and even reached to the back of the house. I felt grounded for the first time since I was a child and like this tree, started going about putting down my own roots. Finally, I was at the time of life I had anticipated and prepared for so long. This was a season of great contentment.

While we saw our extended family regularly, we were starting to feel like our own little family unit. Our days were filled with making friends and exploring this delightful new community. We started establishing our own family traditions, sometimes by accident. Life was filled with playdates, walks, parks, church service, hikes and lakes. Never before had I lived somewhere with such mild weather, and I marveled at the beautiful foliage and palm trees all around. Going to the lake became a weekly activity in the summer. We went for adventures even after I was pregnant again to the trails behind our house. Story time at the library become a habit and reading was a staple in our home life.

While my life at the Center For Change had been very rewarding and invigorating, I found being home with my children a little daunting at first. I was shocked to discover how truly impatient I was. My kids were bottomless pits of needs, draining me of my energy and patience. I remember once my dad told me of my current season, "Parenting is when you have *nothing* left to give ...but you have to anyway." His counsel resonated with me. I threw myself into learning more about parenting and discipline. Reading scores of books and trying to sift through all the advice often left me feeling ever more inadequate over the minimal tools I felt I was starting with. Though we had little money, I took advantage of free museum days, found "you-pick" blueberry bushes and filled our calendar with playdates.

All my siblings came to visit us in our new home, and it felt good to be settled and thriving. Lenaya came to visit us occasionally with her new boyfriend. We went with her and Forrest on boating trips to Shasta Lake. We really liked him, and I worried about how she was doing, but she was so happy and buoyant that my wariness stayed in the shadows. I felt a lot of sorrow for her plight. They were both wonderful people who would always be at odds when it came to religion. My mom likened them to the proverb of the bird and the fish. Where would they build their nest? During that time my parents were able to rebuild a relationship with her. They talked to her every day, and she was ever bright and cheerful. They played games and ate dinner, starting to make up the lost years.

Nathan still wasn't completely satisfied with his job, but fortunately, the City Manager took notice of him and started assigning him more challenging projects, beginning to mentor him.

A new bishopric was called in our ward, and he was assigned as the Ward Mission Leader, which he enjoyed. Nathan started to feel more satisfaction in his job. He spent a year working on an enormous project and was successful in being awarded a $21 million grant to build a new library in our community. At that point, the City Manager promoted him into the management office and started giving him more supervisory opportunities. With that promotion came a significant raise. I still look back and remember that true riches to me are being able to afford an avocado, olives and nuts at the grocery store.

We started to feel a little less financially strapped around the time our third son, Connor was born. Having three boys felt a little like walking through quicksand, and it often felt impossible to get anything done. Luckily, Connor was a very sweet, mellow baby. He was happy to sit in his bouncy seat while I cooked meals, read books to the boys or attempted to fold and put away laundry. At times I felt pushed beyond what I considered my limits. Connor was a terrible night sleeper, waking me routinely several times a night. My attitude was impacted by the amount of sleep I got. Sometimes, all three boys would appear to be on a sleep strike, and I despaired of having an uninterrupted night ever again. Connor developed reflux, so half of every meal ended up on the two of us, which meant, I had a constant stream of laundry to do.

Winters in Redding brought months of steady rain. Each week, I gathered up the laundry baskets in the house and pushed open the sliding glass door that led to the backyard. I splashed through the puddles to the garage and dumped the loads into the washer, then tromped back through, clean loads in hand. After a few hours, I turned on a PBS program to distract my little ones and spent my afternoon hours sorting, folding, and putting the laundry away. This was one of many chores that I felt at least would stay done until the following week when the baskets magically filled back up. In later homes we owned I always felt a sense of luxury at having a laundry room inside the house and a door straight into the garage.

We held weekly family home evenings with our energetic boys, where we attempted to teach a short lesson and have quality family time. I despaired of them ever sitting still through a lesson, but these evenings eventually became a very happy tradition, generally ending in some form of dessert and a clever game of hide and seek or rounds of Candyland. The same was true of our scripture study. I didn't see the point of reading a chapter each day that our kids didn't comprehend, so we started on what turned out to be a five year long journey of reading and explaining *The Book of Mormon* to our children, discussing its words, asking questions to make sure they were comprehending and clarifying the difficult passages. We didn't read every night but did try to be as consistent as possible. In the evenings we gathered together, sang primary songs, and knelt and prayed as a family. The Spirit flowed according to our consistency.

During this year I savored the precious few moments I had to myself. I painted watercolor portraits of my babies, read books, gardened and joined a community band. I had a tendency to get busier and busier, which added stress to my life, but also a degree of richness. Saturday mornings, Nathan made breakfast and we enjoyed a break from our busy lives.

One chilly winter afternoon I was reading a wonderful article in the Ensign by an Apostle, James E. Faust about our souls, while Brandon and Andrew were in quiet time and Connor was napping. Brandon kicked Andrew after Andrew took one of his toys, but I didn't respond with anger and frustration as was my typical way. Instead I held Andrew and I expressed my love for him as well as Heavenly Father and Jesus' love for him. Then I expressed my love and Their love for Brandon. I mentioned briefly that it made me sad when they were unkind to each other, but I didn't dwell on it. Andrew calmed down and I found him a new toy. As I was walking out, Brandon called me back and wanted me to witness him giving Andrew his favorite toy. I praised him and again expressed my happiness and love for him. Next thing I knew he was giving Andrew all the toys on his bed. I helped Brandon find some new toys to play with, and had no more problems from them for the rest of quiet time. They responded so much to me and my state of mind. I wish that I always reacted appropriately to my children as in this instance, but I did always try.

In the sacrament prayer, I have found comfort in the fact that we promise, "that [we] are *willing*" (D&C 20: 79) to take on God's name, remember him, and keep his commandments. I fall short, but I keep on trying and am willing to strive to be better. He in turn offers His Spirit to assist us.

This stage of life seemed to bring with it chronic illness. I counted the sick days from my journal in the course of one year and found mention of 70 separate days that I actually recorded someone being sick. They shared all their colds, fevers, wheezing, and stomach flus. Andrew still struggled with respiratory infections, while Connor suffered from stomach problems. I perpetually was nursing someone back to health, not always taking care of my own health.

Near the close of 2002 I started feeling spiritually depleted. I missed the spiritual strength that I had felt on my mission and at other times in my life. I started reading *The Fire of Faith* by John H. Groberg looking for some rejuvenation. Partway into my reading, I felt the Spirit course through my body as I pondered the events of the book. I felt a certainty from the Spirit that Lenaya could still live up to the potential within her. I envisioned at a not-too distant date, a new person, full of the Spirit, throwing off the shackles that held her back. I determined to consistently fast for her, knowing from past experience that miracles can happen. I hoped and prayed that Lenaya would experience her own miracle.

Lenaya

It was around this time that trigger number two hammered down on me as well. My eating disorder had been in a remission of sorts for quite a while. Forrest and I were on a drive around the lake and I said something about being 120 pounds. He said, "You're not 120! I pick you up all the time. I'd guess you're about 140." Fuming, I sat in angry silence for the rest of drive. Who did he think he was? Was he calling me fat? Did he think I was disgusting? And furthermore, he couldn't possibly be right could he? I hadn't nurtured my obsession with the scale in the previous months, but I also didn't feel like I'd gained twenty pounds. That night, the second I walked in the door I went straight to the scale in my parent's room. 145!? I couldn't believe my eyes. I couldn't believe that I had gained twenty-five pounds without even noticing. I was stunned and hurt and humiliated and mortified. I sat there with angry tears sliding down my face and vowed to drop that weight. I told my parents I needed to run to the store. I went to my old friend Savon drugs and bought a 100 pack of Dulcalax. I took five laxatives that night, and started my ritual starvation the following day. Forrest left a few days later on a mission trip to Mexico for a month.

The first weekend he was gone, my new friend, Zoe, asked me to go with her to California to visit her mom. It sounded harmless and fun. I hardly knew Zoe, but we worked together, and she was a riot. I was back in my comfort zone, serving tables at Marie Calendars. I was twenty, I'd been sober for just over a year, I was losing touch with my parents despite living with them, and I had begun to sever my relationship with God focusing instead on my weight and relationship with Forrest. I was ripe for the picking. I met up with Zoe and hopped into her car. We got about ten miles down the road when she pulled out a blunt and asked if I wanted to smoke it. I didn't hesitate: "Yes!" Getting high for the first time in a year felt much the same as it had my last relapse....amazing! I bummed cigarettes off her and spent the weekend out of town smoking beautiful, purple, green buds. I smoked cigarettes, went on hikes, lounged in my jammies, hazily pondering the meaning of life. I realized that this didn't feel deviant or scary. Most importantly, the old cravings for meth hadn't popped up like a sadistic jack in the box.

I'd spent my sober year in fear that if I ever so much as looked at a substance, I'd be right back in the black hole of oblivion. Here I was, in *normal* socially acceptable company, having a *normal* experience. There weren't any meth heads, nobody was fiending for their pot fix, or clamoring to get the first hit. It was calm and relaxing, and moderate. Zoe and I grew close forging a constant friendship.

I started smoking a pack of cigarettes a day from that weekend on along with enough pot to sabotage my starvation routine. I got the munchies and couldn't resist food. So, I started taking a fad new diet pill called Metabolife—a supplement only on the market for a few months before the company was barraged with lawsuits. I had already stocked up a six month supply. It was expensive, but it countered the munchies perfectly. By the time Forrest got home from Mexico, I was habitually using and down to 117 pounds. I was so proud of my weight loss, but I hid everything else. I had compartmentalized my life again. My life with my friends was kept completely separate from my life with Forrest. He smelled smoke on my breath often, but I always emphatically denied smoking. His offhand comment had been my catalyst, and yet he scarcely noticed the drastic weight loss even when I pointed it out to him again and again. He'd reply vaguely, "Yeah, I guess I can tell that you've lost weight." I couldn't believe that it wasn't jarring to him. Everyone else I knew constantly gave me positive reinforcement asking me what my secret was as they marveled at my transformation.

I was living so many versions of myself that I couldn't fully commit to any one of them. It wore thin quickly and led to more feelings of guilt. My drug and alcohol abuse was tamer than before, and more enjoyable to me. It was the difference between doing drugs to survive, and doing drugs for amusement. I was encouraged and surprised by my ability to drink heavily and smoke weed regularly without turning to or desiring more hard-core drugs. To much of the world, my behavior was socially acceptable, manageable, and normal. I continued the on again off again cycle with Forrest, and I thrived in school maintaining straight A's. Sunday dinners at home with my parents compelled me to lie about having attended church earlier. Some things in my life felt jaded, while others felt enhanced. When I listened to music, or worked on papers, or read literature, it all seemed more poignant. My social network became the service industry. We went to work, partied all night, went back to work, often still in our uniforms from the day before, and did it all again. I loved waiting tables and did it for a long time. Serving created a desirable stage for me. I performed and told stories, and delighted my guests. And they, in turn, were a captivated audience. I felt important...the ex-drug-addict defying all odds making something of myself. I believed I was accomplishing great things despite overwhelming odds. My past made it easier to decline offers of meth or cocaine. Zoe and I went on adventures exploring the outdoors, attending parties and clubs, dancing, and numerous road trips. We analyzed song lyrics while ditching the various boys in our lives. We lied to everyone, often preferring sitting in the car at a popular make-out spot, climbing down the rocks and smoking bowls. Kid Rock's tape was stuck in Zoe's car earning it the title "the Kid Rock mobile." We'd blast the music screaming out the windows as we drove by other vehicles, "*Only God knows why*!!"

Who?

I am a hostage in the mirror,
so afraid to let you know me. Afraid of what you'll see. They say
the key is communication. AM I the only one
who doesn't understand?
I'm sorry for the tears I let flow freely.
I'm sorry for my jealous rage.
I'm sorry for my stupid fit of anger.
Who taught me these awful traits?
I am guilty and should be condemned
for the sadness I let you see. The crime? I'm responsible for
the heinous eruption of what I feel, please punish me.
There now don't you feel better?
NO!! YOU'VE GOT IT ALL WRONG!
Communication is ugly, it doesn't free you at all.
Crying means vulnerability—
Jealousy means insecurity—
Anger means accountability—
Speaking means I'm a FREAK!
Why is everybody allowed to feel but the prisoner
inside the mirror?

Oh, but you love me. I almost forgot. So tell me
who am I? Who do you love? Oh yeah,
and in my relapse into sobriety could you please explain
what love is.
You tell me love is commitment, or is commitment obsession?
But obsession is addiction. So am I addicted to you?
Our identities collide in a spherical eruption of emotion so that
when I lose you, I fear I'll lose myself.
Whoever that may be.

-Lenaya Frey 1999 (20-yrs-old)-

This period of my life feels very déjà vu: I worked, partied, slept, repeat. Though these years are sharper in my mind than previous times, they remain muddled. I packed so many people and interactions into those years; I scarcely remember faces or names. Before long, I was drinking and smoking weed literally around the clock. A boss once told me he would worry about my job performance if I *didn't* smell like booze. He wasn't the only one who thought alcohol was my puppeteer. Soul searching made me squirm. In therapy, I would later identify introspective analysis as a trigger for binging...on anything. Because I was drunk and stoned around the clock, it was only a matter of time before I got a DUI. It happened shortly after my twenty-first birthday. I was going to a party with friends and we had stupidly brought a bong in the car with us. I wasn't drunk; not even buzzed. I was high, but no more than always. Driving on the freeway, I saw lights behind me. My stomach lurched. "Drop the bong!" I frantically screamed. We each had an open Coors Light in our laps. We hurriedly shoved them under seats spilling beer everywhere in the process. By the time I pulled over and the officer approached my window, it smelled like a bar during the Superbowl. The officer asked if I'd been drinking. "I've had two beers." I politely responded. Apparently that's the worst possible reply; code for I'm-completely-smashed-please-take-me-to-jail-now. The officer asked me to get out of the car and gave me a field sobriety test which I easily passed. He was convinced that I was sober and about to let me go when backup arrived. This other police officer had a breathalyzer. I wasn't afraid to blow in it feeling sober; the half empty beer in my car was the only thing I'd consumed for hours. I blew hard into the tube. No one was more surprised than me when the officer put me in handcuffs and began reading me my Miranda rights. They called for a tow truck when they gave Zoe a breathalyzer, convinced she wouldn't pass. Miraculously, she did permitting her to take my car. My hands cuffed, I heaved a sigh of relief there wouldn't be a full search uncovering the bong, multiple pipes, weed, and open containers. The irony that I was pulled over because of a bad break light was not lost on me as I sat in jail. I was wearing a red corset and black slacks with a chain around my waist and glitter on my a-line blond hair. I was annoyed and embarrassed as they booked me alluding to the glitter in a way that seemed to indicate accusations of being a prostitute. I vehemently opposed the allegations resentful of the man fingerprinting me. I accused him of being out of touch with fashion and then sat in sullen silence. A few hours later when they released me on my own recognizance, I was shocked and celebrated beating the system once again. I naively thought my parents remained uninformed.

Zoe picked me up from jail at about 4 am. By the time I took her home and flew to my parent's house, it was morning. I quietly snuck into my bedroom. Moments later, my mom entered my room in full attack mode. I'd already prepared my defense yelling, "You're just mad because I was out all night, but my friend's cousin's car broke down and I had to drive her there, and I fell asleep...." Incredulously my mom yelled back, "Are you kidding? Do you think we don't know about your DUI? Do you think we don't know you're smoking again?! All you do is lie!" And then, over the banister screamed out, "Nick, she's lying to us again!!" Without any fight left in me, I turned around, flopped on my bed, and pulled the covers over my face. A minute later my dad was in my room standing with my mom at the edge of my bed trying to talk to me. I kept the blanket as a wall feigning indifference. My dad was trying to get to the bottom of things while simultaneously expressing their love for me. What could be done? How could they help? My mom furiously, desperately asked, "Why do you keep lying? Why can't you just be honest?"

"Really?" I retorted, "Is that really what you think I could or should do? And what exactly would that conversation look like? 'Hi mom, Hi dad, I know you're really proud of me for overcoming all my addictions and going back to church and school, but guess what, I started drinking and smoking again. Isn't that awesome? Aren't you proud?'" That silenced them. The gravity sunk, and we all three sat there, pawns in a game with no objective and no ending; the only players in a stupid maze that went on for all eternity. I felt I would never be who they wanted me to be. And their hearts would never stop breaking.

Larissa

"Several years ago Elder Russell M. Nelson of the Quorum of the Twelve Apostles was asked how to balance the demands of family, Church, profession, and personal interests. Elder Nelson first acknowledged that finding a perfect balance is virtually impossible. He then compared trying to balance competing demands to flying an airplane. He explained that at times certain aspects of life will cause the plane to tilt to one side. Later, other demands may cause the plane to tilt the other way—back and forth, side to side, as we address the many challenges of life. The key, he explained, is simply not to crash. He recommended that we invite someone, perhaps a spouse or other trusted friend, to always be there, hands firmly planted on the control stick to help bring us back into balance when necessary. Finally, Elder Nelson stated that everything we do in life—how we spend our time, how we invest our talents—should be connected to bringing us closer to the Savior" (Qtd. by Elder Craig C. Christensen).

Early the next spring, when the world seemed full of blossoms, new shoots of fresh, spring grass, and a swelling Sacramento River, my parents visited. My dad had found a book listing all the waterfalls in Northern California. We set out to explore Potem Falls with them. Hiking with a goal in mind, was easier for little feet. Our boys loved the adventure and we all marveled at the scenic beauty. Cool mist met us as we reached the tall falls and its pool of water, where we pulled out our picnic lunch. This weekend started a tradition of exploring a new waterfall each time my parents came for a visit.

My father was born with a cheery disposition. In his 50's he had an MRI which showed that he apparently had hydrocephalus as a child and should have been mentally handicapped his entire life. The brain is an amazing creation, and somehow his brain rewired itself, creating new synapses and its own unique wiring. He credited the cheerfulness and kindness of his own mother for his upbeat personality. My mother claimed that what first attracted her to my dad was that he thought differently than anyone she had met before. I truly never saw him depressed at any time in my life. Happiness was his gift. Of all our siblings, Lenaya inherited the greatest degree of his cheerfulness.

Often in relationships, we place a steadying influence on each other. My mom felt things more deeply and personally and especially so concerning her children. Where my dad was always hopeful, my mom often sunk into pessimism and hopelessness. I think she felt the need to balance him out somehow.

My parenting approach was impacted by all that I had witnessed and experienced. The words of my patriarchal blessing still haunted me. I looked for teaching opportunities at every step and conversation. I tried to be honest with my kids in talks about drugs or other addictions. I told them the truth that drugs make people feel great, which is why people abuse them. But I tried to help them see the reality that addiction holds a well of sorrow. I taught them what the converted Alma the Younger and Sons of Mosiah had taught that, "Wickedness never was happiness," (Alma 41;10-11) and that their greatest joy came from faith, good works, and prayer. Truly, joy comes from saving souls (Alma 26:30). My kids shared their own insights during our discussions. Black and white in their thinking, as is typical of young children, they uttered condemnation after learning of a car accident caused by a drunk driver. I tried to help them see the gray issues that often accompany these tragedies while still teaching them about choice and accountability for their own actions.

My parents seemed happier in their marriage than they had been for many years. Despite the friction that came from constant worry about Lenaya and confrontation, they were able to start having a healthier outlook on her choices. They were disappointed by her relapses, but they didn't feel as destroyed as when she was younger and blamed themselves less. While she was still living with them, it was more difficult to see her increased lying and poor choices. We all knew by that point that we could love and support her, but we couldn't change her. My parents were able to maintain love and hope for her amid uncertainty for her future. I can't emphasize enough the power of love and unconditional acceptance. She always knew we loved her, though we didn't agree with her choices.

After she moved out, my parents settled into a more

comfortable relationship with her. They felt sad at many of her choices, but their own personal happiness wasn't as tied up in her actions. She was an adult by then and they tried to be helpful and supportive of the good things was doing. As a result, their connection with her and with each other was much better than it had been before. They were never clear on exactly what she was doing, but I think it was easier to not know.

Sometimes she came with them on our waterfall trips, and I was unsure of who she really was. I smelled the cigarette smoke on her, but she was always careful to keep her hidden life separate from us. She was the favorite aunt, ever cheerful and full of delight at every little cute antic or funny spoken phrase from my kids. Lenaya swung them around, got down on the floor to play trucks, turned play into an adventure with her boisterous laugh. She was so full of happiness, I often felt envious of her carefree life with no responsibility. I wondered at her apparent lack of consequences for all her years of abuse to her body.

I read the story of the prodigal son and while I thought I understood the point of the parable, I could often relate with the older brother. I self-righteously resented how much she had squandered from our parents, apparently unappreciative of how much she had been given. In Luke 15, Jesus was speaking to the Publicans (tax collectors) and sinners. His audience were the downcast and sinners. In time I started to understand that we are all sinners. While Lenaya's sins may have been more overt, mine were just as debilitating in my daily bouts of impatience, judgment, and anger.

Jesus chose to spend his time with the humble sinners rather than the self-righteous murmurers. I must admit at that point I had more in common with the Pharisees in many ways. But I truly desired to be less judgmental. I sincerely loved my sister, wanting to help her, yet I still wore spiritual blinders. My perspective was limited by inexperience and impatience. Time was tutoring me to refrain from judging unrighteously. Heavenly Father knew my sister's heart. Harsh and judgmental reaction wouldn't help her. As I tried to follow the Savior's example and draw close to him I would be able to recognize the Spirit to help her.

During this task-oriented season, I often tried to balance the needs of everyone including myself. It felt that I was never quite in a balanced place, and I later came to believe that perfect balance is an illusion. In the mornings, Nathan and I woke up before the kids to exercise, but then we would miss reading the scriptures. I tried to be consistent in reading to the kids and got behind on housework. Staying up late on a weeknight to watch a show with Nathan led to paying the price the next morning when I was grumpy and irritable from packing too many things in. We took on house remodeling projects and slowly removed old wall heaters, replaced windows, painted the house exterior and updated our bathrooms. I worked to teach my kids to help out with the housework, but teaching young kids to clean is really more of an investment in the future. Still, I made the investment with hope that someday they would be more of a help. We were kept busy with church callings, Nathan serving on the Stake High Council and me in Primary with the children and often felt that there were not enough hours to do all that was required of us. The best advice someone gave me was to accept I was never going to get a good night's sleep. I needed to get over it and move on. I stopped counting hours and felt happier.

In April, my dad, an ever appreciate advocate of music, came out for a visit and to attend my community band concert. He was fully present with me and my boys. He got down on the floor with them to play trains and read hordes of books. In the evenings we visited and enjoyed our adult relationship. My dad had a talent for fully listening and loving me unconditionally. Being with him never failed to lift my spirits.

I cycled between taking on too many tasks, becoming exhausted and overwhelmed, backing off, and then adding more to my plate. Learning new skills brought me a lot of satisfaction, but often I bit off more than I could really handle with a young family. I canned boxes of tomatoes and fruit that we picked together, we went on trips, I scoured the community for learning opportunities including swim lessons, co-op preschools, and reading time at the library. We walked the river trail, played countless games, and went to the Kids' Fishing Day at the Mount Shasta fish hatchery. Looking for ways to save money, I learned how to cut the boys' hair and sew curtains for my house. Yearly family reunions with

Nathan's family as well as mine always brought fresh perspective. The years seemed to speed up, and somehow I was already 30. Life was rich and full and so, so busy, turning out to be one great balancing act.

In the fall of 2004, I embarked on my homeschooling journey with Brandon. Our first day of homeschooling was very memorable. As part of a math and science based homeschooling charter school, Brandon went river rafting down the Sacramento River. He attended 2 days a week for 4 hours, and then I got to teach him his reading, writing and math. Andrew attended a pre-school a couple days a week, and Connor and I had a little time at home.

Time passed, and soon I was pregnant with our fourth child, finding this to be my hardest pregnancy so far. Never having a moment to rest, I was exhausted, but my pregnancy went quickly amid so many distractions. At our ultrasound, when I discovered I was having a girl I was in shock, certain I would go on having boys. My thoughts turned to a little girl whose hair I could braid and curl and all the cute clothes I could dress her in. I also looked forward to having a relationship with a daughter who would have more in common with me.

Lenaya

A few weeks after my DUI, I moved in with Zoe. It was time to exit my parents' house, in part because of my lifestyle, but also because I felt a crushing responsibility to be so many different people. I yearned to live away from them so that I could just be me. They were saddened and concerned by my choice. I promised I would come for dinner every Sunday. At first I did, but eventually I reserved Sundays for partying the hardest because they were my day off work. I woke up in strange places, or at home with strange people, and I recuperated from the weekend by smoking copious amounts of weed all day long. When I did venture across town to my parent's house, I was royally hungover, and medicinally high. Forrest and I broke up yet again, but this time, the break up would stick. Though I knew it was a terminal relationship from the start, it was devastating. I buried myself in one night stands and booze, never quite feeling the full effect of the loss I would mourn for years to come.

Zoe and I decorated our apartment with bongs and pipes and thousands of beer caps made into intricate designs on the ceiling. My parents often talked of coming over... something I knew from my past could never happen. My ego was fed by our never-ending ability to make appearances at five parties per night. We never stayed anywhere for long, but we made a big scene everywhere we stepped. It made me feel wanted, famous. We came late, left early, and always had somewhere better to be. Once, while at the grocery store purchasing alcohol and cigarettes, there were some handsome guys in line in front of us. We began flirting with them and they asked where we were going. We were evasive as usual asking, instead where they were headed. "We're going to a party at Zoe and Lenaya's house. Do you know them?" We played dumb biting our lips and hiding our gleeful laughter. "No, do you?" "Yeah, they're like, the coolest chicks ever. Seriously, you wouldn't believe the stories about them! They're crazy!" We ran from the store howling with laughter mimicking their words repeatedly. I scarcely cared that I was building a reputation, only that people knew my name.

Free!

I love you too
Then why are you leaving?
Because somewhere along the way
I stopped loving me.
I am not free.
Free from me?
No! Free
from the bondage of choices
made long ago. Free
from not believing. Free
from hiding behind the desperate minds of confinement. Free
from a memory which escapes me. Free
from a past that taunts my future. Free
from a future that reverberates my past. Free
from self-abandonment. I am not free.
Free from hunger?
No! Free
from addiction. Free
from a life that long ago stopped living. Free
from a state of bewilderment that encompasses the empty shell. Free
from knowing. Free
from facing knowledge. Free
from self-estrangement.
I am not free!

-Lenaya Frey 2001 (21-yrs-old)-

Around this time I started dabbling in cocaine and more prominently, ecstasy. I never got back on meth, but I abused diet pills—a high that parallels speed. Zoe and I started going to raves snorting various types of ecstasy. I had done ecstasy years before, but the new-age version was a very distant relative to its more hallucinogenic predecessor. This trendy drug was regularly laced with meth, heroin, and mescaline. We started hosting "cuddle puddle parties" where we would fill whole rooms with feathers and pillows because the high was so physical with *textural* experiences. We traveled to raves near and far with sequined tube tops and jewels glued around our faces. We'd wear glow in the dark wings and face paint, perfecting the art of glow shows (spinning and throwing glow sticks on strings). We traded our rock for techno, and habitually carried pacifiers and rabbit's feet to assuage our clenched jaws and sensory deficit. One night, before an early morning shift at Marie Calendars, I went to a club and got my hands on some particularly potent blue ecstasy pills. We were dancing, and partying all night. At 4 am, a few hours before I needed to get to work, Zoe and I decided to share one last pill. We left the club at five, and I was chugging beers as I drove Zoe to my boyfriend's house. I have no idea how I got into my work clothes. After dropping her off, I headed to work, downing a beer and smoking a bowl on the way. I was so hammered; I didn't even have the sense to call in. So I went, I took orders, I placed the food items in the computer system. We were slammed, and it felt like everything kept coming at me from all directions. I would go to the computer to put a table's order in and forget what I was doing. Then, I'd remember and look down at my paper and put more orders in so that I ordered about six breakfast plates for every two people. It only took an hour before my manager caught on that things weren't going to be okay, and he asked me to leave. He didn't fire me, which I was grateful for. I was annoyed he accused me of being drunk. He should have known that drunk-Lenaya was totally equipped to wait tables successfully. I left, demoralized, and parked on the side of the road to take a nap before I went home. Later, the experience became another running joke between me and Zoe.

Being single for the first time in a long time was not to my benefit. My promiscuity reached new heights of constantly seeking for something, anything, to make me escape. I'd constantly caution the men in my life not to develop feelings for me; otherwise, I'd have to cut them loose. That happened frequently. I carried this ideology of no commitment for years. Whenever a guy started professing feelings for me, it'd make me angry that he was ruining my fun, and we'd part ways. Perhaps my heart was still healing from Forrest, but I thrived on feeling wanted by more than one man. I believed girls who don't want commitment are the most sought after. If I'm being honest (and I'm certainly and painfully trying to be) I developed feelings for some of them too, though I never admitted it even to myself. I even needed Forrest to still want me. Even though I completely severed ties with him, I was more than a little crushed when he began dating one of my former coworkers. And even though I was with plenty of men, it was one of the loneliest times in my life. Ultimately I developed a new codependent relationship. Right around that time, I had a coworker whom I hated. Steve and I got off on the wrong foot right away. He thought I was a spoiled priss, and I thought he was a nerdy jerk. We went to the bar after work one night with a group, and discovered that our first impressions had been wrong. We would spend the next two years together.

Codependent relationships are always interesting. In the beginning, it's so much fun. You party together, run amok, and wake up in the same bed. For me, Steve was something like a recorder to replay moments from my blacked out night before. At first, he laughed and joked. By the end, it wasn't a laughing matter. Steve liked booze, but not as much as I did. I liked cocaine, but not as much as he did. He drank heavily to keep up with me, and I began snorting a lot of cocaine to keep up with him. It was disappointing to be abusing a powder again. That was somewhere I'd sworn to never return. I felt it was completely different than my previous meth addictions. I was fine without it. I only used because I wanted to be with him and was petrified of being left out of anything. I never looked for coke, and I rarely contributed money towards it. Eventually, like all drugs, I became more and more addicted to it.

Sometime in the midst of this, I went with my parents and extended family to Yellowstone national park. There were a lot of family members and babies there. I love children but began feeling discontented I had no babies of my own. The trip was wonderful and felt restorative to me physically and emotionally. It was fun to see so many of my relatives, and the setting was exquisite. There were canoes and lakes, and waterfalls. My parents have a special affinity for waterfalls, and in one day we went to thirteen! We saw geysers and watched slack-jawed on the side of the road while a herd of wolves took down an enormous elk. I delighted in witnessing a mama bear and her three cubs. The mama was nervous with all the cars and people on the side of the road. She made noises and sent her cubs up a thirty foot pine tree. Once she determined that the people on the side of the road were nonthreatening, she barked up to her cubs and they carefully began making their way back down. The adorable creatures hung from branch to branch stretching their little bodies and pointing their toes until the tips of their claws grazed the one below. Over and over they'd wiggle their furry bodies until they could get a sense of grounding and let go. It was adorable and poetic. This mama protected her babies, even if it meant being apart from them. I realized my parents had protected me at all costs, even sacrificing living with me for those teenage years. There's something about witnessing the earth's miracles that somehow forces you to be closer to God; to be more aware of His great hand in all creation. In the evenings, all the families would come together and share in the cooking and cleaning and end the nights sitting by the campfire playing games and visiting. I realized more than ever the things that were missing in my life. I vowed to stop living such a wasteful life and get off drugs. I realized again that happiness was found somewhere I wasn't looking.

After the trip, we drove back to Utah, flew into Reno where Steve picked me up from the airport. I never even got my luggage home before he whipped out a bag of cocaine and my swimming suit. We're going swimming and hot tubbing, he excitedly exclaimed. I wasn't home from the trip for more than fifteen minutes before I was snorting lines. Disappointed doesn't begin to describe how much I detested myself in those moments. They were fleeting though. Because by the following morning, the insanity seemed not to be in the partying, but in the crazy decision to stop.

We continued on this way for two years. I felt like I came behind coke in Steve's affections which seems fair since he fell after alcohol in mine. With Steve, a sinister and morbid drunk came out. He was never very clear on the details, only that in drunken rages, I would accuse him of disgusting and deviant things. I never had a single recollection of these fights. Typically, I had to be reminded that we fought by him or others, depending on where I woke up the next day. I was deep in the stage of blackout drunk every single night. Of course it had to end. Nobody could continue that way; him trying to avoid me, me, getting crazy every time I was in his presence. Our relationship took its toll on my friendship with Zoe. I hadn't realized that she felt replaced until we got into a fight about in on my birthday. We were wasted, but her feelings came to light, and it added another story to our running stock of funny nights. In the end, it was a moot point because Zoe got engaged shortly afterward.

This relationship took its toll on my weight as well. At first I chalked my weight gain up to the fact that I was going out to eat a lot more than usual. Also, I was either forgetting to take laxatives at night before I passed out drunk, or I was spending the night at Steve's where his bathroom connected to his bedroom. I never felt like I had enough privacy or could make enough excuses to have to use the toilet five times in a matter of an hour. So although it gave me anxiety to start fitting more snuggly in my clothes and then later not fitting in them at all, at least I felt like the weight would drop once I got back on the laxatives. It took several months of being single to learn that in fact, the laxatives had stopped working. I was eating bar food, typically between 4 and 6 am, then taking handfuls of laxatives. It seemed as if they were still doing their job, but the scale climbed and climbed. I stopped trying to starve at all and the binging took on new life. I simply had no understanding of what it meant to eat. Regular meals didn't make sense as I had always attempted to purge in one way or another everything I ate. Because of this, I hadn't eaten a fruit or vegetable or anything remotely healthy in years. I'm not sure I've ever eaten normally. The pain in my stomach compounded until I felt like I was dying around the clock. I ate Tums in bulk and pooped blood by the bucketful for months. Despite these things, I continued to take between fifty and one hundred laxatives every night. And every day, I got bigger and more depressed about my size. Remarkably, life went on.

I continued to go to school and maintain excellent grades. Though my attendance was horrific, I always had some sob story and stayed in close communication with my professors. Although I was absent and tardy often, I tried not to ever miss a deadline. As a professor, I have students like me all the time. I'm not sure I'm as tolerant as my instructors were with me. Only once did I have an irreversible consequence academically. I had a professor who simply wouldn't budge. I got a D on an essay, and when I went in to argue with him about it, it became very clear that my grade was a reflection of my attendance. He had no interest in coming to an understanding, so I cried and told him I'd been terribly sick and had been out for much of the semester after having surgery, and the excuses went on and on. He replied that my health was yet another reason why I should retake his class. I was outraged. The truth is I should have been faced with this consequence far more often. I ended up repeating his class the following semester (the only class I needed still to graduate). Thankfully, I was able to withdraw so I didn't get a bad grade and the following semester, I graduated with a BA in Secondary Education with a focus on English. I was on the honor roll and dean's list. It would be erroneous to give the impression that this is a typical achievement for most drug addicts. I'm not sure why I was so lucky. I only know that I had a strong academic foundation in my upbringing. I imagine I lucked out in the intellectual DNA department, and it was easy for me to compartmentalize. I often put parameters around my social calendar such as, "If you write four pages and read thirty, you can go to this party." I had to write 100 pages of journal for the class I re-took. They were supposed to be representative of a semester worth of classroom observations. In reality, I had attended only a handful of middle and high school classes. I got a notebook, pen, a pack of cigarettes, and sat belly-up to the bar for eight hours where I completed and mostly fabricated 100 pages of observations. As a professor, I'm often torn about how to respond to the students like me in my classrooms. I know they can be successful, so I don't want to completely discourage them. But I also know they're partying far too heavily to be able to manage a career, so I don't want to be too lenient. The truth is, more often than not, I don't have to make a decision either way. Typically, students like me stop showing up, and I rarely hear from them again.

Larissa

"The tender image of [the prodigal son's] anxious, faithful father running to meet him and showering him with kisses is one of the most moving and compassionate scenes in all of holy writ. It tells every child of God, wayward or otherwise, how much God wants us back in the protection of His arms" (Jeffrey R. Holland).

Nicole was born a month after Brandon started 1st grade. With four children to care for and an ever increasing schedule, I started to neglect my own self-care and fell into a sort of funk. I was happy enough, but I started to become more cynical and as much as I fought it, I felt myself become resentful and bitter. Nathan was busier with work and feeling happier and more fulfilled. Enjoying his church service on the High Council, he was gone most Sundays, so I was left to take care of the children on my own. I didn't have time to exercise and was still was in a cloud of post-partum blues that I didn't identify. I stopped reading my scriptures as consistently, was forever sleep-deprived, felt that I could never measure up to my tasks yet kept trudging away. Even though my life was what I chose, I somehow felt that my opportunities to learn new things were behind me, and now I could only help my kids reach their goals. I felt stagnant. One church meeting I sat in the audience, viewing all the perfect families around me and listening to a young, enthusiastic sister missionary speaking. I thought to myself that I was once that girl, but I would just love to see her in 10 years drowning in the responsibilities of young children and see how spiritual she was then. That was a red flag of sorts and a wake-up call to where I was. Soon after that, I took an evening by myself away from home to write down my swirling thoughts and set goals to help myself get into a better place. Renewing the habits proven to lift me time and time again, I started to feel my spirits lighten. The following Fast Sunday I fasted for spiritual guidance and needed direction.

That spring morning, a rare Sunday when Nathan was sitting in church with me, I listened to the prelude music on the organ and while we were singing the hymns I noticed how slow our organist was playing. I felt a wave of compassion for the sweet sister who had played the organ in our ward for the past 30 years and realized that she couldn't play forever. At that moment I felt a strong personal message from the Lord that I needed to learn to play the piano and then the organ, so that I could take over for her. The feeling of warmth and peace was overwhelming and so certain. Never mind that we didn't even own a piano or that this was the least likely time to take up a new responsibility. The Spirit knows us best, and directs us in what will bring us great joy even if it makes no sense in our minds.

Thankfully, Nathan trusted the inspiration that I received and we soon purchased an electric piano on which to practice. A friend who had majored in piano performance suggested I learn from some exercises, and I settled down to practicing. I practiced every day during Nicole's nap or in the evening after I put the kids to bed, using headphones to not disturb them. Throughout the process I felt assurances from the Spirit that I would learn to play the organ eventually. I was called as the ward primary pianist soon after and slowly learned to play the simple primary songs, adding the songs to my practice exercises.

"Line upon line, precept upon precept," I gained a new talent, which was very rewarding and invigorating. Within a year, I was formally called as our ward organist. I practiced 40 hours the week before my first Sunday, first playing the right hand, then the left; hands together, pedals alone, right hand with pedals, left hand with pedals and finally all together. Since, the piano was relatively new to me, adding the pedals was incredibly mentally challenging, but I wanted to learn to play the organ properly. My nature to do things all the way pushed me to perfect it. My first Sunday, I made a multitude of mistakes, but I felt that it was my best, and I started on the path to learn all the hymns in the hymnbook. My experience was exhilarating!

I continued to enjoy homeschooling Brandon through our charter school community and made many good friendships through his friends. New opportunities opened up to us through these friendships, and brought about rich experiences. We all enjoyed having a little girl in the home. The boys doted on her and even used their own money to buy her things. She was talkative, artistic, funny and so sweet. The boys started to help more around the house, slowly taking over some of my chores including the dishes, lightening my burden.

From the time that Brandon was three, Nathan had started telling him nightly bedtime stories which evolved as the other children grew older. His stories starred our children and magic characters with special powers. They were sometimes moralistic, sometimes just plain silly, but always funny. The children loved their stories, and I was relieved after my long day, to turn them over to Nathan and settle into my piano practice.

The boys got involved in soccer and became more independent in their school and play. They started to read on their own. Brandon read the *Book of Mormon* on his own before he turned 8 and was baptized. We started to reach and pass some of those milestones in life with kids sleeping through the night, being potty trained and learning to read. I felt that I was getting more of a handle on my life. Unconventional in our learning, we enjoyed dissecting a squid or traveling to places along the California coast. We loved to go to any children's museum and took advantage of our local museum. Mostly, we developed the attitude of each moment being a teaching opportunity and enjoyed learning along with our children.

The enormous old pine tree in our front yard started to concern us. We found roots in the backyard that were threatening to compromise the foundation of our house. After about seven years of living in its shade, we paid a company to cut down the tree. We dubbed our home Casa Del Tocon or "House of the tree stump." Nathan, jokingly composed an ode to our tree:

> For 54 years I stood
> Mighty and strong.
> I grew and grew with nothing wrong,
> Until one day out of caprice,
> They cut me down into the street.

I remember the moment our own roots were cut very clearly. Brandon, our oldest, had been baptized a month earlier. Spring was in its height with flowers blooming everywhere and the grass a verdant green. Nathan and I were on a date out to dinner, enjoying a break from our little ones. He had a new boss and was telling me about his future at the city. My heart sank when he relayed a conversation of that day indicating that he was stuck in his current position. Feeling suddenly stifled and limited, the thread that connected me to Redding broke, leaving me floating. We went home that night and began searching on the internet for city manager job openings.

A few days later Nathan came into our room and dropped a printout on our bed. As I searched the job description I felt a surge of the Spirit, and later that night wrote in my journal that I knew we were moving to Alamosa, Colorado. This confirmation was like a switch being turned on.

Life turned into a whirlwind for a few months after that. Nathan flew to Colorado for a job interview and was soon after selected as the City Manager. We sold our house to some friends after only a week and started packing up with mixed emotions. Somewhere through the years, I had abandoned my idea that I would save Lenaya with a magic word or conversation. I settled instead on the connections that we had available to us. We saw each other fairly consistently and my kids were common ground. She came out with my parents through the years for baby blessings and other important events. She had boundless energy playing with the kids and almost seemed to be a pied piper the way they followed her around and idolized her. She was the favorite aunt who had time to play endless games and read handfuls of books to them. She loved my children immeasurably, which helped me to love her more. I still felt that I knew very little about her, but I never doubted her devotion toward my children.

Right before we moved from California, Nathan and I celebrated our 10th anniversary with a week-long stay at a dude ranch. I felt a new connection with Lenaya from the time we had spent together bonding, I felt strong assurance from the Spirit that I could entrust my children to her. For the first time ever, I asked

Lenaya to stay with my children for the week. I felt a peace throughout that week, and though it may have seemed from the outside like the worst possible idea, I never worried about her responsibility in caring for them. My children were thrilled to have her all to themselves for an entire week. Nathan and I spent a special week escaping our worries, riding horses, and soaking in the beauty of nature. We thoroughly enjoyed our time together, knowing there would be rough days ahead. Coming home to happy kids, a foundation stone was placed in my relationship with Lenaya that had a significant impact on our future.

After that week, going away parties were thrown, and I flew out with Nathan to find a new house. With the increased value of our home, we were able to pay off our school loan, our car loan, and put down a substantial down payment on a larger home in Colorado. The closer our moving date came, the more fears I felt, but thankfully, I felt certain that we were doing the Lord's will. Early one sunny fall morning we closed the doors of our beloved first home, hugged our friends goodbye and drove east with tears streaming down our faces.

Lenaya

Not long after Zoe got engaged, I moved out. It wasn't volatile, but it also wasn't the most amicable of terms. We'd grown too big for our little apartment, and we both were feeling replaced. Living together is hard on friendships. I rented a room by UNR with some coworkers. Of the seven tenants, I knew two. For a while, it was very much like MTV's *Real World*. There was plenty of drama, parties, drugs, and alcohol. Now single, I could get back into starving myself and lose some of my newly acquired weight. Since laxatives had become ineffective, throwing up was my back-up plan when I couldn't resist the craving for food. I had to share a bathroom with four other people and a toilet that constantly overflowed. I began bingeing, throwing up and taking laxatives in full force, yet I still didn't see any success and the pain in my stomach worsened daily. I never went to the bathroom without pools of blood, and nothing I did effectively helped me lose weight or prevented me from gaining it. I pretended to embrace the change, but the truth was, I was beyond devastated. I buried my pain in booze and promiscuity as I wincingly watched the scale climb. Eventually, I stopped abusing laxatives and throwing up, but I never stopped binging. I simply didn't know how. It was a shocking transformation from 120 lbs to 180 lbs in the matter of a year, but most people were kind. Sometimes, when I hadn't seen someone for a while, they would involuntarily gasp. It hurt my heart, but I felt helpless and resigned.

I got into another relationship. This time, with someone I'd known for a while. He was slightly possessive but kind and generous. I should have known from the start there was no future though, for he was atheist and didn't want children. That was a perpetual challenge: resolving the colossal gap between the life I lived, and the life I wanted. How could I argue with him about the importance of religion when I was morally absent? But somewhere deep down, in my cavernous subconscious, I clung to my religious foundation. I wasn't living it, but I was incapable of abandoning it.

After graduating with my BA in Secondary Education, I needed to do my student teaching. Because I had to pay tuition, work at the school forty hours per week, and live, I moved back in with my parents. They had moved from the house of my childhood and had a separate living quarters which I happily commandeered. I came and went as I pleased, often sleeping at my boyfriend's house, though never admitting it. I continued to wait tables on the weekends, so I rarely saw my parents. Even on weeknights, I stayed out way too late, awakened hungover or half drunk, and then drove the thirty minutes to the middle school where I did my student teaching. My mentor-teacher left me to my own devices early on which was frustrating at the time, but helped me rapidly learn how to teach and manage a classroom. Despite my lackadaisical effort, I really felt I was doing something important. My students liked me. I felt like I was reaching them, and evaluating my work was inspiring. I poured my heart into teaching and brought it home (or at least to the bar) with me every night. I worried about running into students while loaded or smoking, which happened a handful of times. I wanted to leave a lasting impression on them. I rejoiced when they overcame educational obstacles, and I fretted when they made poor choices such as doing drugs or skipping class.

My past created many obstacles in obtaining my subbing license. It seems the school district didn't look kindly at things like possession charges and DUIs. It was enormously frustrating for me knowing that other teachers were guilty of criminal behavior such as DUIs. I wrote countless letters to the superintendent pleading my case. I explained repeatedly how I'd been on good behavior for a number of years, with the exception of my DUI. I explained how attentive I was to my students and how dedicated I was to my career. Eventually, they relented and let me acquire my substitute teaching license. I took it as a complete victory being naive to the future battles I would encounter. I was on my students' level; I got it; and was enthusiastic about teaching. I was doing what I'd always set out to do. I turned a blind eye to the fact that I was still an addict. I failed to recognize what a disservice I was doing to my students. I believe I was a relatable teacher, and I know I got through boundaries others couldn't penetrate. I could have used this gift to change the course of many lives. But I didn't. Instead, I went to the bar.

After my student teaching, my principal attempted to hire me for a one-semester contract. The school had received an allocation for a gifted and talented program that she wanted me to spear-head. It was a huge compliment, particularly when the superintendent specified that she had not given permission for me to get my teaching license, only my sub license. Irate at the bureaucracy of it all, I attempted to accept the fact that perhaps all this hard work had been for nothing. My principal fought for me, and I felt completely justified in her support. A few weeks later I was the GT teacher at the same middle school I'd done my student teaching. This was a push-in pull-out program, so I had no regularly scheduled classes. As a result, I took advantage and often showed up hours late, hungover, without anyone to hold me accountable. I also spent way too much time sitting in my classroom, alone, playing solitaire on my computer. When I engaged students, I found it incredibly rewarding, but when I was alone in my room, I felt nothing short of a failure and a few times drank energy beers in big gulp cups. Had I been more motivated to participate in the regular classrooms, I might have turned that position into future positions. Instead, I felt defeated and afraid. I didn't know where my jurisdiction lay in other teachers' classrooms, and I felt ineffective. I was plagued by feelings of inadequacy. I worried that I wasn't knowledgeable enough or dedicated enough to be what my students and their parents needed. After that contract was up, there didn't appear to be another on the horizon. I don't think I was being overly sensitive when I considered myself blacklisted in education. I was bemoaning my fate to my dad one night when he said something that stuck with me forever after. He counseled, "The Lord has so many blessings for you. He only wants you to be on the path of righteousness so that you may claim them."

While I was looking for a job, rumors surfaced that in Las Vegas they were desperate for teachers due to a deficit. Knowing that there was a much larger Mormon population in Vegas and sensing the end of my relationship, I promptly made plans to move. I didn't have a job or an interview, but I assumed it would be a cinch to make those things happen. I began packing and making arrangements right away. I was going to get healthy, lose weight, stop doing drugs, slow down on my drinking, and even go back to church. I was leaving my world, my friends, and once again, my family, behind. I actually desired a change for the better. I had so much momentum that even upon discovering that I did not and would not have a job, I left anyway. I continued to be unconcerned about the job situation feeling suffocated and overwhelmed in my hometown. I was desperate to flee. My boyfriend kindly drove with me and spent my first two weeks playing tourist with me. We arrived in the middle of the night, moved in to a house with two other teachers whom I'd never met, and promptly hit the strip. We barely slept. We made our way up and down the party venues along the strip from sun up until long past sun down. And then, two weeks later through a tearful goodbye, he left. Once again I found myself alone, forlorn, and filled with regret. Why had I chosen to do this? How could I possibly survive? I decided I would figure out which ward I should go to, make church friends and go from there. Unfortunately, Saturday nights spent into the wee hours at bars meant Sunday mornings I was in no shape to attend church. I justified my decision to continue the lifestyle by assuring myself that I had come such a long way. Though I was still drinking heavily, the truth was, I *had* curbed my drug and alcohol use. Although I'd made steps in the right direction, I was nowhere near setting foot inside a church building, so I put thoughts of getting *that* healthy out of my mind.

Eventually, the money ran out and I had to start looking for a job. I was intimidated by the massive city despite working in a large casino for the last five years. I worried that because I was fat, nobody would want to hire me. Looking at the want ads didn't help assuage my fears either. Job posts like: "must look good in lingerie" or "must be attractive, no larger than a size 6" or "bikini bartenders" lined their pages. Because of this, I put off attempting to get a job until I'd put a few thousand dollars of drinks on my credit card. Finally, it couldn't continue. I applied for and interviewed in two places. I got hired at both. This was a boost to my confidence as well as one of the first steps towards overcoming my eating disorder. I chose to work at House of Blues which ended up being a lucrative decision. I immediately moved to a one bedroom apartment for less than I was paying for a tiny bedroom where I perpetually hid from the strangers I called roommates. I was living on my own for the first time in my life just months before my twenty-fifth birthday. I celebrated with some server friends at a club, drinking copious amounts of alcohol that still paled in comparison to the drinks of birthdays past. At the end of the night, on my way home, I found myself feeling homesick and all alone. I went to my little one bedroom apartment, and slept on the blow-up mattress on the floor.

A year later, I had a demanding social calendar with lifelong friends. I was partying too heavily trying to not worry about my future. I was still abusing alcohol and weed, but I *had* slowed down from my partying in Reno. One fairly drastic change was that upon moving, I'd made a conscious decision to no longer be promiscuous. This promise was easy to maintain largely in part to my intense embarrassment about my size. But I made friends so quickly and easily that I started to slowly understand my value. This, along with getting hired at two desirable restaurants helped me to begin to feel confidence despite being overweight. I discovered that, as long as I didn't hide out in humiliation, my experience in life was virtually the same at 180 pounds as it had been at 110 pounds. People valued me, and my personality was what they saw. This was a shocking revelation. People liked me the same, which ultimately began to transfer my own self-loathing into acceptance and what even resembled love. Another step towards this acceptance was eliminating many of my addictions. I stopped hiding behind intimacy or drugs or laxatives. It was a slow process and I still was sometimes shocked to catch a glimpse of myself in the mirror. My dad used to always tell me that every time he looked in the mirror, he was surprised to see an old man staring back at him. He said he felt the same as he had twenty years ago. I felt like a skinny person shocked to see the opposite in the mirror. Also, I was surprised that men didn't hit on me in bars very often. There certainly were some guys who displayed an interest, and I had a few fleeting relationships, but overall, my days of handsome conquests were over. I no longer had to convince men not to chase me home leaving me conflicted about my self-esteem and sexuality.

Despite small efforts and big changes, I continued to receive praise for my astonishing ability to be a functional addict. Several of my closest friends and the ex-boyfriend who'd moved me there, joined me in Vegas opening doors for new friendships and old habits. I was making the most money I'd ever made in my life, and things were going smoothly. I had minimal responsibilities with fewer people tugging at my time than in the past. Once again, I became complacent. I had zero momentum to make changes in my world. I was stuck... for what I hope will be the last time.

VI. Miracle

Larissa

"Weeping may endure for a night, but joy cometh in the morning" (The Holy Bible, Psalms 30:5).

Moving from the colorful warm climate of Redding, California, to the ruthless weather of Alamosa, Colorado felt a little like leaving the Garden of Eden to go out into the Dark and Dreary Wilderness. Locals say Alamosa has three seasons: summer, winter, and wind. Spring had always been my favorite season amid the blooming life. In Alamosa, if a flower dared to expose its petals in the spring, it was blown away by evening. Alamosa is located in southern central Colorado and is close to the New Mexico border. Originally a railroad town, it is the center hub of an enormous high altitude alpine valley, surrounded by seven 14,000-plus-ft. peaks. With its altitude 7,543 ft., the valley is mainly high desert sage and rabbit brush, where farmers and ranchers fight the elements to grow various crops using irrigation.

My first impression of Alamosa was that it was not a place

that I would have intentionally chosen to live, so it was good that the Lord chose it for us. He often knows what we need as opposed to what we want. I determined to look for the good and make the most of our situation.

Our house was fairly simple, but we had a roomier living area and an extra bedroom located in a nice family neighborhood. What sold me on the property was its view, which looked out on a beautiful wetland where cattails line a pond. Each month brought with it different wildlife and birds. My favorites were the yellow-headed blackbirds, sounding their bright chatter, perched precariously on tall marsh grass waving back and forth in the wind. An enormous backyard provided room for the kids to run and play. Soon after our arrival we remodeled, putting in a woodstove and a new kitchen counter and flooring. I continued to homeschool my two eldest and joined a co-op pre-school for Connor that helped us make new friends. Every month I planned a new adventure into our curriculum, and we explored the nearby National Sand Dunes Park or the frozen Zapata Falls.

Home to one of the original stakes of the Church of Jesus Christ of Latter-day Saints, there was an impressive Mormon membership for a valley with a population of only about 15,000. Agriculture was the primary industry, and it had a moderating effect on the economy of the valley. The highs and lows of house prices and spending were buffered by the farms just as oceans buffer the weather on islands.

Unlike Redding, which had been so welcoming, people in Alamosa were more tentative. They dared you to like the valley. Most long-timers had close family and friends and were too busy to add any new friendships. My greatest challenge those first couple years was painful loneliness. Being so far from friends and a regional airport, we had few visitors and were isolated from shopping other than Wal-Mart and a few little stores. My first week I went to a church-wide women's broadcast and sobbed through the entire evening. Still, people were kind to us, and served us in many ways. The people and places were so foreign to me, and I often asked myself, "What have I done?!" but I still knew it was right.

Though I saw many features of Alamosa as obstacles when

we first moved there, I came to later appreciate their refining effect. With few people to talk to in the first couple of years and not a single station of television, our family bonded as never before. We went on adventures to explore our new home; kept science logs of the changes we experienced at the impressive National Sand Dunes and found a treasure in nearby clear hot springs. We started to meet other homeschoolers at a weekly playgroup which gave me the support and confidence I needed to continue homeschooling. Having few local friends to talk with regularly, I called family more often and grew in our relationships through our conversations. When family did visit, we appreciated these times together so much more.

Nathan was validated in his work as the City Manager, though it took a lot of hours at first and I felt that even he was removed from me. In a small town, our family was often in the spotlight and when Nathan made politically unpopular decisions; our kids sometimes paid the price through exclusion. In many ways, homeschooling was a blessing to insulate them from local politics.

Our children struggled with the change in climate and desperately missed their friends. It was painful as a mother to watch my kids suffer. Still, despite the small size, or maybe because of it, we found compensations. There were two colleges in Alamosa that supplied us with learning opportunities. Available to us were concerts, plays, chemistry magic shows, robotics workshops, a tiny planetarium with free children's shows, and community sports.

Across the street from us were the church and a neighboring park which included an outdoor ice-skating rink. We all bought skates and could go whenever we wanted without a fee or arbitrary rules. All our kids learned to skate and enjoyed playing in the snow. On below-zero days we threw boiling water into the sky and heard it crackle, marveling with wide eyes as it disappeared in the air. Herds of deer bedded down in our backyard at night and we watched foxes run across the frozen pond.

Around this same time, Cami and Cory moved their family to a new law firm in Utah, and Nic and Karla finished up school in Florida with a toddler and baby twins. We gathered every other summer for reunions in order to stay close and help the cousins know each other.

Living in Alamosa felt a little like moving back in time 20 years. As our children grew, they met their new friends at the park to play "groundies" or "capture the flag." They played in the street or built forts by the pond behind our house. They floated down the Rio Grande and swung off the rope swing. In the winter they met their friends at the skating rink or roamed from house to house.

Alamosa was only four square miles and I appreciated being able to get to the store or library in only a matter of minutes. Nathan continued to come home daily for lunch, so our family ate breakfast, lunch, and dinner together which was a wonderful time of closeness. Nathan's hilarious sense of humor rubbed off on our boys and we laughed and talked after working on school all morning.

We instituted Friday pizza night, where we watched movies and enjoyed treats. With only a couple pizza places in town, I mastered the art of making homemade pizza and we enjoyed our traditional time together. During the winter months, we popped corn over the woodstove in a camping popper while playing games in the evening. We continued our tradition of scripture reading, family home evening and family prayer, never perfect but still trying.

Change for me was always a stretching experience. I was pushed out of my comfort zone and was forced to make new friends. My personal support system centered around our homeschool community. We had a wonderfully diverse group from nearly every major religious denomination as well as native cultures and foreign-born families. We also loved our new church congregation, where many giving people mentored our kids and invested in their spiritual growth.

We acquired a dog and cat as we had promised the kids when we moved, adding to the chaos of a homeschool household. Life was filled up with piano lessons, Legos, learning web sites, and cub scouts. Three boys in scouts produced *many* pinewood derby cars. Always making community service a priority, I was appointed to the local homeless shelter board and joined the college band.

Homeschooling gave us the flexibility to travel with Nathan to conferences in Denver or Glenwood Springs, where we made many happy memories. We had to travel a couple hours to receive medical services and routinely took Andrew to appointments for his respiratory issues.

Nathan was sucked into his work, and we saw less of him as work became increasingly stressful. I found myself calling my sisters more to cope. Ironically, my relationship with them grew quite a bit closer as a result of my isolation. I feel now that my loneliness was an essential step to building my relationship with Lenaya. If we had stayed in Redding, my social calendar would have been filled, and I wouldn't have needed to talk to her, but I came to crave these weekly phone calls.

Soon after we settled down in Alamosa, *the call* that I had always waited and longed for came. Having gotten closer and built our trust, Lenaya called me one afternoon. She burst into tears when I answered the phone and poured out the truth of her eating disorder. I just listened, my mind racing, as she spilled out her first horrible secret. I had believed her to have an eating disorder all along, but she needed to be honest and open with me before I could help her. What amazed me was that without years of counseling or an ounce of support, she had stopped her purging and laxative use completely. Having worked in the field of eating disorders, I knew this was almost unheard of, and I marveled aloud at her amazing strength. A new connection was forged, and started to be the topic of our conversations as I became a listening ear and sounding board as well as a source of support for her. This connection was a balm to my own loneliness. I needed her as much as she needed me, and my heart soared with joy for her accomplishments.

We flew Lenaya out over the 2007 Spring Break. She seemed much more mellow that trip and more real than I had ever seen her. Because we already had the basis of a relationship, we were able to talk more deeply about things that really mattered to us. We took her to some of our favorite places in the area as well as an overnight trip to Colorado Springs. She played with the kids as if she were another kid which delighted them, and it was fun to share with someone the life that we were establishing. Finally, I was starting to have the relationship with her that I had always craved and hoped for, though I knew there were other unopened rooms of her life that would open when she was ready. I took what I could get, and I felt like I was really coming to know who my sister was. By then, I had come to simply accept her wholly, and it was much easier to reserve judgment, which was replaced by love.

We cooked meals together, discussed the books we were reading, shared our educational philosophies and talked about different aspects of the gospel. In the evenings, we put the kids to bed and played games or watched movies. It was so restful to have Lenaya in our home in such a casual setting. She seemed to really relax that week, lounging around comfortably and taking naps once in a while during the week. Her path seemed to be turning a corner. I could tell that she was starting to make changes.

Lenaya

Once again, the Lord intervened. He answered prayers I never uttered, pleas from loved ones known and unknown. I didn't know that my life was about to change, but He did. The opulent sun was setting on a vast horizon of addiction and self-deprecation. I was quickly approaching the greatest lesson of my life.

In January of 2007, I made the New Year's resolutions that I would start exercising, eat right (whatever that meant), and quit smoking. No one was more surprised by that declaration than me. I *loved* smoking cigarettes. It was as much a part of my identity as my profession, or my name! When people considered quitting, I'd always say, "Not me! I love smoking, and I have no intentions of quitting. I'll happily smoke until I die!" I meant it too. The very thought of quitting gave me intense anxiety. And yet, here I was, telling my friends, saying it *out loud.* Later I would come to understand this decision as divine intervention.

Quitting smoking was indescribably hard. I was prepared for the physical withdrawal from past experience. I was ill-equipped for the volatile emotional response. On day two, I was bowling and drinking with friends. There seemed to be a cigarette hanging from every mouth in the alley. I sobbed, alone in a bathroom stall, aching for a cigarette. I'll never fully understand why I didn't cave. My inner-self screamed, "Now or never! *Now* or *never!*" The thought paralyzed me that if I didn't quit today, then that was the end of it. I would *never* quit. In my mind it became a literal battle of life and death. For days, then weeks, I agonized over my insatiable desire to smoke. I knew drinking only made it harder to quit, but I couldn't give up alcohol, so I forced myself to take the more difficult approach; and I succeeded. This success motivated me to go to the gym more often since I had less shortness of breath. I also determined that I would go to graduate school so that I could teach college. Surely my criminal history wouldn't be a factor in teaching adults! I took the GRE general and scored more than high enough. Next, I took the GRE literature. I had never had to study much for a test, so I was stunned when I discovered that my score wasn't even close to high enough to get into UNLV. I threw myself into my studies, sacrificing precious drinking time, and took the test again. Though I scored higher, I still wasn't close. It was demoralizing and frustrating. The long, grueling test covered topics I'd never heard of, many of which I wouldn't learn until I actually attended grad school. It felt like an impossible dream. Defeated, I abandoned my goal.

Nevertheless I continued on my quest for self-improvement; I lost twenty pounds from diet and exercise, and I completely quit laxatives and throwing up. They were ineffective anyway. Then, one drunken night in the beginning of February, I had my first one-night stand since I'd moved to Vegas and sworn off promiscuity. I was feeling better about myself, and one of my managers had been flirting with me for a while. Somewhere in my subconscious I knew that the girl he was *really* after had just announced her relationship with a handsome and charming guy. I fell back into old habits where I didn't actually want him, but I wanted to be wanted. I desired the attention, and I wanted to be his *first* choice. Insecurities and ego fed into my actions as I'd never entertained the idea of pursuing intimacy with him in the past. A lot of tequila greatly decreased any inhibition. I blacked out. I only have vague recollections of that night. I woke up in my bed in my apartment next to him with no memory of how we got there. I downplayed the situation laughing and cajoling about the hilarity of it all. I left him in my bed, went out to my living room, smoked a bowl, and wrote some abstract paragraph about how I felt like something was coming...something big. Then I drove him to his car. We talked and laughed casually on the way. I knew for certain this would not happen again, least of all because of the no-fraternization policy at work. We never spoke of it, and our work relationship was unhindered.

Five weeks later I went to a Christina Aguilera concert with my friends. I drank from 9 pm until 6 am the following morning. Two things raised red flags in my mind. First, when my breasts were jokingly slapped by a friend, I freaked out. It really hurt, and I got mad; not joking fun mad, legitimately and uncharacteristically mad. Second, the next day I threw up. I *never* got hangovers. I *never* threw up on accident with the exception of the stomach flu. I knew enough about pregnancy to think the pairing of these two symptoms odd. When, in March I drove down to the store to buy a pregnancy test, it was more of an afterthought than anything. A great friend from Reno who'd recently moved to Vegas called and asked what I was doing. "Should I come over?" he asked.

"Sure," I replied. In my head I thought that I was asking him over just to hang out. Positive, I was overreacting; I just wanted to be sure I wasn't unknowingly abusing a baby with my heavy partying. He came over, and we read the directions on the pregnancy test. It said results could take up to three minutes. I peed in a cup, dipped the stick in, and we both watched in shock as it instantaneously flashed, "pregnant" in hot pink letters. The. world. stopped. It was the single most dreamlike moment of my entire life. "What?! Oh my gosh, oh my gosh, oh my gosh! I'm pregnant!" Disbelief doesn't begin to describe the feeling. I was overwhelmed and terrified and resentful and yet, somewhere deep down I was also ecstatic, relieved, *grateful.*

About a month earlier, I'd gone to the doctor to get my quarterly Depo Provera birth control shot. At the appointment, my blood pressure was 170/110. The doctor refused to give me the shot. A nurse without knowing the situation asked if I was trying to get pregnant.

"No," I explained, "I have elevated blood pressure, but I'm also single, so it's fine."

"Oh good," she replied, "It's going to be a long time before you can start thinking about a family after being on the shot for so long." I scoffed at the preposterous idea.

Giving up booze from that moment on was easy compared to eliminating weed from my life. I knew the threat of fetal alcohol syndrome was real and scary, but I had so many people in my ears reassuring me that smoking weed was harmless. After all, *they* did, or their *moms* did, or their *friends* did, and they all turned out fine. In the end, my intuition won out, and I quit by the end of the week. I would be lying if I said it was easy. But for the first time in my life, I had *someone* to protect. I'm not sure I ever would have quit for myself, but once there was a tiny person growing in my belly, the choice to abstain became much simpler. It truly was a miracle! I was pregnant despite defying odds, but also I was changing. If the Lord hadn't created a desire in me to quit smoking, I might not have been in a place where I was capable of such drastic transformation. Also, because I had not gotten back on meth or powders, I consider each rehab a success! I changed by taking three steps forward, two steps back, so my progress was gradual. Had anything been different, I might not have been able to get sober, or take care of a tiny infant. At the time, I questioned my ability for both. My spiritual foundation, aptitude for children, years of therapy, abstinence from my most powerful addictions, closure on the long and dreary chapter of eating disorders, and my first step on the pathway home worked together to make this transformation possible. Without any one of those facets, I'm certain I would not have been capable of the requirements to have a successful pregnancy and parenthood. Also, it was miraculous that I felt as good as I did. Indeed, it was a tender mercy from the Lord that I could stay sober, could *desire* sobriety. In my world I had watched so many people destroy infants before their birth, or abuse drugs long after the arrival of children. I know that having a baby is not a cure-all. But for me, my tiny baby was an important impetus for change. I chose to follow this pathway home.

Still, the detox was an intensity accompanied by the drastic change in hormones as my body began to create a little baby. It was made substantially easier when, by week's end, I was on a plane to go visit Larissa. I had already decided not to tell her because I didn't want to ruin our much anticipated visit. But being there helped tremendously for me to get all of the poisons out of my system. Larissa and Nathan had generously paid for me to visit for my spring break. I couldn't have premeditated a more beneficial time. It was a wonderful trip! Because of the dramatic changes taking place in my body, I was very tired. I slept a lot and wrote in my journal. It was also a little bittersweet to watch Nathan so carefully and kindly take care of his children. At night he would spend hours telling them made up stories and helping them with projects. I felt incredibly guilty knowing that I would not be offering the same life to the child growing in my womb. At times, I would go into the room they'd set up for me and cry, trying not to begrudge the life Larissa had so carefully cultivated. My emotions were all over the place, and at times I thought I would burst. Pregnancy alone would have been a roller coaster, but the addition of quitting a lifetime of substance abuse simultaneously was unthinkable. I found myself humbly praising God for what I now understood was His hand in my quitting smoking before. I'm unsure I could have endured that withdrawal at the same time. I was beyond grateful. I couldn't believe that I had been blessed in that way despite the defiant choices I had made again and again.

A few days after I found out I was pregnant; I hit my knees for the first time in what might have been a decade. I expected to feel disapproval, anger; I figured the Lord had some serious repenting for me to do. Much like the reparation necessary to rebuild any type of trust with loved ones, I anticipated a long road ahead. Imagine my surprise then, when instead; I experienced nothing of the sort. On my knees I cried and pled with Heavenly Father to help me; to tell me what to do; to make everything turn out okay; to protect this little baby in my belly from any harm. At this point I scarcely knew what damage I had already done. Instead of anger and judgment, I felt what I knew I didn't deserve: love. I felt God's arms wrap around me and I heard and felt Him say, "There you are. I've been waiting for you all this time. I'm so happy you're here. I love you." He could have been standing next to me for how certain I was of His sentiments. I felt His love flowing through me like currents of electricity. I simultaneously felt comforted, and unworthy. I couldn't believe that after I had turned my back on Him for a lifetime; after I had hurt so many people; after I had all but killed myself; that all He wanted from me, was me.

A few days after I returned home, I called Larissa and told her I was pregnant. She said, "I felt like something was off! Why didn't you tell me?"

"I was afraid it would ruin the trip. I wanted to be able to think about something else." She encouraged me to tell my parents which I knew I would, but I had been planning on waiting until after my first doctor's appointment. Larissa had become my soft place to land, my confidante. I trusted and relied on her. I was likely to do what she instructed. She was the only person to whom I had confided my eating disorder. She'd marveled at my ability to stop purging without having counseling. The truth was, like so many other times, she'd been my counselor. And between her, the rest of my family, and the Lord, I had done nothing alone.

"Mom and Dad deserve to know now," she urged. After hanging up with her, I knew she was right. I determined that I would call them the following evening. When I called, I asked for both of them to get on the line. I decided the best approach was the direct approach.

"So, I'm pregnant," I said quietly. Silence.

"Are you sure?" Mom asked.

"Yes."

"What are you going to do?" Dad asked, "Have you thought about giving it up for adoption?"

The dreaded question. I knew my dad, an attorney and advocate for adoption would ask that. I had thought about adoption. I'd thought about it a lot, but I never once thought I could do it. I felt mildly guilty about that. More than anything, I felt in love with the tiny creature inside of me. I didn't even know the gender, but it scarcely mattered to me. If I had been younger, or if I hadn't already been in the process of a change of heart, adoption would have been the *only* option.

"I'm going to keep it. I thought about adoption, but I already love this child too much," I replied defensively.

"Any child who gets you as a mother would be lucky," he lovingly responded. I was prepared for a fight. I should have known that much like the rest of my life, my parents would support my agency.

"Are you going to move home?" Mom asked. Another question I'd already thought to death.

"No, I'm going to stay here and go to grad school. I hope to be accepted into the program by next semester. Also, I make a lot of money at House of Blues, and I will need a nest egg. I prayed about it, and I feel certain that I'm supposed to stay here."

"How can we help?" Mom asked next. I'm not sure how I answered, but I hope I said something like, "You've already helped more than words can express by raising me, accepting me, and loving me." I was overwhelmed with gratitude for their kindness and acceptance. They asked about the father and I explained in uncertain terms that I did not think he would be a part of this child's life. We spoke of my resources and education, of my opportunity and ability. I talked about how I wasn't a teenage girl. I was twenty-seven with a future and a sturdy safety net. I already had more advantages than most pregnant girls even if I was single.

After I moved to Vegas, I had a persistent visiting teacher (an assignment in the LDS church where women visit other women monthly with a spiritual message). I dodged her every chance I got. She was dedicated though, and every month she left the message with a little note, and her phone number. I had actually never met her in the years I'd been living there. If I was home when she dropped by, I'd hide. I've been on the other side of that door many times now, and I always make sure to leave a note. I know how valuable they can be. I didn't know which ward I was in, what time they met, or anything, but I had her number. I called her up, and she filled me in on the times, and picked me up for church the following week. After my first prenatal checkup when I learned that I was high risk because of extremely high blood pressure, she facilitated a blessing for me. Priesthood holders in the church offer healing blessings as well as blessings for comfort. Having been outside the church for so long, it is astonishing that I retained a testimony of blessings. But I had seen miracles in my life from blessings. I was worried about the baby… fearful for its health, and mine. That blessing was another stepping stone propelling me towards an unshakable confirmation that God still knew me. He was still listening.

I started going to church immediately after finding out I was pregnant. It felt almost as if I was trying to make transactions with God. Something like, please let this baby be healthy, I promise I'll do everything I'm supposed to only please make this baby be okay. Initially I was concerned about her health. I'd toned down my partying immensely in the last year, but I'd read once that even a glass of wine could give a baby fetal alcohol syndrome. Still, that was only an underlying reason for my church attendance. More than anything else, I felt such an urgent responsibility for my baby. I knew that it was my duty to raise her up in righteousness. I felt like I could make poor choices for my own future, but never, did I want to answer for making those choices for an infant. A lot of it too, had to do with sobriety. I had such clarity once the initial two weeks were past. My mind seemed crisp like a splash of cold water, and my heart felt clear, productive, able. I felt like this baby was going to save me. But first, I needed to make sure that I saved her. I attended church, I met with the bishop, and I got on the path of repentance all the while telling myself that I was doing it for the baby. Then, one Sunday, as I sat in Sacrament meeting, I felt an overwhelming outpouring of love from God. I felt forgiven, and accepted, and important. But most of all, the Spirit whispered to me that I was there for *me*. I was just as important as this unborn child. Though the baby would benefit from my attendance, *I was there for me*. That moment changed everything. In many respects that was the true start to my path back to God. Later, I'd feel a similar sentiment when my daughter was born. I remember instantly being overcome with the absolute certainty that

she was a daughter of God. And it stood to reason that if she was a
daughter of God, then I too was a daughter of the King. I'd been
taught that my whole life. I believed it. This was the first time I *knew*
it.

Though my lifestyle and circumstance were changing, I tried
desperately to keep my social engagements intact. This meant going
to bars till the early hours of the morning, working late hours, being
the designated driver for my friends, knowing the latest gossip and
gritty details of my co-workers and friends. I could hang with the
best of them. I didn't complain. I hung out all night full of
unwarranted enthusiasm for my bulging belly. People constantly
remarked on how sober-me was exactly the same as wasted-me. It
was reassuring in a time of confusion that my character, cheerfulness
and enthusiasm were the same. My state of peace is the thing that
changed the most: not how I *acted*, how I *felt*. About seven months
into my pregnancy, people stopped inviting me to bars. No longer
was I expected to pick up my drunken friends and drive them
around. After work nobody included me in the drinking plans for
the evening. For a while, I was completely hurt. Once again, I felt
left out. I was outraged and indignant that I had spent all this time
with them. Soon I would be lost in the void of motherhood, but I
wasn't yet. I prayed then too; I was slowly learning to turn to the
Lord in times of need rather than some sort of substance. I was
immediately comforted that I was not being left out of anything.
Those places were not for me; I had no use for that environment.
The Lord was helping me deliberately close that proverbial door and
open a new one. This was a crucial development in my life and
journey because when Xiana was born, I knew that the only place I
ever wanted to be was with her, and that I could never be left out
again.

I continued to work at House of Blues until two days before my
scheduled C-section. I needed to make as much money as possible
before Xiana was born. It was challenging to resolve my newfound
spirituality with such a contaminated environment, but I managed.
Being re-integrated fully into religion was a slow process. First, I
attended only Sacrament Meeting. It took at least a year before I
began attending all three hours on Sundays, and it took several years
for me to make keeping the Sabbath day holy a priority. It was
incredibly foreign for me to worry about not shopping, or going out

to dinner, or attending parties on Sundays. It was unnerving to suddenly feel guilty about not reading my scriptures daily or falling asleep while in prayer because for so long I hadn't felt guilty about my more severe weaknesses. It was confusing while also being so clear. Those months seemed full of complex contradictions: peace while in the eye of the storm, solace and anxiety, happiness and loneliness, remorse and forgiveness, faith and fear, inadequacy and authority. Despite all the confusion, my dominant emotion was complete and utter happiness. I felt peace, and freedom, and excitement to a degree I had never before experienced. Preparing for Xiana's birth was like anticipating every new, rewarding, fulfilling thing on the earth simultaneously. There was no comparison in addiction. These feelings were absent in my previous world.

At nine months pregnant, I moved into a two bedroom apartment on the other side of town. I was nervous attending a new ward, very pregnant, and very single. The blessings never ceased. I was welcomed, fellowshipped, and circled with love. That ward became my family away from home. They looked out for me and quickly Xiana; they loved us, and they fed us in countless ways. Although, my nonmember friends continued to party, they surprised me by remaining singularly supportive. They didn't disappear, the venue simply changed. I began to understand fully what my dad had meant all those years ago when he'd told me that the Lord wanted to bless me but could only do it if I was on the path of righteousness. The blessings poured over me including finally scoring high enough on the GRE literature to be accepted into UNLV's graduate program in English literature.

There were many times in my pregnancy where I felt very alone and confused. I missed the bar and the parties and the scene, but they gave me such a different feeling than church and family. I began to learn that when those feelings hit, it was best to I just let them pass and realize the joy at the end of those feelings of doubt. I wrote in my journal, mostly letters to Xiana. It was cathartic and, in retrospect, a form of therapy for my new life and resolution of my old one.

As the time of your arrival swiftly approaches, I am overwhelmed with emotion and feelings that are so complicated it is difficult to breathe. Before I have even met you, I want to protect you from anything bad that could ever happen to you. My heart breaks with concern that you will have challenges, and difficulties of any kind. Yet, there is something impenetrable about experience that can never be taken from any individual. I recognize the value of every problem you will ever have in your life, knowing from my own life the vast accountability and knowledge that comes from facing your challenges and making your own decisions, even if they are wrong. So instead of worrying about how to protect you from this world, I find myself delving into the duties of teaching you all there is to know about life, the world, inner value, self-worth, and every other tool that will assist you in living a peaceful, fulfilling life. You always hear about what a mother's dreams are for her children... I find that I don't care at all what career you choose, which school you attend, who you marry, etc. I care that you are brave, loved, lovely, happy, intelligent, goal oriented, kind, optimistic, generous, courageous, vivacious, love God, and love yourself always. I hope that, as your mother, I can be all of those things to help guide you in the direction that I know will be profoundly satisfying. And after I have done all that I can do to be an example to you and lead the way, I hope that I am brave enough to step aside when you make those crucial mistakes, always forgive, and always remember that you have been entrusted to me for a reason. With that service and responsibility comes all the blessings of happiness that exist in this world. So thank you, Xiana... I love you very much!

The night before Xiana's birth, I was given a priesthood blessing that offered great comfort. When Xiana was born, my life would never be the same. Though I should have been her protector and teacher, from the moment I laid eyes on her, she was mine. I was completely smitten without the slightest desire to use drugs, easily leaving an entire bottle of pain pills untouched. Xiana's healthy birth with no alcohol-induced developmental problems was just another in a long line of miracles.

The first few months were somewhat a blur, as I'm sure they are with most new mothers. Things were compounded by being in Vegas without family, single, going to grad school, and having a baby who simply didn't sleep. Due to my inexperience, I enabled her to be held around the clock the first few weeks of her life alternating turns with my mom who stayed with me for two weeks. The day she left, I would later refer to as the day the sky fell. I had a touch of the baby blues that seemed to manifest in complete irrationality. I got it in my head that if Xiana so much as cried, she would be ruined; her life would be affected; she would be scarred. My mom left and I held Xiana for the next twenty-four hours solid. I didn't eat, and every time I so much as attempted to put her down, she'd scream and I would hurriedly snatch her back into my arms. I remember crying, tears streaming off my face rolling onto my tiny infant's cheeks. I lacked even the aptitude to call for help; I was so lost in the strange void of motherhood. Answers to prayers never ceased. My first friend in Vegas, Danny showed up with a tuna casserole, sized up the situation in one glance, and took Xiana out of my arms. It was like a sudden jolt of reality that snapped me back into sanity. Days later, just as quickly as the impending luminous clouds rolled in, I woke from two hours of sleep (holding Xiana in the crook of my arm), looked outside and discovered with shocked sincerity that the sky was still blue. My baby blues had subsided. I took to sleeping on the couch so I could more easily prop Xiana in my arms. I could function on the two to four hours of sleep I was getting in a twenty-four hour period, particularly while ward members and friends continually brought dinners, company, and even held Xiana while I napped or showered.

The blessings literally poured in. And perhaps the greatest answer to prayers: despite the most emotionally grueling months of my life, I never once considered using drugs or alcohol. After nine short months of sobriety and attending church, I felt devoid of the demonic throes of addiction. Never in all of life had I imagined the intensity of love for my child. It was simultaneously uplifting and crushing as I understood for the first time how much my own mother loved me. By extension, I also came to understand God's love and my value. My faith in a fair and enveloping Father in Heaven grew, and I continued to develop a deep understanding that I too, was a child of God… of infinite worth. I had often felt that I must have a very important mission on earth. Why else would I be spared while burying so many less impulsive friends along the way? As I grew to know Xiana and see her old soul and sweet spirit, I came to have a profound belief that if this was the only thing I ever accomplished, *she* would be enough. Bringing her into this world was absolutely the greatest mission I could accomplish. For the first time in my life, I wasn't concerned with my own importance or accolades; she was more than enough success for eternity.

I didn't know that I would be feeding you twelve out of twenty-four hours. I didn't know that the color of poop could make me laugh or cry. I didn't know that you would need to be held around the clock. I didn't know that I could feel so inadequate and so needed at the same time. I didn't know that the whole world could change into something else, but that the sky would still be blue. I didn't know that when your heart is finally whole, it breaks. I didn't know that I would love you so much; I would do anything to make sure you are happy. I didn't know how beautiful it would be to kiss your lips. I didn't know that a tiny flicker of a sleepy smile could make my soul laugh inside and out. I didn't know that it was going to be this hard. I didn't know that it was going to be this worth it. I didn't know how long it took to type one handed. I didn't know that late night TV was so bad. I didn't know that nothing in this whole world mattered except the joy of the angel who came to the earth at 8:01 am. I didn't know I would be so proud. I didn't know I could be so trusted. I didn't know that life is astonishing. I didn't know that the most important thing in this whole world is the needs of a baby. I didn't know that serving another human being hand and foot, is the most rewarding thing in life. I didn't know that the present is more important than the future or the past. I didn't know that you would be perfect...I just didn't know.

I soaked Xiana in, morning and night; I breathed the gift of life around the clock. It was overwhelming not getting any sleep, but the Lord intervened again when she was two-months-old and I went home for Christmas. Karla and Nic (seasoned professionals at putting babies to sleep) taught me how to swaddle her and get her to sleep for five hour increments without being held. It was nothing short of a miracle. Karla took Xiana the first night. I woke startled and afraid several hours later to find Xiana wrapped snuggly in her blanket, sound asleep. A new door was opened, and I began to feel human again. There were no shortage of obstacles, but always, solutions were provided. I was emphatically learning I could trust God.

I had to put Xiana in daycare when she was only eight-weeks-old. Words cannot describe how hard that was. I was so worried. I didn't know where to take her. I knew that no one could care for her the way her mother could. Was it an accident that my newly assigned visiting teacher worked in the infant room of a nearby day care? This was evidence that the Lord knew my need, and He provided comfort and answers to my problem. Months later, in the middle of my first semester of graduate school, I found myself one evening feeling defeated and alone. I was a single mom. My family was all elsewhere and I began to question my decision to finish school and remain in Las Vegas. It was all I could do to stop myself from loading my baby in my car and driving home, to my parents. I know that I had been led by the Spirit to make the decision to stay in Vegas, yet I questioned it with frustration and grief. It all felt so impossible. I knelt in prayer asking the Lord what I should do. Had I heard wrong? Had I made the wrong decision? Was this even possible? Surely it would be easier to go home and live with my parents for a time. After my prayer, I heard the Holy Ghost tell me to read my scriptures and my patriarchal blessing. I opened my triple combination to D&C 6:14 which reads: "*Verily, verily, I say unto thee, blessed art thou for what thou hast done; for thou hast inquired of me, and behold, as often as thou hast inquired thou hast received instruction of my Spirit. If it had not been so, thou wouldst not have come to the place where thou art at this time.*"

This was counsel given to another person, in another time, but the context was irrelevant. The Lord, through the Spirit and scriptures, revealed to me his pleasure in the choices I was making. I then read my patriarchal blessing for what had to be the millionth time. Amazingly, there was a line which I had never before seen. It told me that my "family's temporal blessing would depend on my education." The Lord blessed me for seeking His counsel, comforted me, and led me to feel confident that I would make it through this difficult time because I was following Him. Because He knows my name, He would help me to accomplish everything my righteous heart desired.

Though the Lord uplifted me and helped me through, that was a grueling time. I was working at the writing center, teaching two sections of English 101, taking a minimum of nine credits, raising a baby, and studying for my comps. I knew, even in the moment, that the day would come when I would look back at this time and wonder how I made it through. It was a lot of juggling, and it was incredibly hard. But, in time, I began to understand that even though this tiny person had changed my very existence, I was still me. Though I had grown and developed through my life experiences, emotionally and psychologically I was very young still. I hadn't learned how to absorb anxiety, or vulnerability. I had scarcely considered responsibilities or the intense love for my child. I had been numb for so much of my life, that my emotional learning curve was steep. Beyond being thrilled to be a mom, it was crucial for our success that I be thrilled that I was me. The Lord really operates line upon line, precept upon precept. No sooner would I understand something about healthy coping mechanisms, or spiritual concepts, than I would deal with something directly related to those concepts. Sometimes I still find myself trying to figure out ways to escape, to not feel. Emotions are unbearable for someone who never learned how to deal with them. I've discovered I've been blessed with an almost innate ability to decipher my feelings and use them to propel me in healthy directions.

Though I would be lying to claim that I don't have urgings to do drugs sometimes, so far I haven't responded to those cravings by succumbing to them. I've also learned not to say I never will, because I don't know. In the past, uttering those claims has been more destructive than temptations. But I always temper my success with the necessary understanding that I have not arrived. I remind myself continuously that I could relapse. I never thought I would before, and yet I did repeatedly. To be safe, I try to acknowledge that relapse is a real and terrifying force. Through years of therapy, I've grown accustomed to identifying triggers and analyzing why emotions or situations leave me feeling so afraid or desperate. For a long time, every time the sun went down, my insides would churn and crawl as if sensing a lifetime of drug use in the dark hours. Even still, sometimes when I'm driving, and I can see the stars in the sky, I have the overwhelming longing for a lifetime etched in my subconscious. The seasons changing always leaves me with intense longings for cigarettes and joints. The desire gets weaker every time, and over the years, I've replaced much of those associations with happier memories of taking my children to the lake, sledding, or to the park. Still, it never fails, when the cold winds get warm, and the sun prickles my skin, or that first breath at the beginning of fall, the cravings will emerge. Mostly they're fleeting now, but for years they were all but debilitating. Holding my breath, I imagine the hardest and darkest of times and compare them to my brightest joys. So far, I have been successful. I can think of only two times in the last eight years that I legitimately tangoed with the temptation. Both times, I went so far as to entertain the thought that I could easily buy some beer, chug them, and no one would know. Thankfully, that's the extent of those dangerous thoughts. I've experienced relapse enough to know that, if I ever did, I would be in life-threatening trouble.

Most of the time, I am appalled when I recall a moment in my past. I feel so far removed from that former lifestyle that it's a shock to the system to acknowledge that those are *my* memories. Recently, I was driving carpool from gymnastics, and the girls were all excitedly talking and singing in the back of my minivan. I reached my hand out to turn up the volume on a Taylor Swift song when the light caught my arm just right. My heart palpitated, and I quickly sucked in my breath, wincing at the bewilderment of seeing the track marks peppering my arm. They were all but invisible; a tiny train of connect the dots on both sides of my veins. It was foreign to me as I flashed images of shooting up, myself, others, always waiting for that crimson red to indicate the vein had been successfully pricked. How could that possibly have been me? Here I was, a wife, a mom, a college professor, a counselor in the Young Women presidency, and I had track marks on my arm. I understood more fully than ever before the infinite blessings of the Atonement. Not only had I been able to repent and to be forgiven, but the Lord had enabled me to more often than not, forget too. It was as if my choices were no more. And for every craving that I denied, fewer would follow.

My eating disorder, on the other hand, has reemerged from time to time. Thankfully, I've never resorted to true anorexia or bulimia again. But my relationship with food and yo-yo dieting over the years are only a few short steps away. I've seen great success in losing weight while eating healthily and exercising, but it seems to only take a moment before I'm bingeing again. Without purging, the end result is weight gain. I dance this torture again and again. I'm trying to understand better what triggers a binge. Sometimes, like when I'm pregnant or nursing, I seem to give myself complete liberty to eat whatever I want whenever I want. Unfortunately, after a lifetime of deprivation coupled with bingeing and purging, I have no clue how to listen to my body. I'm not sure I even know what it means to be full. I'm working on it. One thing that I've found to be helpful over the years is to concentrate on adding plenty of fruits and vegetables to every meal. Then, if I feel the urge to overdo it, at least I've eaten something with nutritional value. Even that is a challenge though after a lifetime of willfully consuming the fattiest, highest calorie options to satisfy my cravings. What was the point of wasting fresh produce on the sewer? My logic is totally screwy, but it's a serious challenge to undo thought processes that dominated my mind for half my life. I've discovered that I am a highly emotional eater. Whether I'm happy or sad, my go-to is food for reward or punishment. Once, while at a lesson about learning to love yourself, the teacher asked some challenging and introspective questions. It was an alarming discovery to find myself, not only squirming, but immediately planning my entire meal for the evening in my head. It was incredibly eye-opening to recognize that the least bit of discomfort or addressing my self-esteem led me to think of food. I do not yet have all the tools to combat this way of thinking, but I'm working on it. I'm trying to figure out my underlying emotions that lead me to binge. Lack of self-motivation and guilt head the brigade of my overeating triggers. Working on this book has opened unimaginable recesses into my soul. Feeling inadequate as a mom, a wife, a leader, often propels me to the fridge. This is one of the many areas where I'm learning I need God's help. Relying on Him and trusting in Him more fully has been the most successful technique I've discovered.

I grew in my spiritual knowledge tremendously with the birth of Xiana. It was remarkable to me how much of my foundation had stuck which showed me that the loving examples of my family quite literally had sustained me to hell and back. It was like riding a bike: I was hesitant at first only to quickly discover that I was made to ride a bike. My parents had taught me long ago, and though I hadn't ridden in a long time, the ability had not been lost. I was grateful beyond description. I began then to fantasize about going through the temple. At first, it seemed to be a pipe dream. I was single; I was practically a new convert; I'd never had a calling; I'd gone so far in the opposite direction. Still, when Xiana was just a few months old, I was reading my *Book of Mormon* one night and read about Alma the younger. His parents were spiritual leaders, and he rebelled against the church and its teachings taking his peers with him. He went against his parents and the Lord, leading others to believe him, when an angel appeared to him confirming he'd been wrong. He came back to the Lord and went out to teach others about Christ. I identified with him and understanding surged my entire body. I too had been born of and raised by goodly parents. I too had turned my back on the God and mocked those who would follow Him. I too had been lost. Having Xiana was exactly the same as being visited by an angel. And Alma had become a courageous, successful missionary and servant of the Lord. I decided to meet with my bishop and ask him about taking the temple prep classes.

My first lesson was on Mothers' Day—symbolic of the very role that had propelled me there. My family decided that the most central location for me to receive my endowment (a special ordinance done only in a temple) was in Utah. I chose the Timpanogos Temple both for its proximity to Cami's house as well as its significance having been the only temple where I'd done baptisms for the dead. All but Jed joined me in the temple that day. It was surreal and overwhelming and beautiful. I felt of God's love again and again. Beyond everything, I understood the Atonement in a new way because I felt unceasingly forgiven. Also, I understood in ways I never had before, the significance of an eternal family. I was so grateful for the opportunity to have my Xiana sealed to me for time and all eternity someday. For the next few years, I would never enter the temple without someone—an old friend, a teacher, a leader: my village— bursting into tears at the sight of me there.
Every time people expressed their heartfelt joy at seeing me in the temple. Most of them should have patted themselves on the backs for following the promptings of the Spirit to minister to me, pray for me, and never give up hope for my return. As loved as all the attention made me feel, it also bothered me at times. Why should I be celebrated and praised for making poor choices when those who made excellent choices were often ignored or taken for granted? Being the prodigal son gave me great sympathy for those who were not. I always felt guilty for being admired for overcoming things others had simply abstained from. Later I would learn I needn't have felt bad for them. They received blessings and rewards beyond compare.

Larissa

"I would be my brother's keeper; I would learn the healer's art. To the wounded and the weary I would show a gentle heart. I would be my brother's keeper--Lord, I would follow thee" ("Lord, I Would Follow Thee," Verse 3).

"Lenaya is pregnant? Lenaya is pregnant?!" The thought spun around my mind for weeks. I pushed Nicole in her stroller, following the trail of my boys on their bikes as we turned the corner in our neighborhood. We had a rare calm day, free of wind and were taking advantage of the warm sunshine. Confused, knowing that babies are happy announcements, I worried about what would happen in Lenaya's life. Would she be able to handle the demands of pregnancy, let alone motherhood? I knew that she was thrilled beyond measure, but I also knew that she had no clue about what she was actually getting herself into with little support. Would this new life be enough to motivate her to permanently create a different lifestyle? How could I explain to my impressionable young children who adored their aunt, that she was having a baby without a husband in the picture? I wondered about what kind of life this baby would have, worried that the stress might push Lenaya over the edge.

As it turned out my worries for my sister were unfounded. I struggled at times bouncing back and forth between judgmental thoughts and an attempt to love and help her. I wondered about her promiscuous lifestyle witnessing concrete proof of her choices that before I had only guessed at. I wondered what else she hid from us. I recognized the many obstacles she potentially faced raising a child on her own. I knew from years of experience that I had no power to change her, and I wondered how lasting this change would be. I think tempered hope was essential for me at that point. What I didn't know was that I would stand back and marvel at her progress. Not knowing the future, I had to work really hard to banish judgement and simply love and support her. The more we talked and the closer we grew, judgement simply melted away. Now suddenly, Lenaya was coming to me for advice, full of questions and I was finally able to share what little understanding I had gleaned through the years. All the times that I wanted to have the magic conversation were fruitless until she had changed her heart, and now that her heart was open, I was able to support her. To my surprise, I was also able to learn from her.

One common mistake family members can make when loved ones stray is to become very angry and condemning and estrange their family member. They hate the sinner as well as the sin. I can understand the anger. It is very frustrating to have a child disregard the values that you hold so dear. When Lenaya was a young teenager my dad was trying to have a conversation with her as they were driving somewhere. Stopped at a light, trying to convey the difference between friends and family members he stated, "Lenaya, I would step in front of those cars for you." She curtly responded, "Then why don't you do it?" I felt the heat of intense anger toward her and the pain she caused my parents and our family. Yet my parents were unflagging in their expressions of love toward her. I know they felt hurt and angry many times, but they resisted the tendency to turn their anger on her or to reject her and cast her out. This is especially hard to learn how to do when a loved one's lifestyle does not match our own. Balancing loving the sinner without condoning the sin is a constant challenge and has no simple recipe. If our love and happiness are tied to the choices our family members make, then we give all our power to them. Learning to love in the midst of rejection and hurt is one of the important lessons we need to learn in this life.

The other mistake I see family members make is to embrace the sinner *and* the sin. In an effort to grapple with their child's poor choices, I see many parents abandon their own habits and beliefs at the very time they need them the most. Sometimes in embarrassment, they stop attending church or turn their backs on their support systems. At times, in their devastation, they question and reject previously held beliefs. Parents often isolate themselves at a time when they need help and support more than ever before. They let their pride or self-criticism separate them from help. As onlookers to the situation, we tend to judge harshly. I felt very critical of my parents for years in how they parented us and in how they handled those difficult years, but time softened my judgment and I see now that they did the best they could with the tools they had. Many times my parents dreaded facing their peers, full of sympathy and advice. Somehow we need to search for the middle ground between these two extremes. We can neither reject our child, nor rationalize away their actions. In time, we developed a relationship with Lenaya that wasn't contingent upon her changing her lifestyle. With a loving relationship set in place, when she decided to change, she knew we were a safe place to turn, where she would be loved and supported.

Time has a way of speeding up as we get older. My kids continued to grow, and life got busier, though my capacity grew as well. I served in different church callings and continued to improve as an organist. I taught my kids to read one after another and learned with them through the years. My highest priority has always been to seek the Spirit in my life as well as teach my kids to recognize the still, small voice of the Holy Ghost. The vast majority of my spiritual experiences are small and simple promptings that I strive to act on. Those years were difficult but beautiful.

Lenaya's situation was unique in that she always had a belief in God but just ran away from it for years of her life. For her, having a child was the shock she needed to finally start living her beliefs. I realize for some that is not enough or their addictions are too entrenched. We never know what impetus will propel an individual from sin and addiction into a new life. Only God knows us wholly. People really are capable of changing their lives with His help. It is an act of faith for us to believe that change is possible. I am grateful to her ward family for the incredible support they were to her when she was making so many changes. I don't know if she would have been strong enough, alone in Vegas, to change. They embraced Lenaya wholeheartedly, providing a loving, nonjudgmental support network. They pushed her to fully repent, search the scriptures, give service to others and ultimately led her to the temple.

In just a moment it seemed, our family travelled to Utah where I attended the temple with Lenaya. What a surreal experience to sit a few rows from my sister and ponder on the fact that Lenaya's temple promises and blessings were no different than my own. Just as in Christ's Parable of the Laborers where all received the same payment for their work performed no matter the length of time, we were offered the same reward for our Laboring in Christ's vineyard here on the earth. As Elder Holland stated so eloquently, "We are not diminished when someone else is added upon. We are not in a race against each other to see who is the wealthiest or the most talented or the most beautiful or even the most blessed. The race we are *really* in is the race against sin..." (Holland, April 2012).

Lenaya

As soon as I finished my Master's degree, I moved back home. It was a sweet time; a payback for years stolen and borrowed; taken and lost. Xiana thrived in her new environment, redefining "family" as she bonded with grandparents only seen on occasions before. Jed lived there too for part of the time, and he developed a fierce bond with little Xiana playfully entertaining her often. I found Brian on LDSsingles.com only to discover I'd known his brother, and met him, years before. He lived in Sparks, was outdoorsy, active in the church, and had a daughter. We wrote to each other for months before we met in person so I felt like I knew him already on our first date. We had dinner, and then walked around the Marina talking long into the night. He was so relaxed; I found that I already I trusted him. I wanted to learn all I could about him trying to listen attentively to every story he got in between my interruptions. I clearly was more talkative. We had only been dating a few months when it came time for me to make a choice about whether to join Larissa in Colorado or to stay in Reno. Larissa had put me in contact with one of the department heads at a community college in Alamosa and I had been tentatively planning on moving there after the summer.

I tried not to let Brian's presence in my life influence my decision, but I was falling for this country boy with the calm demeanor and easygoing attitude. I didn't trust that I was relying on the Lord for my decision; instead trying to further my own agenda. So I prayed, and prayed. *Lord, I'll do whatever I'm supposed to do and whatever is going to be best for me and Xiana, only please don't make me leave Reno. Okay, I know you won't make me do anything so I'm deciding... I'm going to stay here so please make it work.* I felt I needed to make a decision because I know that's how prayers work. You decide and then you pray about whether or not that decision is right. I began to feel like either way would be okay, but I had no prospect of a job in Reno. I applied for the minimal secondary positions that were posted and then began trying to determine if I had any right to turn down a potential job in Colorado with the economy the way it was. On a whim, I emailed one of my old professors at UNR and asked for a recommendation to the composition department. I thought it was futile since, like other states, Nevada had just taken an abysmal hit in higher education. Then I started to second guess myself. Was I just determining the answer that I wanted independent of any divine counsel? Was I looking so hard for the answer that I wanted that I was blinded to the answer that was? I hoped not! The very day that the job was posted in Colorado, I received an email requesting an interview for UNR. Rather than a coincidence, I know it was an answer to my prayers. Elated, I called Larissa to tell her my good news and discovered that my liaison at that school had quit. Answers to prayers are not always confirmed so quickly, but I was extremely grateful to my Father in Heaven for helping me know that this major life choice was correct. This tender mercy was a response to my heartfelt begging to stay near my parents and pursue my relationship with Brian. I was filled with relief, though I was still anxious about an actual job. So, with a resume, a prayer, and a business suit I went to my interview and got hired on the spot. I'm pretty sure words would do a great disservice to the gratitude that I felt, not only for getting a job, but for knowing without a doubt that the Lord is *always* mindful of my needs *and* my wants and that He allows me agency to choose while simultaneously blessing me for heeding his counsel.

Brian and I had scarcely been dating three months before I felt certain he would be the man I would marry. He made me laugh, listened, and was intuitive and kind. He was an amazing dad to both our daughters. He had returned to church activity as recently as I had, giving us common ground while also providing similar goals. Neither of us was changing for the other. Instead, we'd both set foot on the path and found each other there. Our dates almost always included some outdoor walk or event. I love the outdoors and was grateful to have found someone who mirrored my affection. For a while, I thought he might be a pushover which has never been successful with me; I take too many liberties, dominate. But I worried needlessly because it wasn't very long before I realized he would not be commanded. Larissa asked once if I was worried I would steam-roller him. "No!" I replied, "I'm afraid he's going to steam-roller me!" He is the perfect person to balance me. He's calm when I'm irrational. He's an introvert while I'm an extreme extrovert. He never raises his voice where my normal speaking voice is several volumes above others' yells. I don't agree that opposites always attract, but we are very different in ways that seem to magnify and enhance us both. But we also have enough similarities that we can easily reach common ground. He is a spiritual giant, and he helps me to grow in my belief in and love for Christ. He makes me laugh; we both love the outdoors and family walks. We even like similar foods!

I tried to be patient as I waited for him to realize that I was his future wife. I didn't have to wait long, because by December he had asked my dad for my hand and proposed. All through our courtship, my parents watched Xiana. It was an ideal situation. I recognize most single moms don't have the same luxury; my parents blessed my life in countless ways all through it. They never gave up on me; they never stopped loving me; and they continually supported me through every attempt I made to better myself and my life. When my attempts were in worsening my condition, they were firm in letting me know their feelings about my actions, while maintaining their unconditional love for me. They've asked me on several occasions what they could have done differently for me. The answer is absolutely nothing. They could not have prevented me from using my free agency; they could only be a soft place for me to land, no matter how many times I fell.

On April 17th, 2010, Brian and I were married. Exactly one week earlier we closed on our first house. Exactly six months later, Brian adopted Xiana. It was a sweet experience for my dad to perform the adoption for his own precious granddaughter. The judge was amiable and kind creating a video for us with the court proceedings. When the judge asked Brian why he wanted to adopt Xiana, through tears he explained that the week before he'd had a conversation with her about adoption. He told her a judge was going to say he could be her daddy. "But you already are my daddy," she exclaimed. "Then he's going to say that your last name can be Andersen," he replied. "But my name already is Xiana Andersen," confused she retorted. He choked as he said, "That's exactly how I feel." There wasn't a dry eye in the place. If it's true that the deeper your pain, the fuller your joy, then I can honestly say there are few on this earth to experience a joy as exquisite as this. One year after our marriage, we went to the temple to be sealed for time and all eternity as a family. I was nine months pregnant with our baby boy, Kolton, and we were dressed in pure white. As we looked around the white and gold sealing room, rainbows exploded from the crystal prisms of the chandelier. The mirrors showed smiling faces from here to eternity. Words will never be adequate to explain the degree of love felt there or the expression on our sweet girl's face as she became ours, not just for this life, but for eternity. Our only heart-ache was that Brian's daughter, Ekco, could not join us there. But even that will be remedied if we put our trust in God!

I spent more than a decade without a prayer that my life could be, would be, this beautiful. If you would have told me ten years ago, that today I'd have four kids, a wonderful husband, a career, and be an active member of the Church of Jesus Christ of Latter-Day Saints, I would have laughed. And though I know I'm special, I also am humble enough to know that I'm not. Christ's Atonement applies to everyone. There is not a single person on this earth who can't return to the loving arms of our Heavenly Father. He will move mountains to rescue one soul. I know that's true… because He did.

Although I have a wonderful life previously thought unattainable, it is not without trials. I used to think that as long as I got off drugs, there would be no other obstacles placed in my path. I still have trials. Part of this life is trials. Without them, I couldn't progress. Learning how to have a sober relationship in a *marriage* is intense. Feelings of vulnerability, jealousy, and inadequacy, all without being able to suffocate them with drugs or alcohol have been debilitating at times. Our first year of marriage was challenging, largely in part because of my lack of emotional maturity or ability to express myself sufficiently. I didn't know what my love language was, but I expected Brian to. At times I felt overwhelmed and unappreciated, but Larissa gave me an excellent piece of advice early on. She said, "In time, you will understand Brian better. Things won't change necessarily, but you will better understand him and it will be easier." At the time I thought that was a sexist comment to make. It sounded like, "Don't expect him to change, you change." Funnily though, she was right. In time, we came to understand one another better. Things that hurt my feelings tremendously before came to make sense. Things that I took as a personal assault I realized were unintentional. The day before we got married, my dad gave me a blessing. In it he said, "I caution you to always remember that you cannot change anybody but yourself." It was true then, it's still true now. I'm learning. Brian is patient and calm and rarely reacts to my hypersensitivity or volatile outbursts. It drove me crazy at first, but now I am grateful that he rarely takes my bait. It's more productive to discuss things calmly…. although I am still a yeller.

Another challenge Brian has helped me with is that I am often tempted to use my addiction as a rite of passage, a cool card so to speak. For years after I got sober, I felt like I had to tell every person I encountered that I was a drug addict. Partially I felt compelled to do this because it was so much a part of my identity; indeed for a long time I felt it *was* my identity. Partly though, it made me feel relatable and cool and *popular*. If I had been a drug addict, people couldn't accuse me of being one of those sheltered and closed-minded Mormons. I was active in the church and had a close relationship with my Savior and yet, I still felt the urge to disassociate myself. I'm not entirely sure when this changed, but I have not felt those urges in a long time. Partially it's because Brian was never impressed by my awesome ability to be a successful drug addict. Though he accepted me and loved me despite my past, he didn't love me *for* my past. He didn't celebrate my crazy life or laugh at my antics. Instead, he celebrated my repentance and my potential as a daughter of God. It was humbling, and motivational. I continue to learn from him and his example.

I recognize it's a lifelong process to achieve and create identity. I know it isn't unique to my experience to have identity crises or to evolve. Still, I think it's a steep learning curve to be a drug addict for so long, particularly in the most formative years, and attempt to ascertain who I am. For one thing, I always thought I was so carefree, fly by the seat of my pants, everything is an adventure. I'm far more OCD than I ever imagined. I had no idea that I would be such a micromanager as a mother. It's difficult for me to relinquish control. I get anxiety about the cleanliness of my house. I never in my wildest dreams thought I had those characteristics. I'm impatient and fretful. Though I still love adventure, I am a planner with to-do lists for days.

Sometimes I think I have a pretty solid grasp on my identity, and then something derails me. While writing this book, I received some devastating news. Images of a high speed chase, and suicide by cop flashed on my screen and stung my eyes with confusing tears. I read aloud to my husband, the story of my old boyfriend's death. Earlier that day he had posted on Facebook that he was engaged. I had "liked" his status. This would be yet another marriage, but I was hopeful for him. He was the boyfriend who packed up and left our house while I cried on the doorstep. He had a zest for life coupled with a disregard for death. He was afraid of neither. The images of him as he finally got out of his truck wielding a gun before he was shot to death will probably always haunt me. I cannot conjure images of happiness or peace. All I can think is how helpless he must have felt; how completely and desperately trapped. How he must have thought or known there was no way out of this one. A reporter interviewed his dad briefly. His father said, "It's a horrible thing to watch your son die on the news [but] I'm not surprised he reacted the way he did. He was on heroin. He wanted to die." This notion brought new moisture to my eyes as my heart broke again for his parents. What an absolute tragedy! And yet, I understand that it could have been me. His death left me feeling isolated and strange, questioning where I belong. After a long stint of feeling like I was a righteous Mormon, I suddenly realized I wasn't. I felt exactly the same as I had all those years earlier. That week at playgroup and book group and sitting in my living room with my family, I constantly had the old familiar feelings of, "I am not them. They are not me." Matt is dead. I am *him*. I am not *me*. I *am* him. I staggered between the world I had comfortably embraced; the world that was mine; and the world that I used to know. The comments started pouring onto his Facebook page until I could no longer read them. I didn't want anybody to judge him because it felt like their words were judging me! Should I defend his actions and choices because they were mine or should I feel angry towards his irresponsible behavior because I no longer lived that life?

Resigned, I begged the Lord to let me know who I was and what to do. I instantly understood grace in a way I hadn't before. Christ had paid the ultimate price, and the Lord would judge our hearts. It wasn't my concern. I was missing the most important thing: I didn't have to choose sides. I could have compassion for Matt and his family while still adhering to a higher standard. I didn't have to be addicted to drugs to be able to empathize with him. I didn't have to judge him; but I also didn't have to join him. It was breathtakingly simple. It was grace, and love, and beauty. But it was also challenging. The mantra from AA reverberated in my mind: "Change the things I can and accept the things I cannot." While I strive to progress, I also must seek acceptance. It's easy to be everlastingly forgiving to those around me; the greatest challenge is in forgiving and accepting *myself*. And just like all of life, it's often a roller coaster of highs and lows.

The same is true of my career as an English professor. It is peppered with feelings of capability and inadequacy. Most days, work fuels me with a passion and drive sometimes forgotten in the folding of laundry, the brushing of teeth, the mopping of floors. It's tricky sometimes, remembering that the more important work is not always the most rewarding. I've been successful professionally. I haven't had a lucrative career, but I have seen and felt great success nevertheless. Sometimes, when I give a lecture, or make corrections on an essay, I wonder, when will they figure out that I'm a fraud? When will they know that this is not actually me? I'm coming to understand the fraud is the drug addict with no ambition, but it's tricky sometimes remembering. This happens more often at home where they call me Mommy. Inadequacy can be suffocating, and I throw my hands in the air and silently scream while I sit in trepidation wondering when they will know that I am a hypocrite. I never want them to encounter the life I once created. I plead with God that they will not have to learn things the hard way as I, their teacher, did. But *most* times, most of the *time*, I know that I am an admirable professor, the most perfect mother and wife because I know that God created me that way. And then He saved me, and He saved me some more…. because *I* am enough. I have *always* been enough.

Then, on June 27th 2013, I would begin the hardest trial of my life. The day started like any other. My nieces were in town having a grandparents visit and attending a paper doll camp. I was planning on meeting my mom with the girls and my kids at the movies to watch *Monster's University*. The show started at 2:50 pm so Brian would meet us there to pick up our toddler who didn't sit through movies very well. As I was loading up the car I got a call from my mom. "I'm a little concerned," she said, "I don't know if I should go to the movies with you or not. Dad's truck and car are both here, his bike is gone, but the office has been calling, and I haven't heard from him for a long time." I tried to flesh out the details: how long had it been? What had he said? It didn't take long to understand that he had not shown up for any of his scheduled events and had not said anything about taking a bike ride. Furthermore, if he'd disappeared on the river, as he was known to do, he would have taken his truck as well. He couldn't still be riding around the neighborhood some six hours later. "You call the police station, and I will call the hospital." We agreed and hung up the phone. I called the closest hospital to ask if they had any John Doe's. They did not. Relieved, I called mom back. "I have to go! He's calling on the other line!" Filled with relief, I headed down to the movie theater. By the time I arrived, I called her again; it had been a wicked trick that my cell phone came up as his name on their home caller id. "I found him," she said, "I spoke with the police. He is at Renown hospital." Crushed, my heart skipped a beat as I told her I'd meet her there and take the girls back to my house. Anxious and with tears in my eyes, I explained that my dad had been in a bicycle accident and loaded all three of our kids into Brian's truck for him to take them back home.

I raced to the hospital silently pleading with the Lord for Dad to be okay. I was the first to arrive there since Mom hit every single red light. I rushed to his bedside where the police officer had almost no answers. He didn't know what had happened; he didn't know if a car was involved; he didn't know anything! The nurse was talking to my dad while simultaneously asking me questions: age, health, medication, allergies. She said, "Wow, you're unusually involved in the care of your father." I laughed. He had always taken *care* of me. He was agitated and on life support. He had a tube coming out of his head and a ventilator around his throat. His nurse said, "Nick, your daughter is here." I squeezed his hand and tried to calm him down. He was thrashing about. I said, "Dad, it's okay. I'm here. Oh precious Daddy what have you done? You're going to be okay." I kissed his forehead above his black eyes and tried to catalog the list of injuries the nurse was reporting. Broken clavicle, broken leg, punctured lung, broken wrist, possible paralysis, brain trauma. *Brain trauma.* He'd been in an accident on the street he lived on. He had hit a tree. He had been wearing a helmet. *He had been wearing a helmet.* I was calmed and encouraged. I began to understand that he was going to be fine. He squeezed my hand. I'm certain he knew I was there. I continued to talk to him and kiss him until Mom arrived. She came back just as the neurosurgeon was making his rounds. He explained to us that we would be playing the waiting game. "If he wakes up that will be a good sign." I discarded the statement having seen my dad's movement and response to my presence. I figured he had misspoken, unintentionally said, "if." I went in the hallway to be with my nieces where I called each of my siblings in order. Each asked the same thing. "Do I need to come?" I didn't think so. "I don't know," I hesitantly replied, "If you can. I mean, I don't think you need to. That is to say, there's not really anything you can do here." By 10 pm every one of them had arrived. After calling my siblings I dialed to get someone to come give him a blessing. When they arrived, I listened intently to the words uttered. "You will make a full recovery." A full recovery!!! Ecstatic I clung to that pronouncement over the next several days.

We went on survival mode. We made the necessary phone calls, food poured in to both households and the hospital. We took turns sitting with Dad and talking with each other. His brother and sister-in-law came. We told stories, sang songs, anything to let him know we were there. For the first couple of days, he responded by wiggling toes which left me incredibly optimistic. I didn't know how severe the rehabilitation would be, but the thought that he wouldn't live literally was not even an option. By day three we never saw movement again. That was the first day that I began to understand that he might not make it. I came home from the hospital that night. Brian had already put the kids to bed like all the nights before. He had work the next day, but he tenderly listened to me as I sobbed, "What if he doesn't live? I mean really... what if it's not about how hard his recovery will be? What if he doesn't live?" It was agonizing, the worry and new understanding. The whole community prayed for a miracle including the Catholics, Hindus, Muslims, Christians, and Buddhists. Dad had been a significant part of the interfaith community for over a decade. While begging God to heal our father, Cami said something that will forever stick with me. "We keep praying for a miracle, but the truth is, the miracle already happened some 2000 years ago in an empty tomb. That's the true miracle." Indeed, we each came to understand the Atonement in depths previously unfelt. Larissa also said, "If he lives, it will be no less a miracle than you returning to the Lord." I wrestled with that for a few days. It seemed inconceivable that my dad's physical body being restored wouldn't be the most miraculous thing. Certainly, the Resurrection is viewed throughout religion as the greatest miracle. And yet, Christ's Atonement: His suffering for our sins, our loss, our sorrow, our trials, was truly the greatest miracle. Never before had I been so grateful for the Atonement. What if my dear sweet daddy died and I never got to see him again? Ten days after his accident, on July 5th, Mom, my siblings and our spouses sat in a circle around his hospital bed while the nurse removed life support, feeding tube, and turned off all the machines. We sang songs, talked, and each took turns saying goodbye. His eyes had slightly opened that day, and his head was tilted to his left. We each stood on that side. "I love you dad. I'm so grateful that you were my daddy. You were the best father anybody could have ever hoped for. You were perfect." As we said goodbye, tears slid out of his eyes and down his cheeks. Logically, the nurse had put eye drops in thirty minutes earlier, but I'm certain he was there. His spirit joined his body one last time as we shared the moment that he left this life. It was so surreal. It was heart-wrenching and soul-shaping. It was identity-forming and life-changing.

Fueled by a combination of tasks to complete and loved ones surrounding us, we went on autopilot. His funeral service was perfect and, at the end, I felt his spirit acknowledge his approval. He always wanted his funeral to be a missionary experience. The congregation was surely evidence that it was. Months later my sorrow really hit. This was the first major trial I had ever had that I couldn't trace back to my own choices. I couldn't blame the Lord for wanting Dad's return. I couldn't be mad at Him. But I also found it difficult to pray, to breathe, to go on. It wasn't that I was mad at God; it was just that I didn't want to talk to Him; I wanted to talk to my dad. I couldn't very well pray to *him*, so I just stopped praying. The floor had been ripped out from underneath me, and I didn't know if I would ever feel safe again. For several weeks I felt like I was drowning. Everything made me cry, I was newly pregnant with our last daughter, Argenta, and, though I'd never worried before about miscarriage or death, I found myself consumed with worry. What if this baby died? What if something happened to our other children? To Brian? All my life I'd felt safe and secure. I'd always been optimistic believing the best in other people and in my own experiences. But if Dad could die, surely *anything* could happen. I felt precarious and afraid. Then, I began to worry that this identity I'd worked so hard to discover was false. What if without Dad, my safety net, I would be worried and afraid for the rest of my life? What if he was the only reason I was sober? I called Larissa and talked with her for a long time. After we hung up, I felt a little better for the first time in weeks. The next day, I got on my hands and knees and truly turned it over to the Lord. I expressed all my fears and concerns and anguish. His answer was clear. If my earthly father made me feel so safe and taken care of, why couldn't I feel the same security from my Heavenly Father? It was a powerful lesson; one I continue to work on. From that day forward I began to understand that, though I would always miss my dad, I needed to learn to rely on the Lord and trust Him as much and more than I ever trusted my own sweet earthly father. I also began to understand what Elder Holland said, "Heaven is closer than we suppose." I have felt my dad's presence. I know that he lives. I know that his resurrection, and my repentance, and everyone's salvation are a direct result of the Atonement. I'm so grateful for that knowledge which has gotten me through the eye of the storm and saved me.

Larissa

"And if men come unto me I will show unto them their weakness. I give unto men weakness that they may be humble; and my grace is sufficient for all men that humble themselves before me; for if they humble themselves before me, and have faith in me, then will I make weak things become strong unto them" (Book of Mormon, Ether 12:27).

Nathan and I felt that there was one more child for us and I really hoped for another girl. Danielle was born five years after Nicole. While it was difficult to step back into the baby world along with the diaper changes and sleepless nights, our whole family delighted in her. She brought us an abundance of joy. When Danielle was almost one, Lenaya called me on my birthday, which I shared with Xiana. We enjoyed a comfortable conversation based on years of getting to know one another. I mentioned to her that I had been talking with a friend at a function earlier that week. We had talked a little about her experience, and he told me that she should write a book. I agreed quickly with him proceeding to go on with our conversation, but he stopped me, looked me in the eye and said, "No, really! She needs to write a book!"

Lenaya acknowledged that this was something she intended to do, but grappled with how to share her story without sensationalizing her experience as so many books tend to do. That conversation on my birthday and Xiana's birthday brought about another birth of the idea that I write my story to balance hers out. We started working on our book, collaborating throughout the nearly five year process.

Soon after this conversation, I felt a strong spiritual prompting that would stretch me more than anything I had done to that point. Following this encouragement from the Spirit, I entered graduate school for Clinical and Mental Health Counseling. Sacrificing entertainment, exercise, personal interests and even sleep, I read sometimes fascinating, sometimes dull textbooks, wrote papers and participated in multiple group discussions. Considering I had used a typewriter during my college years, the advanced technology overwhelmed me, and many times I questioned my sanity. Though I still managed to homeschool my kids, our entire family sacrificed for my further education. At times, I wondered if the sacrifice was worth it.

At my low point, I attended the temple, praying for confirmation that I was doing the right thing. My answer came through a gentle whispering in the form of a question and answer, "What is one of Christ's names?" followed by a pause and the answer, "Counselor." I felt such peace after that answer and this new fortitude got me through three years.

We spent a total of seven and a half years in Alamosa. One of my most treasured memories was a visit from my parents for Nicole's baptism. She was baptized in early November. My parents flew into Albuquerque a few days early to have more time to spend with us. We met them in Taos and spent the crisp, sunny day together ambling through the Taos Pueblo, where we strolled through the adobes and felt transported to another age. Later, we took them to the plaza where we shopped and introduced them to our favorite restaurants. My dad insisted on buying me a horsehair pot after I'd gushed over how much I loved them. He bought each of the kids a gift that was meaningful to their personalities.

We shared long visits the next few days, and I had a chance to ply my parents with questions about their past, caring more about it now that I was in the shoes they had already walked in. I listened as my dad described his conversion to the Church of Jesus Christ of Latter-day Saints. He attended the University of Oregon, majoring in philosophy. Many of his classes left him with more questions than answers. Partway into the semester, a friend from his high school mailed him some pamphlets about the church and the book, *The Articles of Faith* by James Talmage. As he read this meaty book, many of his questions were answered, and he strongly desired to learn more. He knew of a professor who had recently transferred from working at Brigham Young University and approached him with requests for more information. The teacher sent some missionaries to help him, coming on a Monday night. They taught him every night that week, and he was baptized on Saturday. He never looked back. The next year he transferred to Brigham Young University and left on a mission a year after he was baptized.

As we sat in my living room, tears choked him up while he testified to the profound change the gospel had brought in his life. He was committed to his God, his church, and his family. That commitment shaped him into the wonderful father he was to me and grandfather that he was to my kids. When I hear of how many horrible or absent fathers there are in the world, I feel supremely grateful that I had a loving, kind father who only lifted me up my entire life. Near the end of our visit, Nathan's parents who have always been pillars of strength for us, arrived and we were all together to witness Nicole's baptism.

Shortly after this visit, Nathan and I felt a strong urgency to move closer to our families and again went through the process of applying for a new job, interviewing and uprooting our family to Klamath Falls, Oregon. I had no idea that only three months after we moved, my dad would be gone. I would need to be closer to home, but for different reasons than I expected.

During the course of my studies I read about some of Piaget's theories of development. One idea in layman's terms is basically that we form a belief about something in our lives based on our experience. Rather than reform the belief when we are presented with new information, we tend to bend that new information to match our current belief. It is only when we are hit hard enough with a new belief that we step back and adjust our beliefs to a new idea. The theory is called Piaget's Constructivist Theory (Broderick and Blewitt 78). I had a belief that my dad would live into his 90's. This belief was created by years of watching him go play racquetball with his friends, jog in the mornings, eat lots of vegetables, live a worthy, productive life and by the stories he told of great-aunts and uncles who lived well into their 90's. All facts pointed to him living a long and healthy life. He was approaching retirement, and I expected that he would take a year to do some family history and woodworking a little bit, before heading off on a mission with my mom, just as he had always talked about doing. In my mom's adapted and assimilated world, she expected that after coming off a wonderful

Alaskan cruise, she would celebrate her 60th birthday with her
partner of 40 years and would probably enjoy a barbeque meal
made by my dad that included many grilled vegetables and a
Costco purchased cake. Sometime between June 25, and July 5,
2013 my family came to a point of accommodation. Past beliefs
had to be replaced with new ones. Past expectations were
substituted by new plans. My mom sat in numb shock as we
celebrated a "brutiful" 60th birthday the day before my dad's
funeral, surrounded by people who had flown in or driven out for
it.

Most of the time my life goes on with the distractions of
children, church callings, school and mundane chores, but every
once in a while a glance at his picture, or a fleeting thought brings
me back to the implications of this new great accommodation, and
I find myself sorting through what this means in the long run.
Nicole breaks into tears after a verse of "Families Can Be
Together Forever." During a quiet conversation, Connor weeps
at all the things that he misses. And I find myself overcome by
emotion that comes seemingly from nowhere. We smile and
move on through our pain, which is a steady tutor. The waves of
grief ebb and flow and I plead with the Lord to please be with my
mom. I strain to feel close to my dad and at times feel his spirit
near. Fortunately, my core beliefs remain unscathed and are, if
anything, now stronger.

What if Lenaya had never changed? What if she never turned
from her lifestyle? I understand how painful relapse is for family
members and 40-60% of addicts do relapse ("Principles of Drug
Abuse"). This story could have gone on forever without change
and it does for many families. Our story could be added to the
pile of casualties. I would hate for people to reach the conclusion
that they aren't praying hard enough, or they haven't done enough
to help their loved ones, because that simply isn't true. Personal
choice determines the course of our lives, and many never are
able to pull themselves out of the bondage of drugs and alcohol.

If Lenaya had never changed, I would be sad. I would be very
sad for the loss of her tremendous potential. Yet, I would never
stop loving her. I would keep reaching out to have a relationship
with her. I would include her in my life as much as possible. I

would try to learn from the heartbreak of watching her life, attempting to teach my own children to avoid her pitfalls. I have empathy for both those individuals chained by addiction and those who love them and want them to change. My experience provided me perspective that enrichens me and expands my soul. I'm so grateful that I got to see her change, but I don't wish away all the lessons our experiences provided me.

My oldest son turns 17 next week. How that can be happening baffles me. Next year he will leave on his mission and start his own life. I work part-time as a counselor with families and continue to homeschool my younger children, while my older ones have started attending high school. I treasure the time I have with my family and make efforts to visit our extended family now that we are closer. I especially value the time that I have with my mom both supporting and learning from her.

In candid conversations with my mom, she has told me that she believed that Lenaya would never change except to keep spiraling downward until she died. Yet, my mom still had spiritual nudges along the way pushing her to be nicer to Lenaya than she necessarily felt like being. We lack perspective on what those around us are capable of becoming. Thus, the need to rely on the whisperings of the Spirit from an all-knowing Father is critical to lead us when we are blind. I've talked at length with my mom about what advice she gives others. She holds to the counsel to never give up hope, as cliché as it sounds. She believe it's important to let the Spirit direct you in dealing with your children. She also emphasizes that it's important to not allow the choices of one family member destroy the rest of your family.

One of the greatest ironies I've witnessed is the relationship between my mom and sister. These days my mom watches Lenaya's children for her when she goes to work. Lenaya, in turn, is the one who has carried the greatest load in helping my mom rebuild her life since my dad's death. They call each other daily, spend time shopping together, go on outings, and take turns hosting dinner for each other. Though Lenaya caused my mom such misery, their relationship has become an immense source of joy for both of them.

I have watched Lenaya and Brian since they were first

married and seen them grow in their relationship. Soon after they were married I worried about whether they would make it work when she seemed full of emotions that she was immature in handling. I have watched them grow and her emotional maturity steadily grows. They have a great relationship now with a sense of humor that has carried them through many challenges and pitfalls. They complement each other beautifully. She is a tender mother who both loves her children without bounds and yet becomes frustrated beyond her patience. She is real.

I have learned a lot about addictions. They are divisive. They isolate us from one another. We feel that no one else understands. We become separated from each other and become preoccupied with our own experience instead of thinking about those around us. Addictions are counterfeit. They imitate happiness but are pleasure without any substance. We invariably feel worse the next day and try to recreate that feeling. The truth is that no one is completely happy all the time. We must have challenges to bring true happiness. We all have addictions to some degree, whether the addiction is alcohol, drugs, food, caffeine, video games, sex, lying, escapism in reading, or earning money. Balance is difficult to achieve.

I have learned that relapse is part of recovery for all of us. We continually fall short of where we want to be and where we need to be. We make repair attempts and then step back up to try again. God's grace truly is sufficient. We are on this earth to minister to one another. And in the process, we grow into who we want to be. Satan's tool is to tell us that we are too far gone, that it is too late to repent. I believe that we are never past the point of no return.

Perhaps what is more difficult for us bystanders to do is allow those suffering addiction to change. Having been let down many times, I was wary those first couple years, while hoping that change was permanent. We all see a "Scrooge" as someone who is stingy and miserly, though the person he ultimately became was generous and kind. I had to learn to see Lenaya with a new identity, giving her space to change.

As I watch her in her struggles with a young family, I am reminded of my own difficulties in that season. We are more similar than we are different. She is not perfect. She still struggles to make peace with food at times. She is learning to work together with her husband in their marriage. But so am I. Increasingly, she is the one who buoys me when I am grumpy or struggling with something. She sets me straight with a story or idea that hadn't occurred to me. She increasingly teaches me by how she lives her life, lifting those around her with her trademark optimism. Where we were so long on unequal footing, I now see her standing by my side as a peer.

Recently, I visited my mom who is recuperating from a knee surgery. She felt up to venturing out in public and we met Lenaya with her daughters at a restaurant for dinner. Sitting outside on a beautiful evening, her baby toddled around the patio as we enjoyed our meal. We lounged around the table after paying the bill, not wanting to finish our conversation and camaraderie. The contrast of pain from past years made the night all the more beautiful. Happily, when we discuss those years now, the pain has diminished, leaving behind only the lessons learned.

I have learned that God knows me personally. In the very moments that I feel alone, He is watching over me. When I feel that my prayers aren't being answered, they are...daily. We are all on our individual journeys of life. Our pathways cross. Some paths dip or rise on unique terrain. Hopefully, in the end, our pathways lead us home to our Heavenly Father. With God's grace they can.

Lenaya

Seven years into sobriety, I began to attend the LDS addiction recovery program to support a sweet friend. Their meetings are very similar to AA except that they make scriptural connections and the homework is centered on the gospel. One evening, as everyone was taking turns speaking, the general theme was unfulfilled restitution or apologies. Each was bemoaning the fact that a mother, a father, a brother, a sister, a friend had died without accepting the addict's sincere and heartfelt apology for the grief they'd caused. When it came my turn to talk I felt the strongest conviction about this topic. I explained that seven years of sobriety and endless apologies and sincere remorse weren't sufficient to fully offer restitution for the grief I'd caused my dad before he died. Even though I got to apologize and feel his intense acceptance and love, the truth is we can never make restitution or heal the hearts of those we've hurt; only Christ and the Atonement can do that. Grace is the only thing sufficient to heal and restore. We are all imperfect. Just because I struggled with drug addiction for so many years doesn't make me less perfect than someone who struggles with something less debilitating. We are all fighting a battle within ourselves striving to be better. But the Atonement can heal us all so long as we repent. That is the miracle.

I know how hard and ironic and desperate this life can be. But I also know that there is *always* hope because Christ gave us this sacred gift. If you're an addict, there is hope. If you love an addict, there is hope. If you suffer from depression, there is hope. If you have an eating disorder, there is hope. If you have lost a loved one, there is hope. The Atonement can save us all, and God hears us. Even if He doesn't answer us in the way or at the time we want, it doesn't mean He doesn't hear. A few weeks ago Brian spoke in church about adversity. He said:

President Uchtdorf said, *"It is your reaction to adversity, not the adversity itself that determines how your life story will develop."*

Sometimes the height of our trials prevents us from being able to imagine ever growing from such turmoil. We are sometimes tempted to shake an angry fist at God, asking why me? It isn't fair! In these instances we could let hate and resentment fill our hearts and consume us, or we can choose to overcome and have faith in the Lord instead. Rather than asking, 'Why me?' we could benefit more from the more difficult question, 'What would you have me learn?' or 'How can I gain Christ-like attributes through this ordeal?' Often in such trials, we gain the experience necessary to be the hands of the Lord and help others through similar struggles.

God told Joseph, in D&C 122:7-8 *"And if thou shouldst be cast into the pit, or into the hands of murderers, and the sentence of death passed upon thee; if thou be cast into the deep; if the billowing surge conspire against thee; if fierce winds become thine enemy; if the heavens gather blackness, and all the elements combine to hedge up the way; and above all, if the very jaws of hell shall gape open the mouth wide after thee, know thou, my son, that all these things shall give thee experience, and shall be for thy good. 8 The Son of Man hath descended below them all. Art thou greater than he?"*

Lenaya and I have been married for five years now. Before marriage, we both had our bouts with adversity and fair share of struggles. There's no other experience that I have had that's more treasured to me than when we were sealed for time and all eternity in the Reno, NV temple. None of this would have been possible if she wouldn't have overcome her demons brought on by adversity, endured through them, and stayed connected with her Heavenly Father. At a young age, she ran away from home, getting tied up with lifestyles that drew her away from her personal spirituality. She got lost in addictions for over a decade, losing touch with her family, and the people who were positive influences in her life. Addictions are not easy to overcome. Just as the scripture says, the very jaws of hell gaped open after her. In and out of rehab, it appeared as though she would never overcome this trial. But, through her steadfast efforts, and her strong desire to steal back her relationship with her Savior from the grasp of Satan, the Lord gave her a lifeline so that she could grab a hold of the iron rod once again.

To this day, she has held a firm grasp on that iron rod, regained her worthiness to enter the house of God and perform ordinances. By acting out the things that she learned when she was primary age, she was able to walk the path that led her back to her Heavenly Father, who led her to me.

D&C 84:88 *"And whoso receiveth you, there I will be also, for I will go before your face. I will be on your right hand and on your left, and my Spirit shall be in your hearts, and mine angels round about you, to bear you up."*

Our family has reaped the blessings of adversity. As well as many people whose hearts could not be reached without Lenaya's experience. There were plenty of dark times, she thought she had been abandoned, but like so many of us have learned, He will NEVER leave us alone!

For a long time, I let my adversity define me. Now, I try to let my reaction to adversity define me. The refiner's fire is real. We are polished and strengthened when we overcome trials. I am blessed, and I am not alone. Every person on this earth is entitled to the very same blessings of Grace. The Atonement is big enough for us all.

A gentle breeze runs its fingers through my hair as the sheer aqua hammock swings beneath the branches of two maple trees in our backyard. I've traded the thrill of the swings in my youth, for the fulfillment of this rich life. My baby girl plays peekaboo from my lap accompanied by the music of the older kids' laughter from the trampoline beside us. Brian is working in the garden, trying to ignore the urgent pleas from our children to join them on the trampoline. "Please!" they beg, "jump us!" He feigns reluctance as he puts down the rake and climbs through his newly constructed playhouse to walk the bridge to the opening in the net. Our children are thrilled, and I smile at the baby intently watching as the older kids squeal with delight at the giant bounces produced by their daddy. The sun sneaks through leaves and between branches kissing my forehead with delicious warmth. Soon, I will need to check the crockpot for our dinner, but not just yet. Instead, I relish this moment; this exquisite, tiny moment offering silent thanks to my Father in Heaven for the cherished gift. Every moment isn't as perfect, but they all are gifts. My heart skips beats as I soak in the beauty, the peace, the joy. This life is not always easy, but the payoff is more bounteous than I could imagine. Urgent chores often give way to sprinklers on the grass or bikes begging to hit the pavement. Bedtime stories and family prayer discreetly propel us forward to each next task. There are plenty of big moments, but the little moments insist on their importance, *pick me, notice me, love me.* And we do. I kiss each child as they head off to bed grateful for some much anticipated mommy and daddy time, and I wake up to do it all again. I try not to take any time for granted, for this life, *my* life is not just a gift. It is a *miracle.* It is *happiness.*

The Pathways Home

My foot sunk deep in the prow of earth,
the path ahead
untamed.
Unclaimed.
But I chose it.

The uneven soil shifted with leaves so beautiful
they knocked me over.
And the prayers took flight and held me
above earth--if only
for an instant.
For they could not carry me to other paths I had
not chosen!

Crimson knees scraped
ground as I crawled,
gasping for a cure.
When I remembered "mirrors have no soul"
they can govern me no more!
This is
MY pathway home.
And I chose it.

Wary eyes focused as they queried,
"Did you choose it?"

And the iridescent
petals
propelled me to the
pathway where
patient eyes acknowledged,
"You chose it!"

And they were there… my family!
And He was there…my Lord!
And they had been there all along.

But my appetite still forced me to my knees
and the splendor broke my heart.
When tiny lashes and pencil brows
gave way
to chiseled expressions.
Exhilarated,
I chose her.

The tiny teacher who helped
me choose the path,
and vulnerably led me to him,
found in the only fork our paths
adjoined. His square jaw asking
"Do you trust me?"
And I chose him.

*And this is **my** pathway home so*
he chose us
too.

When Brown eyes turned to green and
green formed to blue
The little eyes multiplied and grew
And I knew
This is my pathway home.
It always
was.

Their joyful eyes are watchful,
Will you love us? choose us? teach us?
And I show them
Love them
choose them
every day
and sometimes
every minute.

My prayers take flight to hold them
if only for an instant
hoping the pathways they choose
will lead them home.

-Lenaya Andersen 2015 (35-yrs-old)-

Works Cited

"Behavioral Health Barometer." *samhsa.gov.* SAMHSA, 2014. Web. 12 July 2012.

Brand, Russell. "Russell Brand: My Life Without Drugs." *The Guardian.* The Guardian News, 9 March 2013. Web. 5 June 2013.

Broderick, Patricia C. and Pamela Blewitt. *The Life Span: Human Development For Helping Professionals.* Upper Saddle River, New Jersey: Pearson, 2010. Print.

Callister, Tad R. *The Infinite Atonement.* Salt Lake City: Deseret Book Company, 2000. Print.

Capuzzi, David, Mark D. Stauffer. *Foundations of Addictions Counseling.* Upper Saddle River, New Jersey: Pearson Education, 2012. Print.

Christensen, Craig C. *BYU Alumni Magazine.* Salt Lake City, UT: The Church of Jesus Christ of Latter-Day Saints, 2012. Print.

DeCurtis, Anthony. "Rock of Ages: Older Artists Offer Fresh Perspective: Jerry Garcia." *Rolling Stone (515).* Rolling Stone, 17 December 1987. Web. 4 April. 2012.

Dickens, Charles. *A Tale of Two Cities.* New York: Dover Publications, 1999. Print.

Doctrine & Covenants. Salt Lake City, UT: The Church of Jesus Christ of Latter-Day Saints, 1952. Print.

Holland, Jeffrey R. "The Laborers in the Vineyard." *Ensign. LDS.org.* The Church of Jesus Christ of Latter-Day Saints, April 2012. Web. 5 Oct. 2012.

Holland, Jeffrey R. "The Other Prodigal." *Ensign*. Salt Lake City, UT: The Church of Jesus Christ of Latter-Day Saints, May 2002: 62. Print.

Kid Rock. "Only God Knows Why." *Devil Without a Cause*. Atlantic, 1999. CD.

McCloud, Susan Evans. "Lord I Would Follow Thee." *Hymns*. *LDS.org*. The Church of Jesus Christ of Latter Day Saints, 21 February 2012. Web. 5 July 2015.

Melton, Glennon Doyle. "Fifteen." *Momastery*. Momastery, 16 Feb 2012. Web. 17 Feb 2012.

Nelson, Russell M. "Addiction or Freedom." *General Conference*. *LDS.org*. The Church of Jesus Christ of Latter-Day Saints, Oct. 1988. Web. 14 July 2015.

Packer, Boyd K. "Little Children." *Ensign*. *LDS.org*. The Church of Jesus Christ of Latter-Day Saints, Oct. 1986. Web. 1 Oct. 2014.

Pink Floyd. "Mother." *The Wall*. Columbia, 1979. CD.

"Principles of Drug Abuse Treatment: a Research Based Guide." *National Institute on Drug Abuse*. NIDA Drug Pubs, Dec. 2012. Web. 10 January 2015.

Scott, Richard G. "For Peace at Home." *Ensign*. *LDS.org*. The Church of Jesus Christ of Latter-Day Saints, April 2013. Web. May 2013.

Stecklein, Janelle. "Man Shot on Utah Freeway ID'd." *The Salt Lake Tribune*. The Salt Lake Tribune, 26 Feb. 2013. Web. 5 March 2013.

The Book of Mormon. Joseph Smith Jr., trans. Salt Lake City: The Church of Jesus Christ of Latter-day Saints, 1981. Print.

The Holy Bible: King James Version. Salt Lake City, UT: The Church of Jesus Christ of Latter-Day Saints, 1979. Print.

The Pearl of Great Price. Salt Lake City, UT: The Church of Jesus Christ of Latter-Day Saints, 1989. Print.

Uchtdorf, Dieter F. "The Infinite Power of Hope." *General Conference. LDS.org,* October 2008. Web. 2 Jan. 2015.

Uchtdorf, Dieter F. "Your Happily Ever After." *General Conference. LDS.org,* April 2010. Web. 2 Jan. 2015.

Wynonna Judd. "Is It Over Yet?" *Tell Me Why.* MCA, 1993. CD